COMRADES IN CAPTIVITY

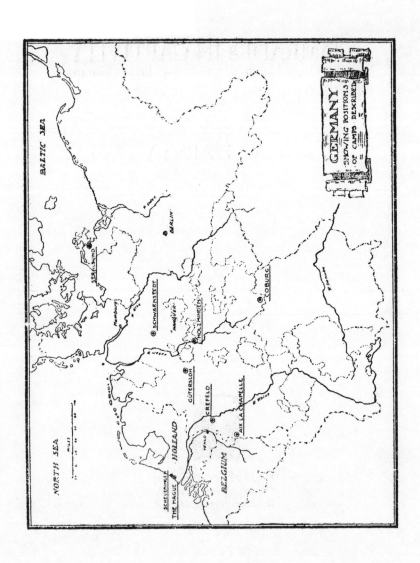

GERMANY
SHOWING POSITIONS
OF CAMPS DESCRIBED

NORTH SEA

BALTIC SEA

HOLLAND

BELGIUM

THE HAGUE

SCHEVENINGEN

AIX LA CHAPELLE

CREFELD

GÜTERSLOH

HOLZ MINDEN

SCHWARMSTEDT

STRALSUND

BERLIN

HAMBURG

KOBURG

COMRADES IN CAPTIVITY
A Record of Life in Seven German Prison Camps

F. W. HARVEY

Douglas McLean Publishing
8 St. John Street, Coleford,
Gloucestershire. GL16 8AR

First Published by Sidgwick & Jackson in 1920

This new edition published in 2010
by Douglas McLean Publishing
8 St John Street
Coleford
Gloucestershire
GL16 8AR

British Library Cataloguing in Publication Data
Data Available

ISBN 978-0-946252-76-3

10 9 8 7 6 5 4 3 2 1

Cover design and typography by Douglas McLean
Typeset in Adobe Garamond Pro 12.5pt /16pt

Printed in Great Britain by
CPoD, Cromwell Press Group, Trowbridge, UK.

Contents

APPENDIX

Foreword to the
2010 edition

Comrades in Captivity is the only published book of prose written by the poet Frederick William Harvey. It is a biographical account of his experiences extending from his capture in August 1916, until his return home following the Armistice in November 1918. Published in 1920, it never achieved the acclaim many thought it deserved. It describes the trials and tribulations of his life as a prisoner of war (PoW), during a period from when he produced some of his best work. It also provides an insight into the philosophy, politics and beliefs he held, most of which endured for the rest of his life. It is at times sad, but also rich with his humour in the face of adversity. He coped with his captivity by entertaining those around him with wit, writing and song. He was called 'The Poet' and observed to be a friend, confidant and inspiration to his comrades.

This foreword sets out some of the context behind the imprisonment of British officers in the Great War and provides the reader with an introduction to Will Harvey's early life.

During the Great War of 1914–1918, some 7,335 officers and 174,491 other ranks of the British Army were captured by the enemy. Of these, about half were captured in the later stages of war between 21 March and 11 November 1918.[1] From 1915, officers were held in designated camps where living conditions were not quite as basic as other ranks had to endure. For instance, officers had beds, the troops had straw-filled sacks. Also, officers were exempted from labour, so spent their days in study or sport.

Will Harvey was captured on August 17 1916, when British officer PoW numbers were relatively low and included many who had been captured in the first days of the war. On arrival at Gütersloh, the first of seven officer *gefangenenlager,* Will Harvey encountered an array of officers of different nationalities, significantly more French and Russian prisoners than British. This variety of nationalities and his experience of them greatly enriches the early part of *Comrades in Captivity.* German policy later changed to providing camps solely for British officers.

The regulations under which prisoners of war were detained were governed by the 1909 Hague Convention. During the conflict there was harsh treatment of many PoWs in Germany and both the British and German governments tested the boundaries of the agreements and adjusted their policies in response to wider political developments and tit-for-tat events. In the early stages of the war the more distressing experiences of some prisoners were fuelled by the opposing sides each attributing atrocities to their enemy.

Towards the end of the war the circumstances of the German civil population deteriorated and living

---

1 British Officers includes those serving in the Indian Army and the colonial forces of Australia, Canada and New Zealand. The total includes those captured at Gallipoli, Salonika and Mesopotamia. The experiences of captives on these other fronts was generally worse than those captured on the Western Front, although officers were generally much better treated than other ranks.

conditions and provisions available to British officers became relatively better than those of the local populace. Such was the hunger and frustration of German villagers that in late 1917 steps were taken to stop them intercepting the delivery of officer parcels.[2]

The camps occupied by Will Harvey were a particular cause of concern and the subject of a special report published in early 1918 by the Government Committee on the Treatment by the Enemy of British Prisoners of War. The committee received reports from escapees and from inspections carried out by representatives of neutral countries under the auspices of the Hague Convention. Information about conditions in the early part of the war were recorded by the American ambassador to Germany (prior to the United States entry into the war), James W. Gerard, who published his findings in *My Four Years in Germany*. Later, the Netherlands and Switzerland played increasingly important roles in inspection of camps, providing internment camps and arbitrating about PoW matters between the belligerent countries. Gerard observed that officer prisoners were generally well treated. They were allowed tennis courts and other amusements, as well as light wine or beer. He recognized that the length of the war had a bad effect on the mental condition of many.[3] The receipt of parcels from home was an officers' right that meant most to officers and allowed them a relatively comfortable existence. Most officers had families with the means to despatch regular provisions and even materials that

---

2 The National Archives F.O. 383/271 Report of Captain Caunter.

3 James W. Gerard, *My Four Years in Germany*, (London: Hodder and Stoughton, 1917) p.129-130

helped with escape. This parcel service meant they had real tea, marmalade and white bread, luxuries that became unobtainable to the civilian population in Germany early in the War.

The quality of camp commandants varied and many were described as excellent, efficient and kind-hearted men. Oberst Court, the commandant of Crefeld had a British wife and allowed Will Harvey to send h is book of poems home to be published. Will Harvey describes him as jolly, a gentleman, and that he treated the officers as gentlemen.

The expectation of gentlemanly behaviour was uppermost in the expectations of PoW officers. Many of the camp constraints leading to complaints involved 'petty restrictions' and 'overbearing conduct' and the officer PoWs were furious at the inability of the German administration to understand the context of a British officer's word of honour.

The best camps from the perspective of gentleman officers were those where parole was afforded by giving one's word. For example in some camps, officers were allowed to wander without supervision for up to two kilometres from the camp if they gave their word that they would not try to escape.

The worst camps were considered to be those with poor facilities for sleeping and recreation and where bureaucratic and authoritarian rules were imposed rather than allowing the prisoners to organize and discipline themselves. The Hanover district, containing Clausthal, Ströhen, Schwarmstedt and Holzminden camps, was commanded by General von Henish, ('Von H' in *Comrades in Captivity*).

Von Henish and his camp commandants (particularly the Neimeyer twins) were much disliked and their treatment of officers reported in the British press.[4] The district was the responsibility of the 10th Corps of the German Army and a significant proportion of British officers were held in camps there from 1917.

The Hague Convention required that officers should retain servants, referred to as orderlies. Ströhen camp had 108 orderlies for 430 officers in July 1917. The orderlies were mostly British soldiers assigned to officer camps, although they sometimes included captives of other nationalities. The comforts available to British officers did not extend to Indian officers who were very isolated and suffered because they were unable to receive parcels from home. The conditions of Russian and Romanian officer PoWs were much worse than that of the British. The British were generally better respected and better looked after by their captors. British officers were supplied with a weekly allowance; 100 marks per week for captains and above, 60 marks for subalterns. Thus they could buy food and services in the camps as well as receive parcels.

They had access to German newspapers and also four-day-old copies of *The Times*. They could even communicate regularly with their solicitors and bankers to manage home affairs.[5]

The conditions and conventions applying to other

4 *The Times*, Thursday, 5 December, 1918, p. 9

5 The National Archive F.O. 383/272 Report of Captain Caunter. He complained that the Germans intercepted his instruction to his banker to buy British War Bonds. He also complained at length about how the deteriorating exchange rate saw a diminishing return for the captured officer whose German marks brought appreciably less at the end of the war when compared to the beginning.

ranks, who were kept in separate camps to officers, were much worse. They were required to work under stressful and difficult conditions and live on the very limited provisions provided by their captors. They were exploited by Prussian landowners and industrialists to provide factory and agricultural work including hard-labour in salt mines and quarries.[6] They were often dispersed to work-centres, which made official inspection difficult. These conditions deteriorated as the war progressed. They also escaped from captivity although, as with much Great War literature, there are fewer accounts by soldiers from the ranks. One early escape account that describes the camp conditions of rankers and tells of a successful escape is by a Canadian, George Pearson.[7]

Despite the relatively good conditions that the British officers experienced, complaints filtered back to London. These ranged from the killing of an officer named Morritt, described by Will Harvey, to the more trivial issues such as the discomfort of paper filled mattresses. All of these complaints were amassed in a report by a government committee on camps in the 10th Army Corps District.[8] Sir George Cave on seeing a first draft of the report wrote that there were 'comparatively trifling incidents mixed up with grave matters without any sense of proportion.' Furthermore he observed:

---

6 Gerard, *My Four Years*, p.133

7 George Pearson, *The Escape of a Princess Pat*, (London, 1918)

8 The National Archive F.O. 383/272

'The public will not consider that it was any great hardship that officer prisoners should have had occasionally to wash their plates and things of that sort, more especially in view of the way other ranks are treated.'

The report was published causing consternation at home but events had already moved on. The prisoner exchange process was bringing more officers home, and in March 1918 the shape of the war changed dramatically and the German offensive that followed saw thousands of Allied soldiers captured. In July the tide rapidly turned, the offensive exhausted itself and exposed the shortage of equipment and men. The Allied counter-offensive saw thousands of Germans captured and the German Army in retreat until the Armistice was declared on 11 November 1918.

The escapers that Will Harvey had joined in 1916 were largely young, junior officers who were committed to escape as a requirement of Army Orders. They were also mainly regular, or career army officers, for whom captivity denied the opportunity of career advancement and recognition on the battlefield. Many of them resisted the opportunities for prisoner exchanges and internment in Switzerland and Holland because they would have been rendered noncombatants under the terms of their release. The consequences of escaping were solitary confinement and imprisonment, tacitly accepted by apprehended escapees. In early 1917, as an extension to the Hague agreements, it was agreed that two weeks solitary confinement would be the standard punishment for escapees.[9] However, this was extended in

---

9 Page 16(C) of the Hague Agreement of 2 July 1917 established reprisal punishments.

Germany by adding extra days if they were in possession of maps, compasses and civilian clothes. Where conviction was required by court-martial, long periods of confinement could take place leading up to the trial. 'Strafing', a term used to describe such punishments as being held to attention on parade, or other penalties imposed on the whole population of a camp, were not allowed under the Hague Convention, but were often applied and deeply resented.[10]

The various arms of the services were all represented in the camps; Naval, Flying Corps and Army. Will Harvey frequently makes note of the differentiation and antipathy that existed between the Regulars, the New Army or Kitchener's Army and the Territorials. The tensions that existed between the largely upper class, public school educated Regular Army officers and their 'temporary' counterparts, from increasingly diverse social backgrounds, were considerable. The need for a mass army to cope on the Western Front, the devastating attrition of junior officers, particularly in the early stages of the war, and the development of a more meritocratic approach to selection undermined the exclusivity of the officer corps. The tensions between the 'amateur' and 'professional' and the associated class issues continued to exist into the Second World War.[11]

Will Harvey seemingly was never affected by these social barriers and he made friends with officers of every background. This may have been in part a result of his public school background as well as his amiable

---

10 The etymology of the word 'strafing' is interesting. The word is an adaptation of *strafen*, to punish, specifically from the Great War. It was later coined to describe an aerial attack on ground forces and used in that form today.

11 See Eric Newby, *Love and War in the Apennines*, (London: Picador, 1983). He describes life in a World War II officer PoW camp in Italy.

nature. Stuart Walker, his great friend, later observed that he had the ability to get on with anyone and other prisoners always relaxed in his company.[12] His early life has been explored by Anthony Boden and Frances Townsend in their respective biographies.[13]

A key point in Will Harvey's development was the entry to Rossall School in 1901. The school was founded in 1844 for the purposes of educating the sons of army officers and the clergy and still has a record of educating the children of those serving in the armed forces. It founded the first 'rifle school' or cadet force on 1 April 1860 in response to the threat of a French invasion and maintains a unit to the present day.

The Rossall Rifle Corps of 1860 later developed into an officer training corps and was regulated by the War Office after the Haldane army reforms of 1906. By 1914, Public schools and universities had become an integral part of army officer preparation. The bond between the officer corps of the British Army, formed in the nineteenth century, continued into the later part on the twentieth century and a public school education was a prerequisite to becoming an army officer. The first and most significant exception to this was the Great War, when the needs for a mass army compromised this exclusive relationship.

The educational experience of Will Harvey at Rossall would have been geared towards his preparation to be a gentleman. The scholastic curriculum although extensive took second place to sports, played every afternoon. He excelled on the sports field and played hockey and soccer

---

12 A Portrait of Will Harvey by his Friends BBC Broadcast 1958

13 Anthony Boden, *F.W. Harvey, Soldier Poet* (Stroud: Sutton, 1988) and Frances Townsend, *The Laureate of Gloucestershire* (Bristol: Redcliffe Press, 1988).

for his school. He complained that he never learned anything at Rossall, but he would have been introduced to the manners and customs of the upper class and the values that prepared scholars for service in the Colonial Service and Army.

Regardless of whether he under took military training, the values and ethos of the school would have formed the necessary preparation for a life in the officer corps of the British Army. There are references to Rossall in some of his verse and the impact of the school in informing Will Harvey's development should not be underestimated, even to the extent of his forming values that opposed some of those propounded by public schools at that time.

Rossall School old boys made a major contribution to the Great War. 1,617 fought in the conflict, 297 were killed and 300 were honoured or decorated. Two were awarded the Victoria Cross.[14] The vast majority contributed their services as officers. The dead were commemorated in the school Memorial Chapel and on a memorial plaque at St George's Chapel near the Menin Gate.[15] There was another notable literary Rossall old boy who became a prisoner of war. R.J. Ackerley, eight years younger than Will Harvey, joined the East Surrey Regiment and was wounded in the Battle of the Somme.[16] He later became a famous author and critic.

---

14 Gale and Polden (1944). *The Centenary History of Rossall School,* William Furness. p. 126.

15 In 2007 The Belgian Government and British Armed Forces allowed Rossall School's Combined Cadet Force to march through the Menin Gate in full British military uniform, led by the school's own marching band and two bandsmen from the British Army garrison at Catterick, North Yorkshire, who sounded the Last Post in a service in St. George's Church.

16 His war experience had many similarities to that of Will Harvey; he was wounded and captured at Arras in 1917 and his brother was killed in action three months before the end of the war. Ackerley interned in Switzerland began his play, *The Prisoners of War,* which deals with the cabin fever of captivity

Will Harvey, a new boy at Rossall, achieved accept-
ance by standing on a chair and reciting Robert Brown-
ing's 'The Pied Piper of Hamelin.' He describes how
at Gütersloh, he endeared himself in a similar way:

'Chesterton's drinking songs set to homely tunes
enabled me to gain admittance into society. After that
I wrote poems, essays and reviews (both of the English
and American variety), played hockey, lectured, and
attended cheery evenings with consistent regularity.'

Given Rossall School's contribution to the Officer
Corps It is hardly surprising that he met a Rossall
old boy in Holzminden; 'Fluffy,' who was the
chief female impersonator in plays and sketches.
It was not just his old public school friends and
comrades in captivity that were endeared to Will Harvey
through his songs and fellowship; these were attributes
that made him a loved member of the mining communities of the Forest of Dean after the war. His appeal crossed
all social classes and he could respond appropriately to
the norms and conventions of wherever he found himself.
At Rossall he learned 'proper English and pronuncia-
tion' but when at the BBC for a broadcast he was asked
to 'speak more Gloucestershire', which he happily did.[17]
Will Harvey's public school education did not necessarily mean he accepted or held the values and beliefs of
the English upper classes. He came from a farming family,

---

and the frustrated longings he experienced for another English prisoner. The
play was first performed in 1925 and after this he became the arts editor of *The
Listener.*

17 Reminiscences of Eileen Griffiths, his daughter.

was born in Hartpury and grew up Misterworth, Gloucestershire. His father was a horse breeder and dealer, specializing in the heavy horses essential to agriculture, industry and transport at that time. In the ten years before the war and after his schooling he formed new and liberal views. His school had been staunchly protestant but Will Harvey had found a faith more comfortable to him in the Catholic Church. This was in opposition to his educational background, his Minsterworth Church and the wishes of his family. He had also developed a view about the need for a redistribution of wealth, so that no one had too much and none too little. His outlook and views on life probably had a bearing on his decision to join a Territorial battalion at the outbreak of war in August 1914.

The culture of the Territorial battalions was less formal than the Regular Army; it attracted a wider social mix. In the Counties the Territorials had attracted the 'Yeoman stock', who had a traditional role in home defence, and also members of the growing professional classes that enjoyed the annual training camps. In August 1914 the 'Terriers' would have been a natural choice for men such as Will Harvey and his two brothers who attended the same recruiting office on 8 August 1914. With his public school education he could have easily sought out a temporary commission in a service battalion, but the 1/5th Battalion offered an ideal solution. They were not an 'Imperialist' army, (Harvey and others were increasingly doubtful of the moral and political basis of colonisation); although to serve overseas Territorials had to sign an 'Imperial Service Obligation'. Enlistment as an ordinary private in a Territorial battalion was consistent with Will Harvey's views about equality and his love of the 'ordinary man'. It also brought him the comradeship of men he knew and understood and whose kinship he valued.

His career as private, and then corporal, were short-lived because the War Office soon realized that the crisis of officer recruitment had been made worse by allowing men of officer quality to enlist in the ranks. Commanding officers, particularly of Territorial battalions, were asked to comb the ranks for men who could be trained and awarded commissions. Will Harvey, Raymond Knight (with whom he won his DCM) and many more who had the prerequisite education and had shown initiative were commissioned from the ranks of the battalion. Will's brother Eric, who enlisted as a private, but suspended his service for a year because of the death of his younger brother, was quickly commissioned on his return to the army in 1915.

Sadly, there is no account by Will Harvey of his war service before capture, although there are several sources that describe the events he experienced.[18] This was the happiest period of his life. Despite the intensity and horror of the enterprise, he cherished the brotherhood of military service. With the editorial help of the battalion chaplain, Revd. G.F. Helm, he contributed to the first and unprecedented trench newspaper, *The Fifth Gloucestershire Gazette*. Harvey lampooned the C.O., the Company Sergeant Major and even army pay. Acts that would have seen him gaoled in most other battalions, certainly Regular

18 A. F. Barnes, *The Story of the 2/5ᵗʰ Gloucestershire Regiment, 1914-1918*, (Gloucester, The Crypt House Press, 1930), W.J. Wood, *With the 5th Glosters at home and Overseas 1914-1918*, (Gloucester, The Crypt House Press, 1925). Both books open with a verse from Will Harvey.

Army units, saw him applauded. The newspaper, allowed because it was seen to raise morale, also became the first place that Will Harvey's more serious work was published.

Will Harvey's humorous work was enjoyed by his comrades in the battalion, an extensive body of over a thousand men. He also used his expressive skills to mourn and commemorate the dead. He was first called on to express the sense of loss felt when one of the oldest members of the battalion and one of its first recruits from 1906, was killed.[19]

In early 1915 Harvey was awarded a Distinguished Conduct Medal when a group from his platoon were patrolling No Man's Land and engaged a party of Germans. Later two of the party, Pte. A.E. Samson and Second Lieutenant R.E. Knight were killed and he expressed his grief in the most moving terms, in the *Fifth Gloucester Gazette*.[20] After capture he contributed to *The Warren*, a PoW camp newspaper. Works he intended for his comrades that were published in the *Fifth Gloucestershire Gazette*, had a wider relevance and were soon appreciated by a larger public audience.

Will Harvey has a varied reputation as a soldier. He was certainly courageous and not afraid of close-quarters fighting. Many years after the war, the writer and poet Leonard Clark, was surprised to find Will Harvey still had his 'trench club' that he had used to fell a retreating German.[21] In *Comrades in Captivity* he reflects upon his

---

19 Sergeant T. Durrett, commemorated in *Epitaph (T.D.)*

20 See *The First Day of Spring* dedicated to Private A.E. Samson, killed 1 November 1915 and *In Memoriam* dedicated to Second Lieutenant R.E. Knight died of wounds 25 July 1916 (September edition of *5th Gloucestershire Gazette*).

21 Leonard Clark, *A Fool in the Forest* (London: Dobson, 1965) p. 109

appearance and lack of a 'heroic stature', but he enjoys being misjudged on his looks. His C.O. later remarked on his untidiness and that in recommending him for a commission he had hoped that a batman might improve him.[22] His performance is judged by himself to have been at times foolhardy. His daring always seemed destined to see him either killed or commended, but in the end saw him captured. The circumstances of his capture were formally reported in 1919, was very much as described in *Comrades in Captivity*. The one point that is less clear, is whether he had the sanction of his C.O. to undertake a single-handed reconnaissance in No Man's Land. He claims to have set the plan out for him, but took his lack of response, as tacit consent to go ahead.

Comrades in Captivity begins at the point of capture and provides a comprehensive account of Harvey's incarceration. It also provides, as he intended, a personal statement of his outlook and philosophy. This is achieved through his examples of prison-camp debates and lectures. He sets out the arguments for and against handing over a British-built escape tunnel for the French or Russian captives to use, applauding the decision to do so in support of the broader allied cause. He uses lectures to challenge George Bernard Shaw's 'Shavian' ideas and to express his own thoughts on the future world order.[23]

He emerges as a much more cosmopolitan figure than he is often perceived. He shows remarkable foresight in predicting extreme ideologies and anticipating the rise of

---

22 A Portrait of Will Harvey by his Friends BBC Broadcast 1958

23 George Bernard Shaw was immensely popular and the term 'Shavian' was used to classify any ideas or philosophies he expounded.

communism and national socialism in post-war Europe. Will Harvey powerfully argues his case for believing in Christianity and romanticism from his perspective as a poet passionate about the natural world and who lived in Minsterworth, Gloucestershire.

In the age of Shavian ideas such as *Superman* and the *Life Force* Harvey's perspective seemed parochial but as the political extremes of communism and fascism failed in the twentieth century and the excesses of capitalism have had to curb themselves to the new ecological imperatives in this century, Will Harvey's perspectives seem particularly relevant today. He shows a remarkable anticipation of the multicultural society when he wrote:

'It is important to remember that we are all the same. It is equally important to remember that we are all different. That is our most interesting quality.'

He caricatures some national stereotypes when he observes:

The Germans, since they are so deadly earnest, have legs better adapted for being pulled than any other people in the world, and are in this respect a very natural prey for the Irish, of which curious people we had a good sprinkling in the camp, both Nationalists and Ulstermen, delightful fellows all.'24

---

24 Many years later after observing the laughter caused by a man slipping over at Whitecroft he observed: 'There you have the difference between us and the Russians. A man slips on a banana skin and the English think it funny. The Russians would write a 700 page tragedy about it.' Ivon Adams on F.W. Harvey *Dean Forest Mercury*, 1 March 1957.

Foreword

So that this book can be read without interruption, an appendix gives more detailed biography of the many interesting characters in captivity with Will Harvey.

The exploits and adventures of the 'escapees' that were published in other accounts and biographies are listed within a postscript, for those interested in reading more.

Roger Deeks
The F.W. Harvey Society, 2010
www.fwharveysociety.co.uk

COMRADES in CAPTIVITY

A Record of Life in Seven German Prison Camps. By F. W. Harvey.

Dedicated to

ALL OLD GEFANGENER FRIENDS
BUT PARTICULARLY TO THE
P.T., AND TO MY FRIEND IVOR GURNEY

INTRODUCTORY CHAPTER:

CAPTURE

IT OFTEN OCURRED TO ME while a prisoner of war in Germany to get my various friends of the Navy and of the Army, taken on various fronts, on so many different parts of those fronts, and in so many different ways, on land, on sea, and in the air, to write out each one a short account of his capture. Undoubtedly it would have made most fascinating reading, but unfortunately it was never accomplished.

This book sets out to give, without the aid of any diary, save those written by others, a fair account of life in seven German prison camps (which will be named) as it was lived by officers in 1916 and 1917. It is an impression rather than a detailed description, and concerns itself with things which stand out in the memory now the whole curious experience is over. Germans will be out of the picture, except where (as in the case of Niemeyer, Commandant of Holzminden, and Beetz, Adjutant of Bad-Colberg) they thrust themselves into it, for the fact is that they seem in retrospect very small by the side of so much varied humanity as gets crowded into a *gefangenenlager*. The great 'strafes' are, unless unconsciously funny (they so often were), less worthy of record and remembrance than the buoyant human spirit with which they were met by men united in comradeship with a fine gift of courageous laughter.

The story does not properly begin until after capture, but since capture is the preface to captivity (a preface often more dramatic than the story it precedes, especially when that story extends over two years) it seems appropriate to preface a book which deals with the latter by an account of the former.

The circumstances of my capture were, to say the least of them, unusual. To put it baldly, I was taken alone in a German front-line trench, which I had entered unseen yet in broad daylight, and was proceeding to explore. It sounds incredibly rash and silly. Perhaps it is neither so incredibly rash nor so silly as it sounds. Certainly it was up to a point the prettiest bit of patrolling I ever did. Certainly it was the identical rashness which got me a decoration in 1915 that got me taken prisoner in 1916.

This is how it happened. On August 16, 1916, our company moved into a new part of the line, with orders that the first night should be given up entirely to trench consolidation, but that on the second night a patrol should be taken out to explore the land in front. Although only a platoon commander, I was entrusted with company patrolling on account of my previous experience. My methods were generally considered unconventional, but the results had been good.

On August 17 it occurred to me during my 'rest period' that, as I knew nothing of the ground we were to patrol that night, I might as well go out and have a look at it. Long unburned grass between the trenches afforded plenty of cover, and it is common knowledge that the hours between two and five were the quietest period of the day alike for German soldiers and English. During that period everyone except the sentry was asleep, and sometimes—well, there have been cases in our own Army, and subsequent events go to prove that probably the Germans were subject to the same demands of Nature. It had been a practice of mine, ever since I was made responsible for patrols, personally to examine the ground before I took my men over it, and this seemed a good opportunity. The particular object of my scouting was to become acquainted with the nature of the ground over which I was to lead a patrol that evening; the general object, to pick up any information likely to be of use to the battalion in general. Because there was at that time no experienced patroller in the company (the battalion being newly out), and because the men were all tired on account of over-night fatigues, I decided to go alone. My company officer had gone off somewhere down the line, taking the other subaltern with him, so I woke up a corporal asleep in a dug-out, informed him of my intentions, and instructed him to warn the sentries, and to replace the wire after me in the sally-port. Then I started.

After leaving the trench, I went crawling along in shadow of the hedge, which ran through our lines and terminated just in front of the enemy parapet, at this point about three hundred yards off. I carried an automatic pistol.

When the hedge ended the grass became short, and before leaving that cover I lay and listened for about ten minutes. A bird sang close by, but there was no sound of digging, talking, or firing, nor, incidentally, was there any sign of German listening posts in the grass.

My primary and particular object was achieved. If I had had a man with me I should now have gone back, but I was beginning to be rather pleased with myself, and, there being no other life than mine at stake, I crawled forward out of cover.

Shell-hole by shell-hole I worked my way cautiously to a little ditch or drain which ran through a gap in the German wire and on to the parapet.

Along this drain, carefully edging my way, I came at last into the projected shadow of the parapet, where I lay (holding my breath) to listen. There was not a sound. I twisted my head sideways, and looked up. Nowhere along the parapet, which here jutted out into a point, was there visible either head or periscope.

I wriggled up a little higher and looked quickly over the top into the trench. There was nobody there.

Reason told me at this point that it would be better to go back. What a little thing in human life is reason! Besides, there were at least three reasons against doing so. These were, first, and of course chiefly, that I did not want to go back, having come so far, without some evidence (*e.g.*, a cap or a rifle) to corroborate my report, and show to the men who were new to patrol work. This would give them confidence, and show them how easy it was. Secondly and thirdly there were two reasons in favour of the trench being unoccupied:

(a) About the same hour the day before I had, in a little fit of rashness, to the consternation of my good sergeant, stepped quickly over our parapet into the borrow ditch at a point just opposite here. Not a shot was fired at me going out, or returning.

(b) Though this was mere hearsay, there had been talk in our mess of a certain officer of artillery who, being sent up to find an observation post, had gone too far, and in fact visited the enemy's lines, putting this parapet (so it was averred) to a highly improper and insulting use ere he returned—and without any hostile response.

These things, added to the evidence which I had personally accumulated, were I sufficient to persuade me that it was reasonable to do what I wanted to do, go on. The Germans, so I argued, being in need of men for the Somme offensive, which was then in progress, had withdrawn troops, leaving this trench held not at all in the daytime, and only lightly at night. A few machine-guns and some trench mortars were probably all they were relying on. To make sure of *this* was not merely sport, but important work.

'Be damned if I go back!' said I, and slipped straightway over the top into the trench beneath.

It is easier to get into a German trench than to get out. I had barely reached the next bay, which was also empty, when I heard footsteps, and a good many of them, coming along behind me. If I turned back to find my hole in the wire I ran the risk of meeting those feet before I got to it. It seemed better to go on. The trench was a good deal deeper than ours, but I expected to find holes through the parados such as our own trench possessed in large numbers.

Through one of these I could creep, finding cover in the long grass behind, and a place where I could watch what was going on around me.

It would be quite possible, so I had told my colonel the day before, for a scout to lie up there the whole night, taking note of the position of trench mortars and machine-gun emplacements, and I had offered to prove it to him. 'Umph!' he had said with a smile, 'we shall see.' This I took as sanction to the attempt which I had certainly not designed to achieve when I set out that particular afternoon, but which, so it seemed, was likely to be accomplished by mere force of circumstances, if my luck held good.

But my luck was out. Nowhere in the parados was there any sign of an exit. The feet were getting nearer. I continued to walk down the trench before them, looking quickly to the right and left for cover. Then, at the end of the bay, I caught sight of a small iron shelter. It was the only place. I approached it swiftly, and was hurrying in when two hefty Germans met me in the doorway. I was seized. My pistol was wrenched away. There was no escape possible. I was cut off from my hole in the wire. The men were shouting something in an excited manner. It was absurd, but—unquestionably I was their prisoner.

It is a strange thing, but to be made prisoner is undoubtedly the most surprising thing that can happen to a soldier. It is an event which one has never considered, never by any chance anticipated.

Yet prisoners are taken pretty frequently. I had myself collared a man the year before on patrol. I had seen German prisoners at work on the river at Rouen. I had heard of our own men being captured, and seen posters in England asking for money to buy food for them.

Yet now I was dumbfounded.

1

DOUAI

THIS BOOK BEGINS THAT afternoon of August 17, three years ago [1916], when I was collared in a German trench by two large soldiers, one of whom looked so ridiculously like a certain labourer I had left working on my father's farm in England that I simply burst out laughing—which possibly saved my life.

Bewilderment and apprehension showed plainly on the faces of both my captors. They took me hastily to their officer. The officer and his fellow-officers were equally surprised.

I had been found in their trench.

Yes.

How had I got there?

Over No Man's Land, of course.

What was I doing?

Patrolling.

Where was the rest of the patrol?

There wasn't one.

Frankly, they did not believe me. Where were we to attack? I must go on to be examined by others, superiors, immediately.

Then a guard was detailed to take me somewhere or other, and a motor-car which had been requisitioned over the telephone met us on a road closely in rear of the trenches.

All this surprised me. Was it merely German promptness, that swift efficiency of which I had read, or was it 'wind up'? I do not know to this day.

It was getting dusk. The car bumped over the cobbles at a rattling pace, overtaking everything we saw which was going in the same direction. Transport was beginning to move. A company of soldiers marched trench-ward, grey in the shadow of the grey poplars which lined the road. It all seemed very queer and exciting. We had wondered so often what it was like on the other side of those German trenches, knowing of course that it must be very similar to our side, yet hardly believing it to be so. Now I was seeing.

The car sped on for several miles, and then stopped in a courtyard before a house of some importance which had apparently not been shelled. Inside I was questioned in excellent English by other Germans, the superiors, and got my one and only glimpse into the working of their secret service. Possibly ours is just as good—I have heard that it is still better—but this, my only first-hand evidence, impressed me. Thus, I had replied quite truthfully to questions as to my name, rank, and regiment, after which I lied (as I thought rather skilfully) to any further inquiries. It was at this point that the affable gentleman in charge of my cross-examination smiled, and, calling for a map, proceeded to point out places, and to tell me quite accurately all I knew about our regiment, its billets, its periods of rest, its history during the war, its superior officers, and much more that I did not know myself. Then he asked me where our guns were. Not knowing where they actually were, I was afraid to do more than smile, asking him if he really expected me to tell him, for I might have spoken the truth out of sheer ignorance!

So far as I could see he knew everything there was to be known except the exact position of our artillery. What puzzled him was, I found, not facts, but motives.

Why, he asked, had the Australians attacked at Laventie in July?

'A raid,' I suggested.

'But you used two divisions' he almost shouted, 'two divisions!'

'Oh, we have plenty of men,' I replied airily.

But he got his own back when I mentioned my suspicion that they were holding this part of the line with very few troops.

'Oh, we have plenty of men here,' he retorted, 'plenty of men; didn't you find them?'

My first night of captivity was spent in a rather large loft over one of the outer buildings. It was both dry and clean. Several German soldiers slept in the same room, and I must not omit to mention gratefully my first and last decent meal as a prisoner of war; sausage, brown bread, and beer being supplied me.

Early the next morning I was taken by train to Douai and lodged in the barracks. There, alone in a lousy little room for (I believe) ten days, I had leisure to think—to think.

All my previous experience of captivity had been so strange and hasty, so kaleidoscopic, that I hardly realized that I was a prisoner.

It was as though I had dropped in to see a lot of rather eccentric strangers, and would presently go back to my friends to laugh over my experiences. I had talked and acted in a queer dream-world, and all the time, interested but slightly incredulous, stood behind myself.

Now I had time to reflect on the reality of it all. 'By God,' I spoke suddenly to the room, 'they've got me!'

Everything,—room, lice, solitude, dirty black bread, bowl of brown disgusting soup—corroborated the statement. I was a prisoner. I should be reported missing. My mother would be duly notified, and would grieve, not knowing whether I was alive or dead. My friends in the regiment would go out to look for me. Possibly they would get killed searching. It was horrible—horrible.

Again and again I asked myself if I could in any way have avoided being taken. Again and again, wise after the event, I discovered ways in which I might have done so. Oh, why did I risk getting into that trench at all? Why, why did I never guess that there were Germans inside that damned shelter which had been my hope of cover when I heard footsteps behind me? and so on and so on—the whole torturing cycle of vain questions which come tormenting prisoners at such a time, and even long after, as they prowl round and round their wire cages, and long after that too, when they have arrived, by various roads, at the truth of the whole matter, which is, 'I being I, and the circumstances being what they were at the time, it was quite unavoidable.'

In such straits I found some comfort in writing the

poem later included in my book, 'Gloucestershire Friends,' under the title of 'Solitary Confinement.'

It was done in pencil on the flyleaf of an old French book which I had discovered lying in the cell.

As it is quoted in a later chapter of the book I will not give it here.

Afterwards I bribed the guards to buy me some writing-paper, and I wrote a long letter to my mother, carefully avoiding anything which might cause it not to be sent on by my captors; but it was kept back nevertheless, and arrived about a month after the letter which I wrote from Gütersloh.

In the cell next to mine was, I discovered, a French girl. When the guards were not about we were able to talk a little. I pushed her my last cigarette through the keyhole, and received therefrom in return her best thanks. She had been put there, she said, a week ago, for distributing cakes to hungry British prisoners who were being brought through the streets. It was a custom of hers to do so.

How long was she to be imprisoned? She did not know: she must trust in the good God. That was about the extent of our conversation, and I never saw her.

Once I harboured an unworthy suspicion that she might be a spy put there to gain information which the Germans had not been able to extract; but she never asked any questions, and I am ashamed that I doubted her.

Suspicion and a morbid distaste for talk are things quickly acquired by a prisoner of war.

I lay on my bed reading a trench-soiled Shakespeare which had been everywhere with me since I came out first in 1915.

I learned several of the sonnets by heart, forgetting for a

while the lice which bothered me. When darkness fell and I could no longer read, it became more difficult to forget, but fortunately it had always been my rule since I did much patrol-work to carry in my pocket sufficient morphia to finish myself off in the event of my being left out in No Man's Land, a dying torment to myself and a living danger to such as might be tempted to drag me in.

This morphia I took in small doses sufficient to induce a nightly forgetfulness of my troubles, physical and mental.

Shakespeare for the light, morphia for the night, was my motto at Douai for ten days.

On two occasions English aeroplanes came over the town. The guards got very excited and threatened shooting when I cheered from the window. Anti-aircraft drove the aeroplanes off.

On the eighth day was brought into the barracks an English patrol which had been captured.

X, an officer in the R.B., shared my room for two nights, and then we were all sent off together into Germany. The two guards who were in charge of X and me were good fellows. Both had been to the front. I believe it is not usually the front line men who hate, ill-treat, and kill prisoners, except when frenzied with battle-excitement, or under pressure of cold necessity. The farther you get from the front line the worse become the people, until upon the mixen of a *gefangenenlager* you discover the maggots of Europe. That at least has been my experience.

I was to meet at Gütersloh many officers captured at Mons and early in the war, who had been struck, spat upon, and herded for days, whole and wounded indiscriminately, in cattle-trucks, not being permitted to go outside even to perform the natural functions of the body. But times had changed.

Now the Somme offensive was going steadily on, and though it is characteristic of most people to bully when they are on top and to whine when they are under dog, it is very specially a German trait. Civilians glowered at us, but they did not spit; nor were we molested by them or by soldiers during our long journey.

After the English soldiers and their guards had split away from us—I believe at Cologne—we travelled (for the most part by ourselves) in a clean, comfortable carriage, and when towards the end of our weary travel we were compelled to enter a carriage of German soldiers, not one of them did more than stare at us.

Our guards, too, were quite ready to buy us food where possible, at a slight, profit to themselves, and to chat amiably about anything, including the war.

One of them knew a little English. He described and vividly illustrated a bombing raid he had taken part in somewhere near Armentieres.

'We throw. They throw. Zip! Zip! Bong! Bong! Oh, malade!'

His Iron Cross had been earned for patrol-work on the Russian front. He was a dapper little man, and looked more like a Frenchman than a German.

The Russian front was, he said, better than the French; but notwithstanding that, he concluded that 'krieg' was 'nix gut.' His countrymen in general were of a different belief, or concealed their feelings very successfully, to judge by the train-loads of singing soldiers we saw. They had decorated engine, carriages, and trucks with green branches, and were obviously possessed of fine physique and morale. They cheered and laughed and went by.

I thought of them at the front, killing and being killed, and wondered when, though not how, it would all end. My guard was wondering the same thing apparently. 'Deutschland kaput. France kaput. Russia kaput. England kaput. Alles kaput!' was his desperate verdict.

The one thing we found impossible was to convince either of our guards that Germany was not fighting a defensive war.

Germany, they said and believed, was the victim of a plot. . . . Such is the power of the German Press!

We arrived at Gütersloh, the first and best of the seven prisons I was to experience, about three o'clock on the second morning of our wearisome travel. With electric lamps shining at regular intervals, along the barbed-wire surrounding it, it looked a clean large place, and in fact was, being an unused lunatic asylum, built with a typical Teutonic care for health and cleanliness. We were marched into quarantine, buildings wired and boarded off from the rest of the camp, and being dead tired immediately fell asleep upon or under those queer soft bags with which all the German beds are covered. On awaking we found two more new prisoners in the room—airmen. One had been brought down on the land and the other in the sea. The latter (and younger) was still inclined to be annoyed with the Germans for putting three-inch shells at him when he was in the water, and for marching him naked through the streets of Ostend after he had been taken out. They were bad sportsmen (how delightfully British!), and he had told them so.

2

GÜTERSLOH

'Walking round our cages like the lions at the Zoo,
  We think of things that we have done, and things we mean to do:
  Of girls we left behind us, of letters that are due,
  Of boating on the river beneath a sky of blue,
  Of hills we climbed togetherɪ—not always for the view.

'Walking round our cages like the lions at the Zoo,
  We see the phantom faces of you, and you, and you,
  Faces of those we loved or loathed—oh, everyone we knew!
  And deeds we wrought in carelessness for happiness or rue;
  And dreams we broke in folly, and seek to build anew—
  Walking round our cages like the lions at the Zoo.'

GÜTERSLOH IS A HEALTHY spot in Westphalia, 'on sandy soil,' and all that sort of thing; but I'm not writing a guide-book.

The camp as seen from quarantine—and indeed from anywhere else—represented a large pine-shadowed cage. Round it, generally in couples, prowled the prisoners, a mixed community of English, French, Russians, Belgians, Irish, Scotch, and representatives of the colonies classed

45

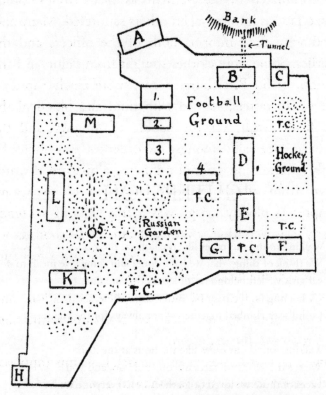

SKETCH OF GÜTERSLOH CAMP.
(Dotted areas represent pinewoods.)

REFERENCES

A.	Camp Offices	*L.*	Russian House.
B.	English House.	*M.*	Civilians.
C.	Mixed House.	*T.C.*	Tennis Courts.
D.	Russian House.		
E.	Russian and Overflow.	*1.*	Canteen. Restaurant, and Kitchen.
F.	French House.	*2.*	Dining Hall.
G.	French House.	*3.*	Laundry, Theatre, Parcel Office
H.	Quarantine and Prison.	*4.*	Private Kitchens.
K.	English House.	*5.*	Band-stand.

indiscriminately by the Germans as 'black troops.' Some walked fast, as if for a wager; others sauntered. Many and varied were the uniforms both of the officers and the orderlies. Some wore clothes straight from tailors in Paris, London, or St. Petersburg. Some, more newly captured, were yet in tatters, stained with mud and blood of the battlefield. Great was the babble of tongues, and the language, especially amongst the orderlies, was often of a highly entertaining description, being a mixture of words drawn from all the various languages of the camp.

'Après la bloody krieg,' was a fragment of a French orderly's conversation, overheard almost as soon as we arrived. He was arguing with a German, and I feel sure that the German understood.

After baths, fumigation, medical examination, and more questions, we were released from quarantine and given rooms in the main camp.

Here is a little sketch of Gütersloh Camp (opposite page), which is easier to draw than to describe.

The barracks of the various nations were separate, but overflowed into another building, to which I was detailed. I slept in a large room accommodating also Russians and French, sixteen of us in all. Their unwillingness to open any of the windows was my only real objection to the place, but I was nevertheless glad to be moved across to the British barrack a week or so later.

Comradeship is, on looking back, undoubtedly the best and most salient feature of my prison days, and especially is this true of Gütersloh. Yet comradeship was not particularly in evidence during the first three or four weeks, except of the sort indicated by Mr. Bernard's drawing. All the foreigners were most anxious to learn English, and a new arrival was simply mobbed by them as soon as he entered the camp.

Later on I was myself to experience the green mouldiness consequent on captivity (besides, the English are naturally reticent), yet I was surprised, and thought it strange at the time, that the first friendly advance should come from a Russian, who offered me his deck-chair whenever I cared to sit out-of-doors.

New arrivals were not ignored by the British. There was a system whereby they were fed (German food being totally inadequate) until their own parcels began to arrive. Clothes, too, were served out to those who seemed in need. And there were invitations to tea with senior officers and officials.

Such preliminaries accomplished, however, one was dropped like a hot coal—for a time, that is, until one had proved oneself.

It was the prison equivalent of that characteristically English custom, 'eating one's way into mess.'

Thus for about three weeks after arrival we were suffered to wander about the camp, and round and round the wire, while not a soul spoke to us save in the voice of officialdom. I am convinced that there was no intentional unkindness in this. It was just the national tradition.

At Gütersloh, the inevitable battle of Regulars versus New Army had been settled sensibly and for ever; and let me add that the settlement was due very largely to one or two (not senior) *Regular officers*. But in this matter the attitude of Regulars, Terriers, and Kitchener's Army, was identical. A polite but icy demeanour was generally

"WILL YOU TEACH ME THE ENGLISH—YES?" A NEW
ARRIVAL AND THE FOREIGN OFFICERS.

acknowledged to be the bearing proper towards new prisoners.

It was for them to break the ice or thaw it, and it usually took about a month to accomplish.

For myself the time was a little less, because I was able fortunately to approach the task from several sides.

'What use are you to this camp?' That was the unasked question which had to be answered by every new arrival.

It was hard, rank Socialism, but very successful. You lived for the State, not for yourself.

Could you write? There were two camp papers needing contributors. Could you sing? There were concerts. Could you play games? The inter-barrack matches would give you the opportunity. Could you act? There was the little home-made theatre built to produce little home-made plays. Could you drink? There was the canteen, and those birthday evenings.

Something you *must* do to keep the life of the camp alight. *Something* you must do, or be damned.

Chesterton's drinking songs set to homely tunes enabled me first to gain admittance into society. After that I wrote poems, essays, and reviews (both of the English and American variety), played hockey, lectured, and attended cheery evenings with consistent regularity.

'The Poet' was my camp title, and though my duties were held to include the writing of topical verses to order, and the carrying to their dreadful conclusions half-recollected songs of George Robey's, I know that never again in this life shall I hold so high and happy a position amid my fellows.

But there were other activities open to or incumbent

upon one besides those binding one to the camp, and first and foremost among these was that binding one to one's country—escape.

It is true that the most dreadful part of captivity is not its physical hardship. In any well-conducted camp, where men are working properly together, and parcels are arriving regularly, the hardship is certainly less than that endured by a soldier in the field. There are exceptions to this, of course, and they occur mainly in men's *lagers,* but these have received sufficient Press notoriety. Generally speaking, the bitter cross of captivity does not lie in any physical hardship.

Hardships there were, and it was no fault of the Germans that they were not double as many! Hardship is a condition of the soldier's life in or out of prison. He is ready to put up with it.

When he grouses it is because it is unevenly distributed.

Comparing his case with that of German prisoners in England he is annoyed; not that he would wish his own country to sink to the Hun level! Therefore he grouses, but puts up with things cheerfully enough.

The whole sting of his position, that which makes it so intolerable, is quite another matter. His friends and brothers are 'out there' killing and being killed. *He* cannot help them. He is futile. He cannot join any more in that dreadful and glorious fight for England and her liberty. Yes, he is futile. There is no more terrible reflection for a man.

He may be a prisoner through no fault of his own. He may have endured much hard fighting prior to capture. He may have carried himself bravely, won coveted distinctions, and so forth. He may have already 'done his bit,' to quote that foolish and vulgar phrase. The 'bit' is not enough. The 'bit 'is *never* done. England is still fighting. Her enemies are still unbroken. *He* is idle. That is the essence of his trouble, the true agony of the prisoner-state.

To walk round and round a wire cage with this thought in your brain, knowing nothing of what is happening at the front save what may be culled from the German reports; knowing nothing save that at best all is in doubt; knowing nothing but that one is powerless, shut up, futile; hearing reports of British and French reverses, revolution in Russia—this is flaming hell!

I do not know what can be worse than to be kept idle in company of such thoughts. And this is precisely what is done to us. Herein at least soldiers, brutally forced to work in factories or salt-mines, or more pleasantly on farms, score over their officers compelled to idleness, except they make employment for themselves and for one another. 'God give me forgetfulness!' has been the prayer of many a man driven morbid and mad by this terrible inactivity: and in some cases the prayer has been answered.

Doctors cannot tell us the cause of barbed-wire disease, but scientific proofs are hardly necessary to show that minds so wrought upon are unlikely to retain their normal balance.

Escape is no simple matter even to men working on farms near the frontier. To officers more closely guarded in strong prisons, hundreds of kilometres away, it is very much more difficult. On arriving at Gütersloh I was told that from this camp only one officer, a Russian, had ever succeeded in getting 'away and over.' The prisoners, and especially the Russians, said the interpreter, frequently tried, but were always caught and punished for their foolishness, in addition to getting restrictions put upon the freedom of the camp generally. The Russians were particularly foolish. The French also occasionally so . . . 'And the English?' I inquired. 'Ah, they are good—so—like sheep.'

It would probably have surprised this insolent Hun to learn how at that time certain of the sheep were patiently engaged night after night in driving a tunnel from under their fold, a tunnel which would, when completed, be sufficient to liberate half the camp.

3

TUNNELS

IT WAS CHARACTERISTIC OF the Russians that they 'took no thought for the morrow,' and escaped out of the camp however and whenever possible, without adequate preparations for travel or a clear idea of where the frontier was to be crossed.

It was characteristic of the French to be more deliberate, but yet to follow the nearest road and mar the success of a venture by impetuosity.

It was characteristic of the British to allow themselves to be thought sheep while they worked night after night, for months driving their tunnel.

It was very characteristic of the Germans completely to misunderstand this apparent tranquillity, and to taunt them with it.

The main British tunnel (for there were several) started from a disused cellar beneath the English barrack.

The Germans may possibly have suspected that the

cellar was being used for illegal purposes, for on two occasions they caused suspension of the work, and the second time by means of heavy concrete.

But they had reckoned without their host, or more accurately without their 'guests.'

A dinner knife and infinite perseverance persuaded one of the heavy granite steps leading to the cellar to slide to and from its place. From beneath these steps work was again begun, and continued with interruptions for over nine months.

Tunnelling was at first carried on only at night, but it was afterwards considered safer as well as more convenient to post sentries and have day shifts.

A certain whistle or a few bars of a song was sufficient warning that the Huns had finished dinner or were in any way dangerous.

Progress was necessarily very slow, because it was not possible to work more than a couple of hours each day, and because the digging implements were improvised out of wood and bits of iron discovered in the camp. The roof of the tunnel was supported with bed-boards and the wood of packing-cases bringing food to the camp. These cases were retained by the Germans, but were constantly stolen back out of the parcel office. The periodic disappearance of bed-boards, and consequent discomfort of that sleeper from whose bed they were abstracted, was indication that a further few feet of tunnelling had been completed.

Abstracted sand was carried away in home-made bags and dribbled about the camp from under cover of Burberrys at dusk when the wearers took their exercise. It was also found that the Church of England chapel, being unused during the weekdays, made a very excellent place of storage. Between the roof and the rafters there must now be several tons of sand waiting the hour when they shall fall upon the heads of a congregation of lunatics to convince them of the Day of Judgment.

Moreover, the discovery by the Germans of one or two tunnels less cunningly concealed was of advantage in this single sense, that it undoubtedly accounted for some of that sand which must occasionally have struck the notice of the dullest sentry, as being of a different and darker colour than that which covered the ground round about it.

The underground shift consisted of five men, and their order down the tunnel was as follows:

No. 1, the digger.
No. 2, the man behind the digger.
No. 3, the pitman.
No. 4, the sandbagger.
No. 5, the fanman.

Their functions are pretty clearly indicated by their names. No. 1 dug out the sand, stabbing the tunnel with the sharpened leg of an iron bedstead. It was found that this implement had in nine months worn down several inches!

No. 2 knelt behind No. 1, raking back the loosened sand and putting it on 'Westward Ho!' which was the name given to a small sledge fitted with wooden runners, which No. 3 dragged painfully on hands and knees to the shaft where No. 4 packed the sand in bags ready to be disposed of. The fanman worked the fan, keeping the air fresh and cool in the tunnel.

The tunnel was carefully designed to end outside the

wire on the opposite side of a high bank standing in the shadow of pine-trees about forty yards away. Between this bank and the wire was the German sentry's beat, and great care had to be taken that he should not guess what was going on beneath his feet. This necessitated a system of telegraphy from the English observation post to the digger at the end of the tunnel, notifying him when he must stop working and when he might go on with it, for the sentry was continually walking backwards and forwards over him.

Especial care had to be taken in roofing also, for if the German sentry should slip through, the tunnel would be discovered and months of labour be made vain. Also it was the malicious custom of Huns on the discovery of a tunnel to fire down it, a proceeding likely to entail unpleasant consequences to the digger, the man behind the digger, the pitman, the sandbagger, old Uncle Tom Cobbleigh and all!

Great delay and difficulty in working was occasioned by the heavy rain and snow of Christmas, 1916, which caused the tunnel to fill with water and to threaten complete subsidence, which latter was, however, averted by dint of much hard and ingenious labour on the part of R. and his followers. About this time the underground workers would arrive up dripping with water and fairly caked with mud, which fortunately could generally be brushed off as soon as dry.

The P.T. (such was the title of the tunnelling party, which had originated in a small characteristic joke and stood for 'Pink toe,' not 'Party of tunnellers') was frequently troubled by the unwelcome attentions of strangers, and very especially by those of a German of such gloomy demeanour as to entitle him to the name of 'Mouldy Death.' Therefore it was with particular pleasure that a member of the party, finding him on an eve in a drunken and sombre sleep amid the pine-trees, emptied over his face the whole contents of his sandbag, and vanished.

A P.T. diary during the winter and autumn months of 1916 would, I know, be full of most exciting and humorous reading, and it is a matter of keen regret that I have not been able to come by one. How, when Huns were momentarily expected, old P. got stuck in the exit and could move neither out nor in; how O. and Ony, the two strongest but shortest-tempered men of the party, were followed and made carry hundredweights of sand round and round the camp beneath their Burberrys; how old P. diverted the attention of the stolid youth who strolled in upon them round a corner at the very moment when the step was being shoved back into its place: these are things which I crave to hear related in the words of those most intimately concerned. Alas! It is not possible.

It was expected that the tunnel would be finished early in the spring of 1917, when travelling would be more convenient and cover more plentiful, and by the end of March it was within a few yards of completion.

Its existence was not suspected by the German authorities, for the general behaviour of the P.T. did not subject its members to any suspicion. They continued deliberately to play games, and to take prominent parts in the social, intellectual, and artistic activities of camp life. To these we will now turn, leaving the P.T. and its subsequent fortunes for a later chapter.

4

LECTURES

THE British Amateur Dramatic Society, having pressed into service as scene-painters such artists (professional and amateur) as the camp possessed, and as manager of lights, stage carpenter, dresser, prompter, etc., such other gentlemen as seemed by nature or experience especially fitted for such tasks, decided to give a really magnificent production of 'You Never Can Tell.'[1] But first a Shavian interest must be created in the camp.

The Lectures Committee took up the cue, and W., one of the most interesting and industrious men in the camp, schoolmaster, Scottish international, delightful companion, who added to his tunnelling activity a class of Russians, part management of games, and joint editorship of one of the prison papers—W., I say, came forward with a fine appreciative lecture on G.B.S.

I regret I cannot quote it instead of my own to illus-

1 [Publisher's note] *You Never Can Tell* (1896). a comedy by George Bernard Shaw that covered the issues of 'feminism and the Church.'

trate the flavour of our prison lectures. W. has disappeared
since the Armistice to the aid of his friends, the Russians.
There is no old prisoner I want more to meet, so if he
should ever see these lines let him note the fact and visit
me at Minsterworth in Gloucestershire. Meanwhile, all I
can produce as a sample is (I hope he won't mind)

'THE CASE AGAINST BERNARD SHAW.'

'*Introduction.*—I must apologize for beginning this lecture
with a few remarks which have, so you may think, little to
do with my subject.

'If this war were over and we were at home, about this
time I should probably have put on my heavy boots and
be tramping along one of those little Gloucestershire roads
which I know so well.

'Facing the sunset, I should be making towards a hill
which is as romantic as its name. I should probably be
singing (softly or loudly, as I pleased), for in my county,
and more especially in such parts of it as are remote from
those ulcers of civilization, the great towns, it is possible
for a man to sing along the highway without provoking
the astonishment of passers-by and the unwelcome atten-
dance of that blue puritanical figure, the policeman.

'So I should take my way, and when I had gained the
summit of the hill I should rest a bit, watching the sun go
down in a great ball of fire. But I should not wait till it had
disappeared. While the front of my hill was yet splashed
with sunset, and the reverse slope a maze of purple shadows,
I should pass downward to a little house which is called
the Red Lion. As I went, white-tailed rabbits would flash

and disappear like Nature's witty and whimsical thoughts, and in the last notes of the birds I should find expressed the contentment and quiet joy which are in Nature's heart.

'I should go down to the little inn, and I should call to the landlord, "Bill Harry, bring me some of your oldest beer in one of your largest tankards!—and if there is one who would care to drink with me, why, bring him the same and we will sit down together." So we would sit down, talking of the things we knew. We should not discuss doubts nor problems; still less should we mention those books about problems written by women who ought to have been men, or men who ought to have been women.

'But having talked of such things and such fields and such men as we had known, we should doubtless sing a song or two, songs old and born in the county? or perhaps, by way of change, a newer song I myself had made up about the good cider and perry to be found in the little village of Minsterworth close by.

'Then when we had had enough of good songs and good beer—which you would say was impossible, but I must disagree, since there is and must be a time for all things—I should again take the road. If it were an autumn evening such as this, the delicate ferns of the frost would lie spread: the road would echo to the heel, and the hollow sky should echo a song as I inarched.

'And when I had got home, why, I might sit awhile trying to make a poem out of the sunset I had seen, or the silver-tailed rabbits, or the mauve shadows on the hillside, or the flowers of the cold which bloom in the mud of the road, or the jolly talk at the inn—all, or any of these; or I might do an even wiser thing, and go straight to bed.

'You will think that this has nothing at all to do with Bernard Shaw. You are mistaken. Attitude is the essential thing in criticism. A man's first duty in lecturing is to get his audience looking at the subject through the same microscope or telescope as himself. Whether that telescope or microscope is a right one or a wrong one is another matter, and one that the audience must decide for itself.

'Now my attitude towards such things as "the life force," "the superman," "the new woman," and all other newnesses of Shavian creation, is this—such things are less important than a single sunset, less worthy of deep, thoughtful consideration than the scarlet cup of one poppy.

'Yet because a man never cuts himself away from his own age without maiming himself; because it is not good for man to live alone, especially in belief; and because he is ever more himself in company of his fellows—for these reasons, I think that whatever problems and questions perplex and, vex our age should vex and perplex each man of us until we have arrived at decisions. After that we may keep them in mind or put them out of it, following the way of our hearts.

'This being so, the study of Bernard Shaw is especially valuable, since upon him the idiosyncrasies of this age hang thick and black like hats on a hat-stand.

'Now it is easy to sneer at Shaw, but it is not so easy to disprove what he says. And it is the more difficult thing which I prefer to attempt to-day.

'*Three Different Attitudes to Shaw.*—There are a good many people who dislike Shaw and call him insincere, egotistical, and unscrupulous, but who at the same time believe (however reluctantly) much of what he teaches.

'"Awful chap!" one can imagine such a man soliloquizing, "but I suppose there must be something in what the damned fellow says. I never did believe in marriage myself."

'Now my own attitude to Shaw is exactly opposite to that. I respect Bernard Shaw as a gentleman. How angry he would be to hear me say it! ('Sir, to be facetious, it is not necessary to be obscene!') Yet if a gentleman be one whose courtesies are not regulated by his interests (and that is, I think, the best definition I have heard), then Shaw is most certainly one, for neither his courtesies nor his discourtesies are regulated by his interests, or ever have been. I respect him (this he might not dislike so much) as a fearless, sincere man, full of almost savage love for humanity—love which takes the form of beating it to school against its will, and often in hours when humanity and (I must confess) I myself also consider that it might well be engaged in healthy games and innocent amusement.

'For Shaw as a man I have only admiration. For his philosophy, his idiotic Life Force, his absurd Superman, his silly disregard of all which has survived the test of time, I have only abomination.

'Most people detest Shaw but think that he is right. I like Shaw but know that he is wrong.

'When I say that most people think Shaw is right, I refer to the inhabitants of a rather small and fashionable world whom, for want of a better term, we will call the intellectual aristocrats.

'There is a larger world of simpler people—a world upon which the fashionable Shavian intellect is accustomed to throw contempt; a world from which we, if we

are fortunate, will take the greater number of our friends—
the world of "the average man."

'Now the average man (we must use this expression for
want of a better) does not know much about Shaw, and
certainly does not start with any prejudice against him;
yet commonly, when he reads Shaw's books, hears his
speeches and sees his plays, he is intensely irritated. Nor
is this irritation that of the schoolboy being "told off," but
rather, I think, lies in the fact that, feeling himself quite
incapable of bowling out Shaw on his own pitch (I mean
of meeting his clever arguments with better ones), he is
yet convinced that some of those detested conventions
and many of those detested dogmas which Bernard Shaw
dismisses so neatly are not getting fair play.

'Thus, while his intellect is forcibly convinced, his heart
is not. Why is this? I have an explanation. It is the subject
of this lecture. Whether or not it is the true explanation
you will decide for yourselves.

'Analysis of the Shavian Attitude.—Let us examine the
character and opinions of Shaw as shown in his work.
That is the only fair way to judge any artist, and it is a particularly good way of judging Shaw. He is so very personal
in his art. Even his dramas are full of himself. Shakespeare
merges himself in the characters he creates: it is impossible
to discover his personal opinions. But you have only to
read a play by Shaw to find out exactly what he thinks
of all his characters, himself, you, the Prime Minister,
and everybody else. Far be it from me to quibble about
objective and subjective art. Let us be grateful for good,
clean, witty plays, however they come to us. Shaw's plays
are always clean, generally good, invariably witty, and they

reveal a good deal of the author which is entirely to our present purpose.

'Probably the most noticeable thing in Shaw's work is something to which I have already referred. I mean his attitude to the average man. Roughly it amounts to this, that the average person is always a fool, generally a knave, and, if an Englishman, also a hypocrite. I do not think Shaw hates him. He does despise him. This accounts for two more things: (1) Shaw's disbelief in democracy, and (2) his belief in the superman. But it is in itself accounted for by something very much bigger, very much more important, very much more significant—I mean the fact that Shaw is, both in the wide and in the narrow sense of the word, anti-Catholic.'

'It is amusing to hear people refer to Shaw as an immoral influence. He is the most moral thing in existence, a Puritan. It is funny to hear Shaw called modern. He is about the oldest thing in history, a heretic. And this Puritanism or heresy, if you so regard it, is the key to his life, the foundation of his views, the explanation of his attitudes to nature, to man, and to God.

'A Puritan is a man afraid of his passions, striving to regard everything by the light of reason *and only by that light*. He may have very fine reasoning powers: Shaw has. He may see things very clearly: Shaw does. The Puritan is a man who sees things through one window only. But Life has many windows.

> '"Within this dim five-windowed house of sense
>   I watch through coloured glass
>   The shapes that pass.
>   Soon must I journey hence,

> To meet the great winds of the outer world
> And see,
> When God has turned the key,
> The true and terrible colours of that scheme
> Which now I dream."

'And besides these five windows of the *senses*, and the clear glass window of *reason*, there is also *tradition*, a window which looks out upon the past, and the window of *faith* which faces the future.

'Now, since by use of all these windows it is impossible to know God's mysteries, manifestly it is yet more impossible so to do by looking through one window only. But that is just what the Puritan tries to do. He tries to put God into his brain. But God (Who made the brain) is too big to go in.

'That is what Shaw tries to do. In his revolt against "the superstition and sentimentality of the Victorian era" (*vide* newspaper) he will trust and accept nothing of which his own clear intellect does not assure him.

'So it is not very wonderful that with all his great intellectual powers and strong sincerity of purpose he should often fall short of the average man in wisdom.

'It is not wonderful that he should fall shorter than the average man in understanding mankind. That sympathy with human nature, that love of men as they are, which Shakespeare possessed so abundantly, Shaw does not possess at all. Whereas Shakespeare enjoyed men, Shaw only enjoys improving them; and the irony of the situation is that the poet without any apparent attempt does improve them, when Shaw, deeply conscious of his duty to do the same, as often as not only succeeds in annoying them. It could hardly be otherwise! In the intensely concentrated light of his intellect, God has dwindled out of personality. He has become "the Life Force." It is always dull work being reformed. Men only suffer it for the sake of someone whom they love. How can one love a "Life Force"? When the history of this age comes to be written I believe the most extraordinary phenomenon will seem to be the fading out of men's belief in God's personality.

'Not only Shaw, but most clever men of our time, together with many who are not at all clever, have chosen to put personality out of mind. It is supposed (goodness knows why!) to be scientific. The adoption in theory at any rate of Christian morality, and the scrapping of Christian tradition, is an illustration. How utterly absurd it is! Why, personality is simply everything. How can a man be moved by anything else? It is the essence of attraction in God and man. The personality of Christ drew all men to Him and enabled Him to perform miracles. It is the personality of men and of women which makes us love them and willing to do anything for them. It is the personality of God which is behind evolution in the plan of the world.

'Men talk of evolution as if it were the motive rather than the manner of life. But evolution is no more than a great clock devised long ago in the imagination of God and wound up by His hand.

'This inability to realize any more than the brain shows is the chief characteristic of all Puritanism. It is the same disease which prevents a man from drinking wine with his fellows, loving beauty, daring to trust his own senses. It is the foundation of the Shavian philosophy. It accounts for Shaw's contempt for the average man. It accounts for

Shaw's inability to appreciate marriage as a sacrament. It accounts for Shaw's distrust of democracy. It accounts for Shaw's dislike of romance.'

'*Some Things which the Average Man knows and which Shaw does not.*—It has been pointed out that most of Shaw's failures are due to ignorance of things which the average man knows quite well. Shaw knows many things which the average man does not; but there are a number of things, simple but important, which the average man knows, but which Shaw, in spite of his intellect—perhaps because of it—does not.'

'The man in the street knows perfectly well that Wednesday is not necessarily a better day than Tuesday, nor Saturday than Friday. But Shaw thinks that modern things are necessarily better than the old things.'

'When Shaw joined the Socialist party he was considered a great asset, and so he was intellectually. In those days the movement was revolutionary, virile, full of a generous passion for humanity and of faith in its destiny. Illogical as were its views, vague as were its aims, Socialism yet possessed a personality passionate and romantic. Consequently it possessed a popular appeal. The world's attitude towards it was, generally speaking, this: "Socialism does much credit to the hearts of those who hold it as a creed, but very little credit to their heads. It is ideal, but alas! it is unpractical. The present system is not ideal but it works." Bernard Shaw changed all this, and in characteristic fashion. He did not fall to proclaiming the rights of man, the hatefulness of tyranny. To people who remarked gravely that the present system was not ideal but it worked, Shaw replied just as calmly, "It does not work," and proceeded to prove it.'

'He was more than their match. His cold reasoning cut through their armour like cold steel. His sharp wit pierced their complacency like a sharp dagger. His epigrams dazzled their eyes. They fled to science, and found that Shaw knew more about it than they did. They took refuge behind economics, and Shaw was again their master.'

'The Socialist party almost screamed with delight. It saw Shaw as a Perseus descending from heaven to rescue their fair Andromeda from that acquiescence in evil which was threatening to devour her. And it is to Shaw's great honour that he did succeed in killing the beast of complacency, or at least in driving it to hiding. But—alas for the Socialist party!—the same dazzling stroke which accomplished the deed also cut off the head of poor Andromeda. The final result of his valour was to turn Socialism from the living and passionate thing it was into a cold problem of the intellect. He found it captive but alive. He left it freed, but a corpse.'

'The leaders of the Socialist party discovered too late that corpses could not fascinate and were not popular. To Bernard Shaw it is due that the Socialist movement in England is what it is to-day. I never think of it but my mind turns to a stanza from "The Ballad of Reading Gaol"':

> "'Each man kills the thing he loves—
> By all let this be heard;
> Some do it with a bitter look,
> Some with a flattering word;
> The coward does it with a kiss,
> The brave man with a sword."

'Certainly Shaw killed the thing he loved. Certainly he did so like a brave man with a sword —the sword of his hard, keen intellectualism. The basilisk eyes of his brain, with power to change a personal God into an impersonal force and to dehumanize man into superman, had turned Socialism, from the breathing, passionate thing that it was, into a puzzling piece of intellectual machinery. Its personality is gone, and with that all its fascination and appeal. It is due to Shaw that everybody now knows Socialism to be a perfectly practical remedy. It is due to Shaw that nearly everybody thinks it a bad remedy—or rather, the beginning of a new disease.

'Another thing which Shaw seems not to understand so well as the average man is the singular truth that two and two do not always make four. Shaw believes it possible to produce supermen in the same way as we produce prize dogs. For the good of mankind he would introduce a human stud. It is not immorality, but inefficiency, and in addition a sense of humour, which would make the scheme impracticable. The fathers and mothers of geniuses have almost invariably been ordinary people. This leads us on to Shaw's idea of marriage. Marriage is, Shaw considers, a rather poor economic arrangement for populating the world.

'The average man, both because he has not the faintest doubt that the world would be populated without marriage, and also because he is at heart, in spite of special creeds, a Catholic, cannot look on marriage in that way. He is compelled to regard it as a sacrament. Shaw cannot possibly regard it as a sacrament, since the sacramental idea (which is founded on faith) is outside the intellectual pale.

'Here, I think, the average man shows more wisdom than Shaw. And I believe also that he is nearer to wisdom in looking upon love as a romance rather than a business. Shaw looks upon it as a business—a bad business.'

'To the average man one woman at least is a princess. To work for her is his romance. It has been said that if Shaw were to rescue a princess it would not be from motives of romance but on principles of economy. My own belief is that Shaw would never rescue a princess. He would not rescue a princess because he would never see one. What he would see would be a female citizen, and in tenderly urging her to perform her duties to the State he would certainly address her as comrade and not as darling.'

'This brings us naturally to the superman. Shaw wants supermen because he has lost faith in democracy, which, he holds, is not able ever to "rise above the level of its material."'

'To this I have two things to say: (1) By 'level' do you mean level of intellect? If so, I must submit that intellect is not the whole nor the better part of the material of democracy. (2) Whatever you mean by level, I deny the proposition. Democracy can and in many cases has risen above itself—*e.g.*, the French Revolution, and the abolition of slavery in the face of big vested interests. There are times when a crowd is greater than any of its component parts; when its soul is, on a gust of high feeling, whirled to ends far greater than anything it could intellectually conceive.

'As to the superman, we have at last to decide what sort of thing he is going to be, and I am not certain that the being Shaw has in mind is a person the rest of the world would at all care to live with. Therefore the idea that they should proceed to manufacture him is unreasonable. But were he ever so desirable, I believe it is impossible to produce him in the prize-dog way. The only way to make the world better is to make ourselves better. People will be changed gradually by the influence of personality administered through religion, through life, and through art.'

'Shaw despises art, but no cold reasoning will turn the world from its ways as art is able; and Shaw is glad enough to use it while he affects depreciation. Man does not live by bread alone, but chiefly by dreams. The first thing to do is to supply the world with fine dreams. Of them will be fashioned destiny.'

'Pleasure in art should be a by-product, thinks Shaw. But pleasure is of many kinds. There is the pleasure of the pig eating its food. There is also the pleasure of a man uplifted by a poem or a piece of music. There is the beauty of the flesh. There is the beauty of holiness.'

'I believe that art without pleasure is not art. Whether the laughing pleasure of Shakespeare's comedies, the terrible pleasure of Shakespeare's tragedies, the high romantic pleasures of poetry and music, of Coleridge and Chopin, in all great art is pleasure. The true aim of art should be to raise the standard of pleasure. A man may not add a cubit to his stature by taking thought. By the influence of pleasure he is radically altered, and in art gains such experiences as life has forgotten to give him. The beneficent pains and pleasures of tragedy and comedy are the growing pains and pleasures of the soul. Therefore the wisdom of art is steadfastly to perform its mission, and not to usurp the function of the pulpit. I have never heard a sermon to compare with the poetry of Shakespeare or the music of Bach.'

'To proceed, it is very characteristic of Shaw that he should imagine that the problem of prostitution is capable of being solved by adjustment of social relations, and the payment of a fair wage to women. It is typical of his keen sight, his fearlessness, and his limited vision. Many people never recognized the fact that women were being driven on to the streets because they were grossly underpaid. Shaw recognized it at once, and pointed it out with his usual fearlessness. But the problem will never be solved in the way he suggests. Prostitution would be stopped in the sense that a woman would not need to take any money: that is all there is to be said about it. Behind that evil is a far deeper one—harlotry. No adjustment of social relations will alter that. No payment to women of fair wages will reform it. It is in the soul, and will be driven out only by that which touches the soul. Indeed, Shaw himself must have realized the inefficiency of his remedy, since he refers somewhere, I think, to the band of enthusiastic amateurs.'

'Thus once more having detected evil by means of his keen sight, and exposed it with his fearless tongue, he fails to find a remedy by reason of that quality of mind to which I have already referred many times in this lecture.'

'A great bugbear to the average person is Shaw's attitude towards patriotism. Bernard Shaw is a Socialist. He thinks that patriotism depends on private ownership of land. Therefore he considers patriotism a bad thing. Against him are two classes of people (1) those who agree that patriotism does depend on the private ownership of land, but are not Socialists; (2) those, whether Socialists or not, who feel that patriotism does not depend on ownership of land, but is rather a passion whose root is in the soul. To this class I belong. I see Shaw's point of view; I admire his fearlessness in expressing it. And I think he is wrong. The fact that he is transparently sincere does not affect my opinion that he is wrong. The most sincere man I ever knew lived in a lunatic asylum. He sincerely believed himself to be a teapot. But he wasn't.'

'I confess that I consider a teapot quite as useful as a superman. It is not as a superman that I admire Bernard Shaw. It is as a sincere, courageous man. I admire his wit, his fearlessness in exposing evil, his cleverness in stabbing our complacency. Yet because of his outlook I cannot help believing that his opinion on any deep matter must necessarily be inconclusive or wrong.

'This is not an appreciative view of Shaw. I do not intend it to be. It is an attitude. And it is an attitude which enables one to read and admire while not agreeing. Also it is an examination of those beliefs and dogmas upon which such an attitude is based; I mean the beliefs and dogmas of the average man.'

'I have but one more thing to say. It is, as the lawyers say, of a personal nature. The other night, after killing some of the tedium of captivity during an evening with Russian friends, I returned to B house humming a song I had sung. Seeing a light in W's window, I went in. We discussed Shaw, and afterwards sang more songs. So it was that when I went to bed and fell into a dream the figure of Bernard Shaw came to visit me in this manner. I was sitting again with my friends, and D.S. had just ended a certain rollicking sea chorus which runs:

A - ro-ving! A - ro-ving! since ro-ving's been my ru - i - in, I'll
go no more a - ro - ving with you, fair maid!

when suddenly a knock sounded on the door, and before anyone could say "Come in," entered the tall figure of Bernard Shaw. Whereupon D.S. addressed him: "Hullo, old thing! Have a drink of bad mulled." Bernard Shaw strode across the room, and taking the wine D.S. offered, swallowed it to the last drop, after which he began to sing in a loud voice the chorus we had just finished. What followed after that I do not remember. Perhaps we spent a jolly evening and Shaw sang more songs; perhaps he disappeared as suddenly as he came. I only know that when I woke up in the morning I said to myself, "What a peculiar dream!" and thinking that Bernard Shaw would never have drunk that bad wine nor sung that nonsensical chorus, it suddenly occurred to me: "Why, I expect that is the very reason he cannot understand Englishmen." To Shaw that "bad mulled" would have been a drug, that rowdy chorus would have been mere vulgarity concerned with a rather confused sex problem. This bait of national rowdyism I fling out to be swallowed by those who do not like to consider themselves Catholic. At the bottom of my own heart I believe that Shaw's failure to understand certain phases of English character, and to appreciate common men in general, is due solely to the thing which accounts for all other of his failures—the thing which I have emphasized and perhaps over-emphasized all through this lecture of mine: I mean his anti-Catholicism.'

W.'s lecture and this reply of mine both appeared in *The Warren*, one of our prison papers.

The Shavian controversy spread. The case against Bernard Shaw, which I had already at W.'s request given to his class of Russians, was patiently translated by a Frenchman for *La Ronde*—'Bill Harry, apportez moi la plus grande bouteille,' etc. It was all very funny. But our object was attained. 'You Never Can Tell' was produced with very conspicuous success, although the scenery had all to be done again to fit a fresh stage, as we were suddenly moved to Crefeld.

The following fantastic snapshot of myself during the Shavian controversy I take from the Gütersloh monthly magazine on account of its humour, and to remind myself of the fascinating personality of the author, whom I shall probably never see again. The 'Jack-Daw' was a great supporter of Shaw.

'On hearing these notes the Jack-Daw flew to ground and, sitting among some dead leaves in a small hollow, burst into tears.'

'He wept for the next day and the following night, during which there was a very hard frost, so much so that the pool of tears in the hollow had frozen in the morning, and he was unable to move from it, and in fact seemed on the point of death.'

'A few hours later a little round human being came wandering through the woods, singing and laughing to himself as he went. Birds flew about his head, rabbits frolicked at his heels, and on his passing the trees pricked up their leaves and smiled. And it happened that his path crossed the hollow in which the Jack-Daw lay in the agonies of death.'

'He bent down as if to help it in its misery, but suddenly stopped and muttered words of great displeasure: "It's a damned Jack-Daw, and the curse of the average rook, and the disturber of all peace, and the enemy of Nature"—and something else about a thing called anti-Catholicism which we couldn't understand. And passing on, he threw back his black head and began in a funereal tone an original, curious, and obscene song.'

'The birds flew away horrified, but the rabbits came still closer, for they revelled in such things.'

'And so the Jack-Daw died.'

Now some of my readers may ask why I have thought fit to give a whole chapter to Shaw in an account of prison life in Germany. Others may disagree with what I have said of him. Others may argue that what I have said is not original. But anyone can skip the chapter who cares to do so; and as a matter of fact, Shaw does come into the story. He shows what some thousand prisoners of various nationalities were thinking, talking, and quarrelling about for a month in 1916. It is from a psychological standpoint that the matter is interesting, not from a literary. What happens inside prisoners is, I believe, just as important as what happens outside them.

If I thought this book had to be a list of disagreeable details concerning the body, I would not write it.

Those things are not worth remembering. Besides, they have been done—and overdone—already.

5

GÜTERSLOH: SPECIMEN DAY

AFTER *APPEL*, OR CALL-OVER, came a rush for the first queue of the day outside the parcel office.

Prison life is largely made up of queues. At Gütersloh it was not so bad, but at some of the other camps—Holzminden, for instance—it is no exaggeration to say that standing about in queues took up five or six hours of each day.

People of England who for a short while in 1918 experienced the sensation will sympathize with the feelings of weariness and smouldering rage generated in the minds of prisoners of war by the mere mention of that word 'queue.'

The list of parcels would have been put up for inspection the previous night by Bobbie or another worker in the parcel office, so that anyone who had a parcel would know that he had, and how many, and when to call for it or them.

At Gütersloh the Germans allowed English officers and orderlies (on parole) to work in the parcel office: which was a great convenience to all concerned, and suggests to me the thought that the whole success of Gütersloh as a prison camp was really due to the fact that it was run by the prisoners themselves and that the Germans seldom interfered with them.

It was not possible (usually) to take away one's parcels whole from the parcel office, but all tins were stored away in a locker labelled with the name of the owner or the number of the mess he belonged to. These tins were opened by the Germans before being given out, as a precaution against the smuggling through of forbidden articles, such as wire-cutters and compasses.

Cakes also were cut in half, but bread, coming under the Red Cross and therefore on parole, was not. And indeed some of the bread was not at all easy to cut after a delayed journey; in proof of which I might relate how, in attempting so to do, 'Jacko,' one of the prisoners—a man over six feet tall and more than proportionately broad, who had played Rugby football for Ireland on several occasions—put his shoulder out and afterwards broke one of his teeth over the same loaf.

This was considered by everyone to be a very good joke, for camp humour tended towards the grim, and poor old Jacko got his leg pulled over it long after his shoulder had been pulled into place.

Jacko was a dear. He messed with Jock (who was also a dear) at the table next to my own. Here is a scrap of their conversation at breakfast:

Jock, producing small pot of porridge: 'They're here-re! Have ye no brought along the milk, laddie?'

Jacko: 'And phwhat for should I be after bringing along

the milk on the morning of your duty, and I not knowing where the tin was at all?'

And the funniest part of it was that they would both spend the hour following breakfast walking round the camp learning French with their particular Frenchmen, *and teaching them English!*

In spite of the recognized Army convention of keeping silence and a liver till about 10 a.m., breakfast was a friendly, cheerful meal. Camp gossip took the place of the morning papers. Had the Germans yet discovered that Peck (not Teck[1]) was not a member of the royal house, and would they hasten to take away the room they had given him on arrival when they did so? How had D's tunnel been discovered? Perhaps there was a spy in the camp. It could easily be arranged in a large mixed community such as this. The Commandant was straight here, though. 'Straight!' (This from an Australian) 'He'd break a snake's back following him.' Besides, that wasn't the question. It was part of his duty to spy if he could manage it. Others have done so, says someone, and relates how the Ruskies in another camp suspected a man, and at last got sufficient evidence to prove him guilty. He was invited to a room where a rope was hanging from a beam, and tried formally by court-martial. The court convicted him, but unfortunately gave

---

1 [Publisher's note] This refers to the Duke of Teck of the German Royal House of Württemberg and Queen Mary's father. The King's paternal grandfather was Prince Albert of Saxe-Coburg and Gotha and the King and his children bore the titles Prince and Princess of Saxe-Coburg and Gotha, and Duke and Duchess of Saxony. There were several other relatives, British subjects, but who bore German titles. In 1917, the King changed the name of the British Royal House from Germanic to the House of Windsor and relinquished the use of all German titles in favour of British-sounding surnames. His cousin, Prince Louis of Battenberg, became Louis Mountbatten, and the Duke of Teck became Adolphus Cambridge.

him a few moments for devotion before carrying out the sentence. During this time the prisoner made a desperate dash to the window, which was on the second story of the house, and succeeded in jumping out. He was terribly cut with the glass and had broken a leg, but the leap saved his life, for he was picked up by the Germans and carried away. He was never seen again inside the camp.

Had the Russians a better knowledge of how to treat the Hun than our own people? ' Yes,' thought somebody, ' it was a good dodge picking out all the most high and mighty among the German prisoners, and sending them into Siberian mines till Russian prisoners got better treatment, and it soon had the desired effect."

"Eee!" breaks in a rich Lancashire accent (the subject is evidently looting), "you can talk of what they did, but by gum! The Fusiliers were the boys that day. Nothing to do but drink Boche wine, smoke cigars, and cut fingers off for rings. Eee! They did have a time for sure. One chap had fourteen watches!"

What were the odds on Ireland beating Scotland in the Barrack match? Men bounced off Jacko like pips off an orange. He would be certain to get three or four tries. Steve offered six to four—not worth taking. The Rugby matches always amused the Germans so. They thought (and said) that the English were all mad. The Germans themselves — how much less amusing they would be if they had a sense of humour! Someone thought they had one. What about the great search for hidden articles when they stripped poor old grey-haired Major W., and he dancing about naked and sovereigns falling out of him? 'As good as Maud

Allan[2], and much funnier,' suggests someone. Exactly, but the point was that the Germans never laughed. No, but neither did the Major. He was purple with anger.

After breakfast there were the letters.

They were the most delightful, though parcels were the most necessary, things in prison. I find it hard to this day to remember without tears the first letters I received from home after they had discovered that I was not dead, and one sent on chance before it was known for certain whether I was dead or not. Letters were generally pathetic or funny, and sometimes both. I thought it most kind when one of a circle of pious people, almost hourly expecting the end of the world as a result of prophecy fulfilled during the war, found time to write to me, contrasting the pettiness of all human troubles with the mightiness of the Doomsday which was to end my captivity. Very different but equally kind was the letter written by an old nurse to my mother and sent on.

> 'DEAR MADAM (so it began),
> 'Please accept my very humble and hearty
>   congratulations to God over the safety of your son.'

I fear she over-estimated my value to the Almighty, poor dear!

---

2 [Publisher's note] Maud Allan (1873-1956), was a famous entertainer celebrated for interpretation of the Dance of the Seven Veils. She was was Beulah Maude Durrant, but became Maud Allan after her brother, Theodore, was executed for the murder of two women in San Fancisco. In 1918 she was to be involved in a scandalous libel writ she took out against a British MP, Noel Pemberton Billing who had published an article that implied that Allan was a lesbian associate of German conspirators. She lost the case.

The following letter arrived in time for my first Christmas as a prisoner, and was a greatly appreciated gift.

'DEAR WILL,

'Your book has gone into the third impression. Congratulations! S. wrote me the news to-day. He also sent the following killing extract from a letter sent him by another new poet to whom he had given a copy of "A Gloucestershire Lad." I think it will amuse you.

'I have looked through "A Gloucestershire Lad," and find to my surprise that I know the author. I was in the same division in my lance-corporal days. I met Harvey when I was going home on promotion. Someone pointed him out to me as a D.C.M. I never saw anyone less like a hero in my life. Imagine a small, dirty, nearly middle-aged man, wearing glasses and an apologetic air, trudging along the -pave under a huge pack (he looked more like a learned tortoise than anything else I can think of), grasping a huge hard wood bludgeon—the bludgeon he did the deed with.

I remember saying to a Gloucestershire private, "Your D.C.M. looks as if he stuffed birds in civil life," and we called him "the bird-stuffer" all the way to Blighty.

He was, I think, taking the bludgeon home to his mother, and was most apologetic about his medal when I congratulated him. So he is a poet into the bargain! This is a wonderful army of ours!"'

* * * *

It is always interesting, and sometimes salutary, to 'see oursel's as others see us'!

'A damned clever letter, which ought to be put into a book,' said everyone; so to please them, and for my own amusement, I am doing so.

But perhaps the most valued letters of all were those written in rich Gloucestershire dialect to tell me, with an eagerness contemptuous of all stops, the news of my dear little village. These letters, which kindled homesickness, and satisfied it in doing so with pictures of fields, and men well known, and their characteristic words—these letters did more to alleviate the lot of prisoners than ever their kind writer could know.

And here, to the credit of the Germans, is a story told (with what truth I know not) of a poor Russian orderly who wanted 100 marks very badly, and knowing no other means of getting it, wrote a letter to God asking that it should be given him. The letter was naturally- censored, and it occurred to the censors, and friends to whom they showed it, to make a collection among themselves, and to send the amount collected (which was 50 marks) by post to the Russian. The result was that the Almighty promptly received another letter telling Him that it was 100 marks which had been asked for, and petitioning that He would be kind enough to send on the other 50 without delay.

Breakfast and letters disposed of, most of the prisoners at Gütersloh did a couple of hours' French or Russian, walking round with their teachers, who would be pupils on the following day and learn English. Finding sufficient interest in my own language, I usually wrote in one of the little gardens, using the deck-chair so kindly lent me by the Russian.

To these gardens, and the English flowers growing on that foreign ground, one of the poems in 'Gloucestershire Friends' has reference.

'Snapdragon, sunflower, sweet-pea.
Flowers which fill the heart of me
With so sweet and bitter fancy;
Glowing rose and pensive pansy,
You that pierce me with a blade
Beat from molten memory—
With what art, how tenderly,
You heal the wounds that you have made!

'Thrushes, finches, birds that beat
Magical and thrilling sweet
Little far-off fairy gongs:
Blackbird with your mellow songs,
Valiant robin, thieving sparrows,
Though you wound me as with arrows,
Still with you among these flowers
Surely I find my sweetest hours!'

Here and all about the camp were numbers of crested larks, which occasioned the remark of an orderly that 'even the blinkin' birds wore spiked helmets in Germany!'

Various animals (wild and otherwise) found their way inside the wire, and were a source of pleasure. There was a friendly ox who carted rubbish from the camp, and allowed me to strike matches on his great horns. An event in K House was when the cat had kittens. They played very prettily in the gardens for a time—that is, until mother and children were put into a pot to be eaten by hungry Russians.

On several occasions squirrels were chased from tree to tree, but I am glad to say that I never saw one caught. Small birds and even rooks and hooded crows were trapped by the French and eaten, until this 'sport' was stopped by the prison authorities.

One day H. somehow caught a young rabbit. When it was picked up it kicked its hind-legs and looked very frightened and funny. He let it go, much to the disappointment of our Allies, who would have liked it for dinner.

Over the question of food the British and French fared much better than the Russians, since they could more easily obtain parcels from home.

British prisoners often ordered food for their foreign friends, receiving a cheque in exchange for the cost. This, I imagine, was the reason why prisoners' parcels were latterly put under control of a central committee in England, and only a certain amount of food allowed to each soldier, for finally, it is to be supposed, the country could not afford to feed the prisoners of other nations.

How they managed then I don't know, for the German rations were hardly sufficient to sustain life, but in mixed camps (like Gütersloh), of course, they got in addition the rations intended for the British and French.

6

SPECIMEN DAY (continued)

After lunch there was generally some inter-barrack game to play or watch. It was the wise policy of the Games Committee, and of the camp committees generally, to fight "mouldiness" by filling every moment of the day with some beneficial activity or interest. These well-organized games were very largely responsible for the good health of the prisoners at Gütersloh, and their general fitness. International matches, inter-barrack contests, and games between the officers and the orderlies, were played with the greatest keenness, and generally occasioned a small amount of betting. As soon as the whistle blew for no side there was a great rush for baths, for they were not enough to go round, and hot water was very scanty. Afterwards, tea was drunk by those who had it.

The time between tea and the last meal of the day was filled in with lectures and classes of various kinds. After evening *Appel* and a last prowl round the wire, the prisoners were locked up in their various barracks, but that by no means ended the day's activities.

We will suppose that it is somebody's birthday, or that the K.O.Y.L.I.s[1] desired to show their friendliness towards other less favoured regiments. Imagine a room tightly packed with people who are sitting on beds, on chairs, and on the floor. A large kettle of punch is brewing on a spirit-lamp. The punch is composed of bad German wine, tinned fruit, and smuggled cognac, raisins, cloves, cinnamon, and a spot or two of Worcester sauce—for bite. Each guest has brought his own mug along, (for that is the prison custom), or shares his neighbour's if he likes to take a chance.

By general request 'Boats' is singing, for perhaps the 109th time in captivity, an old sea-song concerning

> 'A girl called Mary
> Who lived in Drury Lane,
> Whose master was unkind to her,
> Whose mistress was the same.'

After this a Frenchman who has been smuggled across from C. house, and may or may not be able to get back past the German patrol and in through the window, recites with gusto a poem by Olivier Basselin.

---

1 [Publisher's Note] The Kings Own Yorkshire Light Infantry or 'the Koylis'.

Specimen Day (Continued)

A SON NEZ.

'Beau nez, dont les rubis ont cousté mainte pipe
    De vin blanc et de clairet,
  Et duquel la couleur richement participe
    Du rouge et du violet:

'Gros nez! qui te regarde à travers un grand verre
    Te juge encore plus beau;
  Tu ne ressembles point au nez de quelque biere
    Qui ne boit que de l'eau.

'Un coq d'Inde se gorge à toy semblable porte
  Combien de riches gens
  N'ont pas de si riche nez! Pour te peindre en la sorte,
  Il faut beaucoup de terns.

'Le verre est le pinceau duquel on t'enlumine,
  Le vin est la couleur,
  Dont on t'a peint ainsi plus rouge qu'une guisne,
  En beuvant du meilleur.

'On dit qu'il nuit aux yeux; mais seront-ils les maistres?
        Le vin est guarison
  De mes maux; j'aime mieux perdre les deux fenestres
    Que tome la maison.'

OLIVIER BASSELIN *(XIVth Century)*

Then perhaps the Canadians give us some potted stories
from Scripture, and everyone joins in the somewhat mysterious chorus, to the best of his ability, after each verse.

93

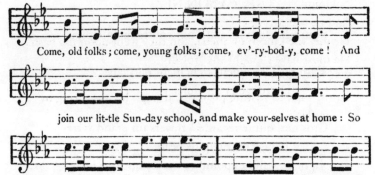

Come, old folks; come, young folks; come, ev'-ry-bod-y, come! And
join our lit-tle Sun-day school, and make your-selves at home: So
take your stick of chew-ing-gum, and squat up-on the floor, While we

tell you Bi-ble sto-ries that you nev-er heard be-fore.

CHORUS.

Hey, wig-gle, wig-gle, wig-gle we! Chickory-i-chu pom, pom!

'David was a shepherd-lad,
A husky little cuss,
And he and old Goliath kicked up an awful fuss.
Goliath tore his hair and swore
He'd kill the kid or bust,
But David took a pebble and flung it through his crust.

> *Chorus.*

'Now Samson was a fighter
Of the Johnson-Sullivan school,
And killed three hundred Philistines with the jaw-bone
    of a mule.
But then Delilah caught him
And filled him up with gin,
And then she cut his hair off and the coppers ran him in.

> *Chorus.*

94

'Solomon was a wise man,
And he had lots of cash;
He met the Queen of Sheba, and they went upon the bash.
He must have thought that royalty
Was very poorly paid,
For he took to writing proverbs, though he was a king by
    trade.

                  Chorus.

'Jonah was a prophet,
And he set out to sail,
And travelled nights and day, they say, in the belly of
    a whale;
But by-and-by it seemed to him
That dry land would be best,
So Jonah pressed the button—and the whale he did the rest."

                  Chorus.

Another Canadian song, more ancient and of innumerable verses, which demanded expectoration for emphasis of the crochet rests, was this, coming yune and all from Northern Canada and apparently designed to pass away the long winter in snowed-up shacks, wherein fishermen were huddled around the stoves.

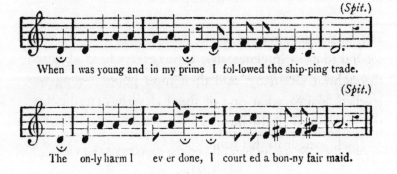

When I was young and in my prime I fol-lowed the ship-ping trade.

The on-ly harm I ev er done, I court ed a bon-ny fair maid.

'The name of the ship was *Nancy Jane*,
The Captain's name was Lee;
For forty years or mebbe more
He'd sailed upon the sea.

'We sailed away down Fundy Bay,
Passed Grand Machias Isle,
Passed Pussamagarddy on our beam—
And the cargo was of oil.

'About four of the clock the wind got up,
And she began to blow:
Old Cap. Lee said it was the worst
That ever he did know.

'The old ship shook and shook and shook,
The riggin' was crackin' and snapping;
The Captain paced the quarter-deck,
And the mate in the cabin napping."

The tale (like the ship) seems heading for some bright romantic disaster, but precisely what and where we never found out, for at this point a burst of well-judged applause invariably stopped the singer.

The Scots, in spite of their national reputation, were second to none in generosity, as was everywhere admitted throughout Germany; and their most popular song was levelled against what one of them cleverly described as ' the meanest of all the human virtues—thrift.'

'Jock' sang it to this tune:

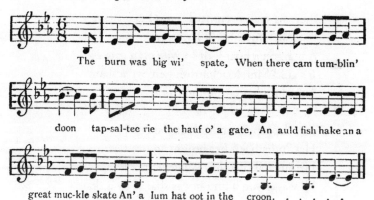

The burn was big wi' spate, When there cam tum-blin' doon tap-sal-tee rie the hauf o' a gate, An auld fish hake an a great muc-kle skate An' a lum hat oot in the croon. . . . . .

'The auld wife stood on the bank
As they gaed swirlin' roon;
She took a guid look, and syne says she :
"There's food and there's firin' gaun to the sea
An' a lum hat oot in the croon!"

'So she grippit the branch o' a saugh,
And she kickit off ane o' her shoon,
An' she stuck oot her fit astride o' the gate
An' awa she went, wi' the great muckle skate
An' the lum hat oot in the croon.

'She floated for mony a mile,
Past cottage and village and toon;
She'd a terrible time astride o' the gate,
But it seemed to 'gree fine wi the great muckle skate
An' the lum hat oot in the croon.

'A fisher was pacin' the deck
By the licht o' his pipe and the moon,
When he sees an' auld body astride o' a gate
Come bobbin' alang on the waves wi' a skate,
An' a lum hat oot in the croon.

97

'"There's a man overboard,"cries he.
"Ye leear," quo' she, "I'll droon."
  A man on a board! It's a wife on a gate—
  It's auld Mrs. Mackintosh here wi' a skate
  An' a lum hat oot in the croon.'

  'Was she nippit to death at the Pole?
  Has India bakit her broon?
  I canna tell that, but whatever her fate,
  I'll wager you'll find it was shared by a skate
  An' a lum hat oot in the croon.

  'There's a moral attached to my song:
  On Greed ye should aye gie a froon,
  When ye think o' the wife that was lost for a gate,
  An' auld fish hake, and a great muckle skate,
  An' a lum hat oot in the croon."

  Chorus: 'An' a lum hat oot in the croon!'[2]

Between the songs scraps of tales are overheard out of the babble of voices. 'One great Hun,' we are told, 'went round smashing all the rifles. Pie caught hold of the barrel, and bashed the butt down on the ground. 'Wouldn't it be damned funny if one went oft'?' said one of my men. And just after one did go off, and blew all the inside out of the smasher. On the top of everything else it was a bit too much for my nerves. I shouted with laughter for about

---

2 [Publisher's note] Will Harvey may have slight misinterpretation of Scottish dialect here. The chorus and song title is actually 'The Lum Hat *Wantin'* th' Croon.' David Rorie MD, composed this song in the late 1890s and later said: '… I wrote the song one fine summer night nearly forty-five years ago . . . It was sung in Ladysmith during the siege, and amongst Scots troops in the Great War.'

five minutes. Even the Belgians looked a bit shocked, for it wasn't a funny sight at all, but I couldn't help it.'

A Canadian is heard complaining that someone has 'a point of view about as broad as a hen's face,' and is abjured by his countrymen to 'cut out the rough stuff.'

Then an Australian officer obliges the company with a song called 'Waltzing Matilda,' the words of which are, he proudly asserts, Banjo Patterson's. He adds that a jumbuck in bush parlance means a sheep, and that 'Waltzing Matilda' is simply another term for 'humping bluey,' or 'carrying a swag.' Shouts of 'Now we know!' greet this explanation, and the singer 'carries on' with Matilda, who dances prettily enough to this tune:

Once a jol-ly swag-gie came to a bi-la-bong

under the shade of a coo-li-bah tree, And he

sang as he sat and waited till his bil-ly boiled,

"You'll come a-waltz-ing, Ma - til-da, with me.

Waltz-ing, Ma-til-da, waltz-ing, Ma-til-da.

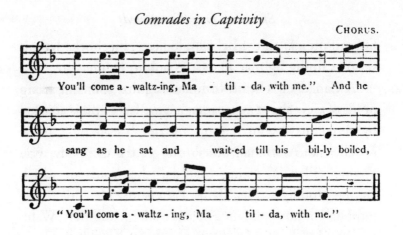

CHORUS.

You'll come a - waltz-ing, Ma - til - da, with me.'' And he

sang as he sat and wait-ed till his bil-ly boiled,

" You'll come a - waltz - ing, Ma - til - da, with me.''

'Down came a jumbuck to drink at the billabong,
  Up jumped the swaggie and grabbed him with glee,
  And he sang as he put that jumbuck in his tucker-bag:
  "You'll come a-waltzing, Matilda, with me."

'Down came the squatter mounted on his thoroughbred,
  Down came the troopers, one, two, three:
  "Who's that jolly jumbuck you've got in your tucker-bag?
  You'll come a-waltzing, Matilda, with me."

'Up jumped the swaggie and sprang into the billabong.
  "You'll never catch me alive," said he.
  And his ghost may be heard as you pass by the billabong:
  "You'll come a-waltzing, Matilda, with me!"'

Sooner or later in the evening comes 'The Old Bold Mate,'
the most frequently sung song in *gefangenenshaft*. The
words are by John Masefield. The tune, which echoed
through a dozen prison *lagers* in various parts of Germany,
is by Ivor Gurney, then a private soldier in the Gloucester,
but now a public character in English music.

Henry Morgan was the celebrated buccaneer who for his services to the Empire was afterwards appointed governor of Jamaica. 'The Old Bold Mate' is a fine rollicking song, fit company for 'Rio Grande,' 'Spanish Ladies,' 'A-Roving,' and the rest of the great sea chanteys, and can be found amongst Masefield's shorter poems under the title 'Captain Stratton's Fancy.'

'Some are fond of red wine and some are fond of white,
   And some are all for dancing by the pale moonlight;
   But rum's the only tipple and the heart's delight
      Of the old bold mate of *Henry Morgan.*

'Some are fond of Spanish wine and some are fond of
     French,
   And some will swallow tay and stuff fit only for a wench;
   But "I'm for right Jamaica till I rolls beneath the bench,"
      Said the old bold mate of *Henry Morgan.*

'"Some are for the lily, and some are for the rose;
   But I am for the sugar-cane that in Jamaica grows:
   For it's that that makes a bonny drink to warm my copper nose,"
      Said the old bold mate of *Henry Morgan.*

Oh, some are fond of fid-dles and a song well sung, And some are all for mu-sic for to lilt up-on the tongue; But mouths were made for tank-ards and for suck-ing at the bung, said the

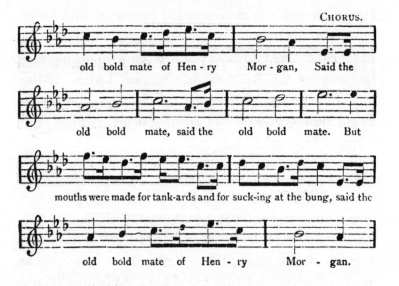

CHORUS.

old bold mate of Hen-ry Mor-gan, Said the

old bold mate, said the old bold mate. But

mouths were made for tank-ards and for suck-ing at the bung, said the

old bold mate of Hen-ry Mor-gan.

""There be good and godly ones as thinks it is a sin
    To troll the jolly bowl around and let the dollars spin,
    But I'm for toleration and for drinking at an inn,"
        Said the old bold mate of *Henry Morgan*.

""There be sad and wretched folk as goes in silken suits,
    And there be mort o' wicked rogues as lives in good reputes;
    So I'm for drinking honestly, and dying in my boots,
        Like the old bold mate of *Henry Morgan*."

The sentry appears, shouting: 'Lichts aus!' He refuses to sing the Hymn of Hate. We give him glasses three to drive him home, and chant the tune on page 103 till he goes.

In five minutes he will reappear with a guard. Then we shall disperse to our rooms. . . . Silence will creep over the barrack. The P.T. (still on night shifts) will recommence work.

DRIVE HIM HOME.

The picture drawn by Mr. Bernard overleaf will show what is happening in other rooms. 'Lights out' is the signal for temporarily covering such lights as are made possible after hours by the use of candles sent out from home, or tapped German electricity.

LICHT AUS!' A NIGHTLY PERFORMANCE
COMMENCING AT 10 P.M.

7

PRISON MUSIC

Perhaps what I missed most at the front, and certainly what most I craved in captivity, was good music. Books, thank God! can be carried in the pocket.

To suppose that the British are unmusical is wrong. I have never been in a prison camp where there was not made an attempt, generally successful, to form an orchestra and perform good music. Nor was this interest in music the work of a few enthusiasts (though they are always necessary whatever the object), as is proved by the fact that when at Holzminden I delivered a lecture on so technical a subject as 'The Relations of Music to Poetry,' a dining-hall large enough to accommodate two hundred people was packed, and people turned away, so that the lecture had to be repeated:— this in spite of the fact that I was by no means an authority.

In large mixed camps like Gütersloh and Crefeld the orchestras were very good, and I do not need the old programme now before me to remind myself of the burst of sweetness and light which fell upon me at the hearing of four 'cellos playing together very softly that aria of Bach for strings; and the strange, sudden sense of exultation over circumstance called up by Schubert's 'Unfinished Symphony.'

Nothing has the power of music to lift one out of one's surroundings; and to none more poignantly than to prisoners-of-war does Music bring her valiant reminder of things 'outside,' the refreshing comfort of a world of realities transcending human chance.

It was kind of the Germans to allow us to buy musical instruments, and to hire a piano on which Chopin could be played. The folk-songs of France and of Russia, and that divine prelude and fugue of Bach in E Major (surely the talking of angels overheard), was a joy hard to overrate. A very old carol, sung to a fine tune which I had never heard before my first Christmas in captivity, is this:

'Le petit Jésus,
Sauveur adorable,
La nuit de Noel
Naquit dans l'étable;
Des bergers vinrent bientôt
L'adorer dans son berceau.
Et Ton vit trois mages
Offrir pour hommages La myrrhe,
Tor et l'encens,
Ah! quels beaux présents!
Car Jésus à leurs yeux
Est vraiment le roi des cieux.

Prison Music

'Les chœurs angéliques
Ont chante Noël!
Mêlons nos cantiques
Aux accents du ciel!
Noël, Noël, Noël!
Chantons tous Noël!

'Le dieu tout aimable
Est ne dans l'étable
Gracieux et beau!
Sur la paille humide
Charmant et candide
Comme un doux agneau.

'Le petit Jésus Disait le rosaire,
Penche sur le cœur
De sa tendre mère:
C'est lui qui fit le Pater,
Le divin Pater noster,
Et sa voix bénie,
Saluant Marie,
Disait 'Ave Maria'
Et puis 'Gloria.'
Il faut donc chaque jour
Imiter ce Dieu d'amour.

'Les chœurs angéliques, etc.

'Allons, ma pauvre âme,
Que l'amour t'enflamme,
Et ne pleure plus!
Marie est ta mère,
Et ton nouveau père
S'Appele Jésus.'

The British also contributed their share; and the Church of England choir sang another quaint little carol, which begins thus:

As it fell out one bright morn-ing, All in the month of May; Child Je - sus asked of His dear mo - ther If He might go and play. "To play, to play, swe - et Je-sus shall go, And to play now get you gone; And let me hear of no com-plaints at night when you come home!"

It goes on to relate how the child Jesus was slighted by the proud children of rich neighbours, and of His refusal to take vengeance on them in spite of His mother's urging, and the request of the angel Gabriel that he might

'Take away their sinful souls
And dip them deep in hell.

'But "No!" but "No!" sweet Jesus said,
And "No, that may not be.
There are too many sinful souls
That yet have need of Me."
Then spake the angel Gabriel
pon a good set Steven,
"Though Thou art but a maiden's son,
Thou art the King of Heaven"'

But the Russians were, taken all round, the acknowledged musicians of the camp. It was not one or two, but all of them that sang, and nearly all played an instrument, if only the balalaika. It was inspiring to hear an excited crowd of them after some mad escape marching round the camp, singing national songs, several hundred voices blended together in ' Volga, Volga,' the tale of one Stenka Rasin, who sacrificed his bride to keep peace among the 'bold free men' of his army.

Sailing homeward with a Persian princess, the hero at the head of his fleet in a coloured ship 'celebrates his wedding merry and drunken.'

'Now a rumour runs around him
Like a roll of sudden drums:
"One night to this slim girl wedded,
He himself a girl becomes"'

Stenka Rasin hears the taunt, and his black brows, says the song, 'move together like thunder-clouds' ; 'with dark blood are filled the eyes of the ataman.'
The princess, who may be pardoned for having fallen into some sort of fainting fit, silently hears his impetuous and frenzied words: 'I regret nothing, but I will give you my

all!' and his address to the river, which was the Russians' favourite verse, and often sung, like one verse of 'God save the King,' to do instead of the whole thing.

VOLGA, VOLGA.

'To avoid a quarrel amid the bold free men' (so runs a literal translation), 'Volga, Volga, dear Mother, let you take this beautiful thing!'

> 'Then the Persian girl he raises
> High, and in one giant sweep
> Swings her overboard and headlong
> Down into the billowy deep.'

'Dance now, you devils, and sing!" he shouts. "Give her a merry requiem!'

This old song, but particularly the address to the river, was sung by the Russians twenty times for every one time they sang their national hymn. It was their equivalent of our 'Old Bold Mate'—whom I hold to have been a much pleasanter fellow.

Here is 'The Workmen's Song' (later referred to in an account of the Russian concert), so far as I have been able to squeeze verse out of a very rough translation to fit the memory of its fine melancholy tune. It was one of the songs forbidden in Russia before the war, but everyone seemed to know it.

SONG OF THE SERF.

Oh, man-y and man-y a song did I hear in my home-land of joy and of pain. I re-mem-ber them not, for al-ways the song of the serf is haunt-ing my brain.

CHORUS.

Woe to it, the big log! Curse it! On-ly song can help us roll it. To-geth-er! To-geth-er! Heave all! Ugh!

'Oh, wise are the English who harness their loads on machines
    which are tireless and strong!
But we, falling under the weight, find nor help nor relief save
only in song.

Chorus:
        'Woe to it, the big log! Curse it!
        Only song can help us roll it.
        Together! Together! Heave all! (grunt.)

'And so for our lifetime of toiling and hardship and want, to
    our children we grant
But the labour unending which kills us, and this immemorial
    labouring chant.

Chorus :
        'Woe to it, the big log! Curse it!
        Only song can help us roll it.
        Together! Together! Heave all! (grunt.)

'From father to son and to grandson, again runs this heritage
down through the years:
A song for the solace of sorrow, and only a song, for the
comfort of tears.

Chorus:
        'Woe to it, the big log! Curse it!
        Only song can help us roll it.
        Together! Together! Heave all! (grunt.)

'But my father, now stark on his board, bade me go to the
    forest to find, not a song,
But a club, and he bade me to break it on tyranny's back for
    our servitude's wrong.

Prison Music

Chorus:
'Woe to it, the big log! Curse it!
Only song can help us roll it.
Together! Together! Heave all!' (grunt.)

THE RUSSIAN CONCERT.
An Impression

'Beauty has as many meanings as a man has moods.'

'Withinside of a rich great garden—in what country I could
not know, since luxury is much the same all the world
over—the morning dew was scarce dry on close-shaven
sunny lawns, and within the shadows of tall trees flowers
as yet unnoticed by the sun stood in rows, begemmed,
and swaying a little to the breeze like impatient, pretty,
dancing girls. Bird-song was in the air, and the plash of
playing fountains. Terribly close to earth, constellations of
green stars shone in the foliage of trees, changing colour as
the wind's fingers adjusted leaves to the light, or in a silver
flash turned them upside down.

'Out of the shadow of these bright things stepped presently the forms of human beings. Men and women they
were, and by their dress foreigners, but of what century I
know not, since elegance remains almost unaltered by the
flight of Time. So, stately as trees and brightly clad as the
flowers, these men and women came with laughter and
the sound of lutes from out the chequered shadow, and
on the smooth lawn ranged themselves in the order of a
dance.

'"Was a lady such a lady,
  Eyes so bright, and lips so red,
  And the breast's superb abundance where a man
      might base his head!'

'They danced; and with bird-song and the sound of their dancing, the walled garden was brimmed with sweetness as a great cup with wine. Shorn of the blare of brass was their music, uttered sweetly by curious shapely instruments of polished wood beneath the caresses of the musicians, and so mingled it was with the movement of the dance that one looked at the feet of the dancers, expecting a breath of sound to rise glittering in visible mist of music.

'It seemed that the earth was but a sweet unsteady bell, to be set a-ringing by the beat and rhythm of those twinkling feet.

'And after they had danced, they laughed together and sat down on banks and sunny patches of the ground. . . .

'Then arose a dark man of melancholy features—a singer. Tall and handsome he was, but with always-hungering eyes; in the company but not of it; and from his songs I learned how impossible it is that adventure and passionate longing should ever be put to sleep in the unquiet heart of a man; how beneath the glitter of all bright things lurks sadness; that a walled garden, howso lovely, is a prison, and the dancers within it exiles.

'And upon that note of sadness (since sorrow is ever soaring) I took flight, and was borne without the walls of the garden. The shimmer of satin and of pearls gave way to that of snow. Brows of men and women shone no more with jewels, but with a nobler crown and tiara—sweat. The century was my own. Out of that song-sweet place of flowers I had come at last to Holy Russia. The gypsies' song floats free on the frosty air, as they wander under heaven, poor yet wanting nothing, homeless but with the horizon for walls and the changing sky for a ceiling. I watch them tramping, tired, to the evening. I see them dancing about their fires.

'Meanwhile (for in music this miracle is wrought) sounds on my ear the "Song of the Workmen." Its sombre loveliness breaks over the heart in a wave of feeling so tragic that (this is the test of great tragedy) the result is sheer exaltation.

'On such a cry a soul is lifted to see (as Moses saw from the mountain) the far-off destiny of man.

'The music stops. Again I am in the garden. Darkness has fallen like a garment, and delight of nightingales embroiders it with faint stars. Lovers serenade with sweet melancholy their own desires.

'There is sweet music here that softer falls
    Than petals from blown roses on the grass,
    Or night-dews on still waters between walls
    Of shadowy granite, in a gleaming pass:
    Music that gentlier on the spirit lies
    Than tir'd eyelids upon tir'd eyes,
    Music that brings sweet sleep down from the blissful skies.'

Save this there is silence beneath the moon.

'Then suddenly, both stars and moon are quenched in the blaze of lanterns carried by gallant gentlemen and fair ladies. Laughter and music break like a flood upon the garden. The dance recommences. Gayer and yet more gay becomes the tune.

'Gaiety, a coloured moon-bright bubble, is born, and grows; swims gigantic, opalescent, wonderful, upon the dark waters, . . . grows, . . . grows, . . . yet more wonderful! . . . Ah! will it ever break? . . .

*　　*　　*　　*

'The Russian Concert is ended. My wandering is done. Again at Gütersloh, and in room 65, I sit to write this review of the evening's enjoyment.

'After an exhaustive study of Wagner's music, Mark Twain came to the conclusion that it was ' better than it sounded.'

'All I can say about Russian music in general, and about this concert in particular, is that it was as good as it sounded—and that is the highest praise.

'Music was to Dr. Johnson "the least objectionable of noises." To me it is not less than a passion. If the gods were moved by such human prayer I should certainly be a musician. Alas! The arts are not chosen. Creation of music is denied me. But not, thank Heaven! appreciation. From a Queen's Hall concert or such evening as this last, I come away literally crammed with *new experiences*—richer by so much *life*.

'Why has this Russian music so much power to affect me? I think the answer is:

'1. Because it is Music

'2. Because it is Russian.

'The chief interest of life is other men and women. The chief interest of our prison life is other nations. But the particular interest of each nation is its nationality, just as individuality is the interest of a man. These are truisms, but like most truisms they are very little realized. Therefore I say: "Oh, you Russians, Caucasians, French, and you Irish, English, Canadians, and Scots, give us of yourselves."

'It is important to remember that we are all the same. It is equally important to remember that we are all different. That is our most interesting quality.

*   *   *   *

'When the Russian revolution broke out most of the Russian officers were overjoyed. "Now," they said, "the army will no longer be betrayed by the Court-hirelings of Germany. Russia will be Russian, and victory must soon reward her!"

To-day a chill comes over me wondering how many of those true-hearted patriots, whose whole thought was for Russia, lie callously murdered because (disregarding the invitations of their English friends) they bravely and foolishly insisted on returning to their own country in 1918 after the Armistice.

8

GÜTERSLOH: THE P.T. AGAIN

A FEW CHAPTERS AGO I was bewailing the fact that there was no available diary through which I might give the reader a keyhole-view of the working of the most important Gütersloh tunnelling party—the P.T.

That it is better to be born lucky than rich is shown by the fact that a week or two after that chapter was written, I was standing with several thousand more people in Trafalgar Square, to see (one certainly could not hear it) a proclamation about peace read by a gentleman who resembled Oliver Goldsmith, when my eye was caught by a sphinx-like familiar profile, and there, within reach of my boot, stood 'Mossy,' a prime mover in the P.T. He was, it appeared, loitering about on his way to India, but before he went he promised to send me his notebook of the history of the Gütersloh tunnel. And here are some extracts.

'On July 7' (this was about three weeks after the sap

had been started in the cellar) 'we discovered the doors of our cellar locked with enormous padlocks. We had now to find a way into the cellar. P. suggested cutting a way in through the floor. This would have meant a trap-door in the cellar roof. My idea was to cut a panel (à la Arsène Lupin) in the cellar door. To prove its possibilities I cut out a panel of the door in Humf's room, and swung it on hinges, sealing up the cut with plasticine. It wasn't my door, anyway.

'These suggestions were rejected, and D. was put to work making keys for the padlocks.

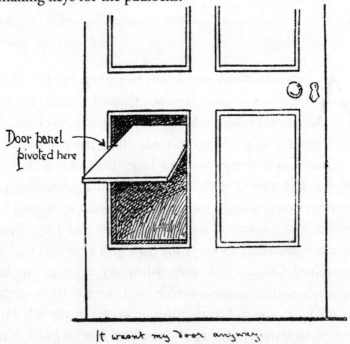

Door panel pivoted here

It wasn't my door anyway.

'He did his job extraordinarily well, and within a fortnight we were free to enter the cellar again.

'*The Making of the Keys.*—An orderly worked in the

Hun porters' room. We gave him a piece of plasticine, and told him to take an impression of the cellar keys. This he managed easily, and so we had fine impressions of both keys to work from.

'D. had got hold of a trench looking-glass, a strong metal affair, and this he bent round a steel rod the same size as the keyhole.

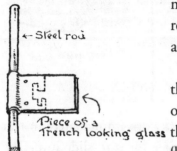

'The measurements from the impressions were scratched on and the key shaped out with the stolen chisel and file, two flanges were riveted together with brass nails.

'When the key was completed it was tried in the lock, having first been held in a candle-flame and covered with soot, so that the marks left on it showed what additional

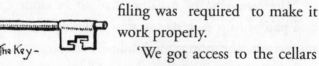

filing was required to make it work properly.

'We got access to the cellars again about July 24, but the Germans had been very active, and as if to make sure that nothing should go on had put down a floor of cement in the little chamber under the stairs, thus completely blocking the entrance to our sap.

'So here was another problem.

'The solution was a daring piece of engineering work planned by R. He decided that if the bottom step could be moved by sliding it under the others, it would leave a gap nine inches wide, through which we could squeeze into the pit which we had already made. His scheme was,

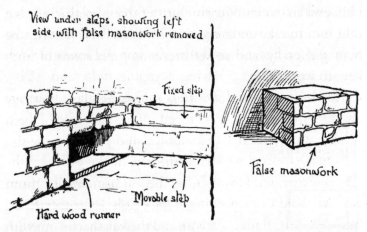

View under steps, showing left side, with false masonwork removed

Fixed step

False masonwork

Hard wood runner

Movable step

therefore, to cut away the brickwork immediately in rear of the step, so as to leave a space for it to slide into. The step had then to be cut away from the masonry on either side and underneath. Hard wood runners had to be placed, and the step to be lowered about half an inch so as to allow it to slide under the next step.

'The removing of masonry had to be done carefully, and patched up each day so that it would stand German inspection. The mortar was gradually cut away with knives, and the bricks removed whole, and false mason-work was made for each side to fit into the holes thus made.

'. . . On July 30 we started to work on the step, commencing about midnight. . . .

'It was at the end of September that the great day arrived, and we had everything ready to move the step. Four of us stood on the step and jumped high in the air. It sank down on to the runners. Following a scraping away of loose mortar, etc., it was pronounced ready for moving. Six of us then got down on the floor, two with their feet against the step, two with their backs supporting the first two, and a couple more supporting them, so that a living ram was made stretching from" the far wall to the step. Several good heaves—and then the step slid smoothly over the greased runners, leaving a gaping hole; and gazing down into it we could see dimly the old neatly cut passage and its supports.

'Again we were free to go a-tunnelling. . . .

'On October 8 we were surprised in the cellar by the French carpenter. However, we tackled him, and he promised he would say nothing. His words were something like this: "Sir, I am a Parisian, and we are accustomed to keeping secrets in Paris. There are people who talk, but I am the soul of discretion." And apparently he was; but the watcher who allowed him to enter the cellar got hell.

'On October 13, the step being open and the sandbags lying out in the cellar to be carried away by the whole P.T., the alarm was given by O., who was on watch. There was no time to quit or even to lock the door before the Boche had entered the house and made straight for the cellar steps. It was a plumber with tools and some piping. Poor O. was just about to fling his arms round him and hold him till we escaped, when he quietly put down his tools and went upstairs instead of down.

'On October 19 we installed our ventilating gear. It consisted of a large pair of bellows made by R. Attached to the bellows was a length of garden hose, and, acting by suction, it exhausted the air in the chamber and forced it up a tube which had an outlet under the outside steps of the house. The good air came in from the movable step. But it was found, after tunnelling a yard or two up the sap, that the candles refused to burn, no matter how hard the bellows worked.

'We got out nine bags of sand the first day, but on the second only four, the party being in darkness and the air very foul.

'The next day we took down an electric torch and got out seventeen bags.

'On October 22 we had gone seven feet. The bellows had been overhauled, and for three days we averaged forty bags a day. Then (as we got farther from the pit) the air got worse and worse, so that it was difficult to breathe. Another result of working in bad air is that people are inclined to be panicky. In the beginning of November we were getting out between twenty and thirty bags a day.

'On November 10 there was a big search, which commenced immediately after *Appel* at 9.30 a.m. This caused a big rush in our room, where the new ventilating gear was in process of being made.

However, we got away everything of a suspicious nature—sandbags, civilian clothes, the fan and the driving-

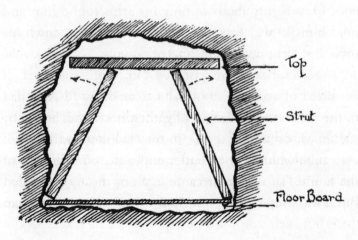

wheel—into the Church of England chapel, and stowed them under the altar. The search passed off satisfactorily.

'The sap continued slowly because of the bad air, and as the tunnel was pushed out from the house it had to be timbered.

'The timbers were put up in the following way: You first put down a floor-board, which could be of light wood, then a top of strong wood, supported roughly by two stout struts {*see p. 124*).

'The struts were then forced back towards the sides of the tunnel, and finally hammered back, so that the whole structure was tight, thus:—

'On November 23 we installed the new ventilating gear. This meant a lot of sand out to make room for it, as it was a good deal larger than the other. We took out 162 bags in four days.

'On December 1 we put in our first air-boxes, and from that time the ventilation became so good that we could again burn candles.

'From December 8 to 15 we averaged forty bags a day. But this was too good to last. An English tunnel had been started by another company from a small copse at the other end of the camp. They had completed their downward shaft, and had a cover over the top very neatly concealed with pine-needles, etc.; but we soon found that they were throwing their sand into our special hiding-places, and a

pit that was three feet deep one day would be level with the surface the next morning. Also, whereas we had learnt by experience the best places to put the sand, the new-comers were making all the mistakes that we had made at the beginning.

'On December 16 the ground was in a terrible state, and our scouts reported that 'Whiskers,' the Hun tunnel-hunter, was seen staring at a pit near the new tennis-court which was overflowing with bright yellow sand.

'We decided to stop work, and warned the rival company of our suspicions.

'On December 24 the rival concern told us they were going to carry on. Sure enough, that evening the Boche rushed the wood, and the workers only escaped by the skin of their teeth, leaving the hole badly closed. Next morning the Boche had the hole opened up. He was now thoroughly awake, and we could do nothing but wait for him to calm down again.

'On December 29 two English cut the wire but failed to get away. We had an *Appel* at 8.30, but no one was missing. The New Year opened with rain and snow alternately, till the ground was a vast lake.

'On January 9 a Russian sap was discovered in another small wood.

'It was decided to set a strict watch for a week, and then to start work again if it was possible.

'On January 18 we found that the tunnel was half-full of water, and the sides falling in. We tried to drain it by digging a sump-pit, and a nasty cold, wet business it was. We had a chain of men passing out buckets of muddy water up the cellar-stairs, and pouring them down the drains.

'When at last we had cleared most of the water out of the tunnel we found that a lot of sand had fallen from the roof, and a great many of the support timbers had fallen in. We couldn't quite clear the water out, so we built a pontoon bridge from the pit and up the tunnel, which made crawling up the sap extremely uncomfortable. To add to our troubles, we found that the floods had poured down our air-chimney and filled the fan and air-boxes full of sand, so that the whole concern was out of order. Owing to this we had to build an entirely new ventilating gear.

'We had been stopped from work for over a month, and when we got going once more it took us nearly three weeks to repair the damage done by the floods. However, on February 5 we were doing better than ever, and averaging fifty bags a day.

'The question of where to put the sand that came out of the tunnel was one of the most difficult to solve. We could only work at midday (during the Hun dinner-hour), and the sand removed had to be stacked somewhere in the house till nightfall, when it could be removed and deposited outside.

'The sandbags were made of curtains and any material

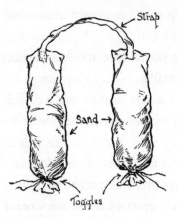

we could buy or steal. We removed the bags from the sap at the end of work, and stored them in boxes in the rooms of O., W., D., and H. Immediately it was dark the whole P.T. assembled to carry off the sand to specially selected dumping-grounds, and to sprinkle it round the camp.

'Carriers went out in pairs, carrying their bags under their Burberrys. The bags were beaten flat so that they would not show too much. Finally someone invented a special carrier whereby he could carry two bagfuls at a time, in long sacks joined together and supported by passing over the shoulders. In this way his arms were free and he was less noticeable. On arriving at his dump he had only to pull a string and the sand shot out from under his greatcoat.

'An adaptation of this patent was also used—a pair of trousers worn over the shoulders, each leg filled with sand.

'January and February were very cold months, and we had hard frozen snow on the ground the whole time. It was therefore impossible to distribute sand about the grounds. Fortunately we had found another excellent place of storage. When the planks which formed the floor of the attics were lifted up, a space of about three inches was discovered everywhere between them and the lath-and-plaster ceilings of the rooms below. By raising the runners that the planks rested on to the top of the beams, we increased this space to about six inches in depth. We put down large sheets of cardboard to keep the wet sand from making the ceiling damp, and scattered the sand over this, completely filling up the space. After replacing the planks we had raised the floor all over the attics by three inches, but to anyone but the architect and ourselves it appeared the same.

'Of course this made the floor unsafe to walk on, because the weight of sand was pressing directly on the lath-and-plaster ceiling of the next floor. In one room which was immediately below the attic the ceiling bulged like a sail, and was cracking so quickly that we had hastily to remove the sand for fear of the whole thing coming in on top of us.'

'I have already mentioned the Church of England chapel.

'On February 26, as we were carrying the sand from the cellar to O.'s room we were surprised by a dirty little boy who used to work with the civilian carpenter. He somehow got between the carriers and cellar-door, and went wandering down apparently in search of food. At the cellar-door he was caught by "Puck," who had been down the sap and was in consequence covered with sand. "Puck" (what a funny old man was "Puck"!) with much presence of mind immediately marched him off upstairs to a W.C., talking volubly about drains in German all the time. Meanwhile the step was closed and the cellar locked.

'"Puck" was awarded the P.T. medal, "The Copper Toe," for his devotion to duty, but as we were all very anxious as to how much the boy had seen we decided to watch events for a week, and so took place the famous "Boy Watch," in which members of the P.T. relieved each other every two hours throughout the day for a week.

'A book was kept, and all movements of Huns in or near the house were carefully noted. At the end of the week this book, which had been passed on from one watcher to another throughout the day, was read out. Here is an extract:

'Sunday, 10th.—E.J.S.
Appel to 10 a.m.—Porter shaving.
10 to 10.30.—Porter goes round house.
10.20.—Visits cellar-door, A house end; tries lock, returns to room.
11.15.—Strange Hun visits porter in room,
11.30.—(Relieved by O.)
11.55.—Langensieben (the interpreter) to Sydenham's room.
12.8.—Strange Hun goes down cellar with porter, A house end. Returns 12.20.
12.25.—Langensieben returns to A house.
12.27.—Porter to lunch with strange Hun.
1.30.—(Relieved by P.)
2.10.—Porter returns to room.
2.55.—Strange hammering in cellar C house end. Find cellar-door open. (Comment "Very bad watching!")
2.50.—Parcel office Hun comes out C house end of cellar, locks door, and departs to canteen.
3.5.—Porter goes upstairs to orderlies' room, talks with sergeant-major, returns to room, 3.20.
3.31.—Porter moving about inside his room.
3.33.—Porter playing fiddle.
3.35.—"Whiskers" walks across footer field, looks suspiciously at B house, stops at goal-post near gardens, examines ground; walks to D house entrance, goes in.
3.36.—"Whiskers" looks out of ground-floor window of D house.
3.37.—Disappears.
3.40.—Strange Hun carrying shovel and bunch of keys approaches B house from A house. 3.41.—Goes past house.

3.45.—"Whiskers" looking out of cellar-window D house.
3.46.—Strange Hun enters C house bathroom-door.
3.50.— Commandant roaring in A house.
4.0.—Russian orderly enters house (C house end), goes up-stairs to top landing, waits there.
4.3.—Hun Q.M. enters (C house end), goes upstairs to top landing, enters attics with Russian orderly.
4.8.—Q.M. comes out of attic, locks door, leaving Russian orderly inside; departs to A house,' etc.

'On March 11 the P.T. met and decided to continue work the next day.

'Work continued until the 18th, when a terrible rumour spread through camp that we were all going to be moved to Crefeld.

'On March 19 we were ordered to pack up, as we were going to leave for Crefeld the following day.

'We had a very stormy P.T. meeting to decide what action should be taken re tunnel. A very bitter meeting. . . [Of this more in the next chapter.]

'During the morning we prepared the end of the sap for breaking out. Another yard was added to it in length, and the roof was excavated so as to leave only a foot of earth between the sap and daylight. A tube was driven through and the end of the sap thus located from the house. The sap was now over 30 yards long, and although well beyond the second row of barbed wire it was immediately below the sentry's beat!'

9

GÜTERSLOH: THE LAST DAY

PERHAPS BECAUSE IT WAS pretty clear that the revolution in Russia was turning out badly and would soon mean a separate peace, and perhaps because the Germans had at last discovered that large mixed camps resulted in firm friendships among the Allies rather than in quarrelling, an order came out soon after St. Patrick's Day, 1917, that all the British prisoners of war at Gütersloh should be immediately transferred to Crefeld, where there were several hundred other British officers imprisoned, and whence they had already sent away a company of Russians in the process of turning the camp from a mixed to an all-British *gefangenenlager*.

It was rumoured that the British prisoners at Crefeld had been given the choice of remaining there, or of coming to Gütersloh, but had elected to stay where they were, and let us come to them. This may or may not be true, but if so they (quite unconsciously) wrung the bosoms of many would-be escapers at Gütersloh, and very especially those of the P.T., whose tunnel was at this time not farfrom completion after the months of delay and difficulty described in M.'s notes.

A day's notice was all we got to pack up and go, so it was quite obvious that the tunnel could not be completed. But on the other hand it was not at all certain that, given good fortune, it could not be used as it was to liberate one or two men instead of the full number.

The question therefore before the P.T. meeting (referred to in M.'s diary as stormy and very bitter) was this: Ought the British tunnel to be regarded as exclusively British, to be ended prematurely with a chance of one or two escaping at most; or ought it to be looked upon as an effort for the cause of the Allies, in spite of the fact that it was planned and executed by British brains and labour? In other words, should it be used for what it was worth at .the moment, or should it be handed over to the Russians, whom it was thought would be the next occupiers of the barrack, to be completed by them, so that the number of escapes might be very greatly increased? It was a hard question for those who had spent their time and energies working upon it day after day—very hard.

Under the banners of 'British prestige' and 'Allied interests' the two parties ranged themselves to decide it. They were almost equally divided, and the resulting debate was undoubtedly stormy—the bitterest in the whole history of the P.T., who had never before quarrelled over any question either of policy or execution.

Remember that no Frenchman or Russian had had a hand in this tunnel. Remember that the English had been called sheep. Remember the labour of body and the anxiety of thought which had been spent on it—this you must do to be able to understand the attitude of those who said: 'If the sap can be used at all, let it be used now, if only for the sake of a couple of British. It is not completed, it is dangerous—very well! If we get shot, let us get shot; but hand it over to foreigners, never!'

Consider the fact that those who opposed this attitude were men equally eager to go, equally daring, equally sharers in the work of planning and performing, and included some of the oldest members of the P.T. Then you will understand the admirable chivalry of their argument: 'What if the British have done the work? The cause of the Allies is the cause of England, and is served only by permitting the greatest possible number of escapers, British or otherwise.'

The reader will probably appreciate these two attitudes, and be able to sympathize with one or other of them; yet since he cannot know the personalities of the men concerned (and since to describe them would take many books such as I am unfit to write), he will hardly realize the truly dramatic nature of this simple debate; and how near to being uprooted were many long and fast friendships; nor the amount of heart-searching and self-conquest which went into that final decision to lay aside all personal and national ambition for the sake of 'the Cause.'

Here is a last extract from 'Mossy's' diary showing 'Records of sand removed from October, 1916, to March, 1917.'

Month	Work Days	Sand Removed	Average per day
October ..	29 days	683 bags	23.5
November ..	30 days	481 bags	24
December ..	11 days	361 bags	32.8
January ..	11 days	227 bags	20.6
February ..	20 days	642 bags	32
March ..	6 days	159 bags	26.5
Total	107 days	2,553 bags	26.3

Length of tunnel, 35 yards.

Dimensions, 2 feet high by I foot 6 inches broad.

Instruments: digger, mason's trowel (stolen while stoves were being built), large hammer with pick.

Accumulators bought from the electrician by "Puck," who said that they were for reading at night.

'March 20.—All British shunted off to Crefeld by five o'clock in the morning. We have failed.'

This is the last entry in 'Mossy's' diary, and the only one which I do not entirely agree with. If that was failure, then to my mind failure is so much like success that I cannot tell them apart.

*   *   *   *

The departure of the British from Gütersloh was a rich mingling of humour and pathos. It was the farewell of friends from many parts of the earth who would never meet again and who knew it. Nevertheless, the manner of parting was in most cases so quaintly humorous that one could only laugh. The sensation of being kissed by a bearded Russian (though as a matter of fact the majority were clean-shaved), and almost simultaneously impetuously embraced by an excited, dapper Frenchman, was very piquant. But my chief delight was to watch the same thing happening to embarrassed senior officers of the very Regular type. Their strategy in avoiding the embrace, and the forced smile with which they faced it when at last it became inevitable, was and is a joyous memory to me in all times of depression.

The march from the camp to the railway station was made difficult, and in some cases painful, by the generally adopted method of simultaneously concealing and carrying *verboten* articles, such as compasses, on the person.

We arrived at Crefeld towards evening, predisposed to dislike it. There was no search, so those who had risked illegal articles in boxes, or carried them openly in their pockets, felt that they had some cause for gloating.

The authorities met us politely, and a few gloomy-faced prisoners looked at us with somewhat bored curiosity when we entered; but the majority continued to walk mournfully round and round the wire, ignoring our presence. Once again we were 'new arrivals.'

IO

CREFELD

In the Minor.

A-mould-ing, a-mould-ing, since mould-ing was my ru - i - n.

CREFELD IS THE ORIGINAL scene of the comedy of the 'Girls of Gottenberg.' Finding amongst the local inhabitants an insufficiency of husbands for their daughters, the burghers of Crefeld petitioned the Kaiser to send a regiment of soldiers; and the All Highest promised and afterwards fulfilled his promise to send them a 'crack' regiment of cavalry, provided they built for their accommodation a suitable barracks.

To these barracks by a pretty irony came we poor prisoners, and we found the atmosphere of the place very different from that we had left.

The atmosphere of Gütersloh had been bracing and

strenuous; its work, its games, and its socialism were those of a public school. But to Crefeld hung rather the mouldy atmosphere of a club—a bad one. The officers of these two camps (with certain exceptions, to prove the rule) never mixed until they had left Crefeld for two really unpleasant camps, Schwarmstedt and Ströhen. Then under German persecution they became comrades in adversity, and at last did justice to one another. Crefeld for that reason will occupy only a very small part of this book, the inspiration of which is comradeship.

On arrival, we were surprised to find that many of the officers had forsaken their rooms in order to hibernate alone in cardboard huts which they constructed on a wooden framework down any passage and in any corner available; and such was the atmosphere of the place that very soon many once-cheery souls from Gütersloh followed their example. But it was not always a distaste for the society of one's fellows that led to this practice, and within a fortnight of their arrival certain of the P.T. had started a tunnel from one of these dug-outs, screening their work with a false wall only evident when one measured the outside of the hut and compared it with the measurement of the inside.

One great advantage which Crefeld possessed over Gütersloh from an escaper's point of view was that it was very much nearer to the border—in fact, only 18 kilometres away. But against this was the fact that it was an extremely difficult camp to get outside.

'Getting outside' is generally the least of the escaper's difficulties—his troubles are then just beginning—but at Crefeld if you were able to get out the chances were about two to one on your getting over, instead of about a hundred to one against. For this reason the German authorities there were concerned to see that no such chance should be given to any prisoner. The camp was searched each day for tunnels; the dust-cart was carefully guarded, and the refuse stabbed through and through with a long spear before it was taken away, and the end of the said spear examined for any trace of gore.

The sentries at Crefeld were always known as 'the earnest men,' because of the following description of them in a camp-notice posted up by the Germans. 'All the guards are to be regarded as superiors to the prisoners. They are earnest men, knowing their duty, to whom the watching is a matter of conscience; and they know what they have to do and what they have not to do.'

But however much they surpassed in earnestness the majority of somewhat flippant prisoners under their control, the guards were no match for them in cunning. The tunnelling went on; and two men also succeeded in getting out of the camp in a tradesman's cart. Unfortunately it was broad daylight, and they were quickly recaptured in the town.

The Commandant of Crefeld was a jolly old gentleman whose nose must have cost him a small fortune to colour; but he was jolly, and he was a gentleman, and he treated the officers as gentlemen. I am grateful to him for allowing my book of poems written at Gütersloh to be sent through to England for publication; although Jackson's beautiful pen-and-ink sketch, intended as a cover design for that book and used on this book instead, was disallowed on the

ground that the decorative barbs had been drawn too big![1]
What the commandant was able to do for the prisoners
he did, or at any rate he tried to do; and it is a pleasure to
pay him tribute in this book, for we did not find his like
anywhere else in our travels through Germany.

Our recreations were walks outside the camp on
parole; and games—football, hockey, and tennis—inside
the camp. The latter-were played on the barrack square,
which was ridiculously small as well as very dangerous,
being composed of stone and gravel rendered septic by
the previous presence of many German cavalrymen and
their horses. Matches were played every Saturday during
the football season between the officers and the orderlies
of the camp. Furious matches were also played between
Gütersloh and Crefeld elevens, and it was as a result of
representing Gütersloh at hockey that I was laid up for
eight weeks with a poisoned knee. The ground was, in fact,
so septic that any slight fall which caused the skin to be
broken was quite sufficient to put you on your back for
months.

The food was better than that given us at Gütersloh,
and more plentiful. I don't know whether it was enough to
live on; I never tried. Certainly the Russians managed to
do so, but since few of the French and none of the English
ate German food, they had an increased ration. Letters
and parcels arrived regularly and were quickly distributed.
The only things I had confiscated while at Crefeld were
packets of cigarettes containing cartoons of the Kaiser by

1 [Publisher's note] A print of the original sketch is on page 25. A colour tinted
version is featured on the front cover of this book. Also see Appendix page 338.

Raemaekers, and I don't much blame them for that. We had a pretty good orchestra which gave concerts once a week, and a theatre rather larger than the one at Gütersloh, where plays, home-made or imported—as, for instance, 'You Never Can Tell'—were performed. Lectures were also given and classes held.

Soon after we arrived, the foreigners were all cleared out in accordance with the German policy of separation then operating. We gave them a great send-off; the camp became all-British, and for a time we thought it damnable.

The truth is that our Allies had been, far more than we realized, an interest and diversion in captivity. They were so very different from ourselves, . . . they were so very polite.

It was a Russian whose room stood in close proximity to the general convenience who felt it proper solemnly to stand up, salute his guests, and apologize, each time the chain was pulled.

Readers who feel offended may count themselves very lucky that I have (reluctantly) censored this book, and left out all the most Rabelaisian of our prison jokes.

II

THE BREAK-UP OF CREFELD

L IFE AT CREFELD WAS much the same as it had been
at Gütersloh, except that it was lived far less spirit-
edly. The men there were for the most part older
captures, more fed up with it all, and less ready to see
misfortunes from a humorous angle. There was no great
strafe, such as invariably unites prisoners in excited fellowship, and brightens life with battle. Crefeld therefore
continued to be one of the best camps in Germany, and
one of the dullest and least sociable.

But this state of things was soon to be remedied. Two
months after our arrival the camp was very suddenly
broken up, for reasons evidently imperative but to this
day obscure, except to those at the head of affairs. It was
supposed that the German authorities discovered plans
of an escape whereby, simultaneously with the arrival of
a bombing party of British aeroplanes, the whole body
of Crefeld prisoners was to break out and march for the

border. The War Office, the senior British officer in charge of us, and the Germans themselves alone knew the true facts of the case.

The camp was sufficiently near to the frontier to make such a scheme reasonable, and a determined rush must have resulted in many getting across, although some (both English and German) would have got killed. But no secret orders had been passed round to us, and to the ordinary prisoner the whole affair is a mystery clothed in many rumours. Another theory is that the townspeople of Crefeld, who were by this time quite friendly, but desperately hungry as a result of the continuance of the war, were planning to kill two birds with one stone by liberating us and seizing our food. All that we know for certain is that the guards were suddenly doubled, and reinforced by a whole battalion of men even more earnest than themselves, and that even on shorter notice than that given us at Gütersloh we were told to pack up and go. Everything was done to expedite our departure, which was to be in two separate parties, and we were told that the camps to which we were going were both very good ones.

To 'Mossy' and other members of the P.T. this news that, we were again to be moved was a bitter disappointment. The sap from the cardboard hut was going on famously. A diagram of it is on the opposite page.

It had been started by some of the Russians who had been moved from Crefeld soon after we came, and it was a fine poetic justice which decreed that the P.T. who had handed over their own tunnel to Russians at Gütersloh should be able to get hold of it almost immediately. A few notes from 'Mossy's' second diary will serve to show that,

as before, the element of humour was not lacking as spice
to the venture.

'Our first attempt to get rid of sand was a hazardous
proceding. We had about six bags of it, and decided to
put them down the open drain that was in the centre

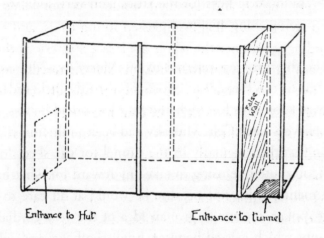

Entrance to Hut   Entrance to tunnel

of the barrack square. So we started off in the dusk,
carrying the bags under waterproofs and Burberrys.
But somebody managed to spill half his bag on the
stone flags outside the barrack entrance, and within
five yards of the sentry; so when we got back from the
drain we were horrified to see a great splash of yellow
sand. The question was how to remove it without
attracting the notice of the sentry, for it would have to
be removed before daylight. A brilliant idea! . . . Here
come two more of the gang returning from the drain.
We dash out and collar them. A terrible struggle ensues
before the eyes of the astonished guard. The vanquished
are dragged over and over the flagstones through the

sand, and the spot is swept clean. The sentry muttered something about "verdampt Englanders," but seeing that we were making no attempt upon the wires, did no more than spit upon the ground in disgust.

But before the work could go on we had to find a place for the sand. This old, old problem was solved by making keys for the attics, and very soon we were going along at a great pace.'

The fine progress referred to by 'Mossy' was due a good deal to the Herculean efforts of a sturdy little orderly. A man about five feet high and four feet broad he was, and I believe a black Celt. Mulcahy had been a miner in civil life, and worked regularly in the tunnel for the sheer love of it, absolutely refusing to take any reward for what he did. I mention this not because he would at all care to have it spoken of, but to give an idea of the very cordial relations which existed between English officers and soldiers in German prison camps. A very large number of escapes (there can be no harm in divulging this secret now that the war is over) were only made possible by this perfect co-operation between officers and orderlies. But where possible this was always avoided by escaping officers, not because the soldier was unwilling to take the risk of punishment, but because the officer was unwilling that the man should get into trouble through his loyalty. Orderlies had their work to do in the camp, and their efforts beyond that were generally confined to helping officers to get out rather than escaping themselves. I know of only one case of an orderly escaping from an officers' camp. The obvious plan for a soldier wanting to get away was to volunteer for work on a farm, where his chances of escape were very much thicker.

It would be hard to over-estimate the help of an experienced miner like Mulcahy in such a venture as 'Mossy's' tunnel. He it was who got out N. and O. after they had been buried. He worked like a demon. His heart and soul were in the work, and no one was more bitterly disappointed than he when it appeared that once again all these labours were to be frustrated by sheer bad luck. To add to the disappointment of the P.T. it was now rumoured that their sacrifice at Gütersloh had been vain, and that the tunnel had been given away soon after our departure as a result of quarrels.

It was decided that one of the party should conceal himself when the others left the camp and try to finish the tunnel alone. His place would be faked on *Appel*, and his name answered by friends for as long as this was possible. 'Mossy' was therefore hidden away behind the false wall, together with the tunnelling tools and a store of food; and the rest of the P.T. and the camp in general carried their tempers down into the barrack square, well prepared for any devilry which should suggest itself.

The thought of concealing themselves till everybody had cleared out of the camp had occurred to several more officers, and so it was found on evening *Appel* that the numbers were not correct. We were counted again, and this time enthusiastic but injudicious faking led to the numbers being not less but more than they ought to be. The Germans, who were now thoroughly suspicious, ordered a third *Appel*, and this time each man as he answered his name was required to march through a small opening in the wire fence which divided the barrack square from two tennis-courts. A large number of these officers, however, contrived to crawl back again under the wire, and to answer other people's names; and as a result of this and the mistakes which the Germans themselves were making a ludicrous result was again arrived at. This last roll-call took so long that darkness came on before it was finished.

Meanwhile, many of the officers who had been counted had departed to bring down such furniture and belongings as they could not hope to carry away with them, and were making bonfires. The idea became popular. Fires sprang up all over the barrack square. While the sentries were beating out one, two others were being lighted. The leaping red flames showed men being chased with bayonets and vanishing in darkness. The fires continued to burn, and increased in number. Finally the alarm was sounded, and a battalion marched in to clear the square. We were given five minutes to clear out. After that, anyone seen about would be shot. The Germans were thoroughly apprehensive; their idea of the rag being that an attempt had been made to burn down the camp. Whether the guards knew the reason of our removal or not I cannot say, but certainly they had the wind well up. Sentries and prisoners alike spent a sleepless night, the former carefully watching, the latter packing and arranging what they could carry with them on the journey.

The strangest company assembled next morning to march down to the station. There were about as many armed guards as prisoners, and each prisoner, determined to leave as little as possible for the Germans, had loaded himself like a Christmas-tree. Such people as were abroad in the streets of Crefeld roared with laughter as we passed, and there was some cause for their amusement.

It was an agonizing march; every fifty yards or so the column was compelled to halt, while bags were changed from one hand to the other and bundles readjusted on the shoulders. There goes one bearing a large English ham, two bottles of cold tea, a chair, a hockey-stick, and on the end of it a canary in a cage. Another staggers onward beneath a cage of live rabbits, a box of tinned meats, and his dirty washing. A third mournfully attempts to pick out of the road contents of some box which has fallen and burst, while the sentry, fearing a trick, urges him forward with German oaths and the butt of his rifle.

Even from Crefeld camp down to the station the road was left littered with breakages and discarded loads, but it was when we had arrived at the other end of the railway journey that the nightmare started. Mile after mile we were urged across country becoming ever wilder and more swampy. The day was exceedingly hot. Weary men hurled aside one by one various loads they had tied to themselves. Finally we arrived into camp furious and utterly exhausted, to find ourselves looking at about four drab, dirty-looking wooden huts roofed with tarred felt. This was Schwarmstedt, the good camp. A barbed-wire fence surrounded, and machine-gun towers dominated, the lager from each end.

If anyone wishes to know where Schwarmstedt is situated—a thing which I cannot possibly conceive—I will refer him to the map at the beginning of this book. There we were. We sank down on to the ground, with what baggage remained to us, and sat quietly cursing amid various venomous insects which infested the ground. Prison life does not make for restraint in speech. 'Well, this is a — — !' said somebody, reflecting the general opinion. 'Oh, a strafe camp, obviously,' replied his friend.

THE EXODUS FROM CREFELD

12

SCHWARMSTEDT

'ACHTUNG!' (ATTENTION) SUDDENLY YELLED the Germans. The Camp Commandant has arrived on the scene to have a look at us. We rise somewhat listlessly, and see with amusement a very magnificent figure approaching. He is old, but tall and erect, and wears with very obvious pride the Uhlan officer's uniform, plastered with enormous decorations gained, I believe, in 1870, when his mind last worked. His manners were theatrical but very courteous. He was what you call 'old-world.' He welcomed us to his camp, which was, said he, not so nice as he would wish for English officers—but there, he had not invited us; we must make the best of it; and he would endeavour to do all that was possible to make our stay comfortable. The rooms held from thirteen to sixteen officers, so that we could be with our friends. He knew all that was to be known about the English, because he had stayed in Scotland. We could dismiss.

Some of us were of the opinion that he was trying to

be funny; others that he was not quite all there.

Personally I believe that he was quite serious, and merely 'old-world'—yes, 'old-world.'

The rooms he referred to lay in three of the long drab wooden huts. The partition between the rooms was of thin matchboarding. The outside walls were thicker, but the tarred felt had come off in places and the boards had warped, leaving cracks almost an inch wide for the rain and wind. A state of overcrowding could not be avoided, and by whatever mode of arrangement, the beds had often to touch one another.

Sanitary arrangements were very bad, and the latrine so situated that the ends of two living-huts came to within ten paces of it. The drinking-water was brownish, and smelt; but filtered water could be bought in the canteen at ten pfennigs a glass, and boiling water at fifteen pfennigs the kettle. There were two pumps in the camp, and at these and in the wooden troughs near we washed our clothes when they became dirty. To reduce the quantity of things required to be washed, and because the camp was filled with a fine dusty sand, very difficult to remove, most of us went about wearing only gym. shoes, a shirt, and a pair of shorts. Bodily cleansing was, we discovered, another question and a more difficult one. The camp baths lay outside the wire, and the Germans required parole to be given before we visited them. This parole, some of us considered, we had no right to give, except for reasonable exercise, in accordance with the Army order. The Germans should have supplied baths within the camp, and had no right to demand parole from us for such a purpose as visiting them. We who refused parole were taken across twice a week by an armed guard, who watched us carefully all the time; the other officers were, I believe, allowed four baths for the same period of time.

Owing to the hot weather, and the fleas which infested the camp, a cold swill under one of the pumps seemed highly desirable, but this was forbidden on grounds of modesty, as the two pumps were in the open. The camp lay in the middle of a large moor, and there was not a house for miles round. The only female I ever saw enter the camp was the dentist's assistant, useful as a smuggler of maps and compasses if sufficiently bribed with dripping, but the last person in the world likely to be shocked by such a sight.

What happened in consequence was that there were frequent rushes from the barracks to the pump by naked officers, a hurried douche, and a rush back. Occasionally two stolid German guards would appear, to march the naked men off to prison; and later on they would call round for their clothes. I recall with some pleasure the time when an 'Inspector of Camps,' or some such personage, was accosted by a naked officer holding up a flea, which he desired to bring to notice. 'Dat,' shouted the shocked Inspector, 'is der most unver-schamter spectacle [with accent on the second syllable] I have never seen!'

But gradually pump bathing was winked at and permitted.

*   *   *   *

When we arrived at Schwarmstedt the camp was quite unlighted except for the great arc lamps shining on the wire, but later the rooms were fitted with electric-light.

The Germans prided themselves, and often I believe with some reason, on keeping their prison camps clean. Therefore our letters home describing the state of Schwarmstedt were none of them allowed through. Finally we decided to include in every letter a perfectly frank and accurate account of the camp, with the object that (1) if the letters did not pass the German censor, then no letters at all would reach home from the camp, and people would, we thought, cause inquiry to be made; (2) if any of the letters did get through they would contain the bald truth. Fortunately it was not long before Captains Fox and Caunter were able to escape, and as soon as we knew that they had arrived safely in England, we felt that further strafing of letters was not necessary. So, evidently, did the Germans, for the censoring became less strict.

Each morning exhibits from the inter-barrack bug-hunting competition were pinned to the doors of the rooms. They were of a very varied description, and a matter of great interest to the collectors. But this sporting and scientific event was soon forbidden by the authorities as 'insulting to the German Kaiser.' Schwarmstedt was one of those camps where something funny happened every day, and I am very sorry that I never kept a diary, because now it is impossible to remember all the things.

The food provided by the Germans was exceedingly scanty and bad, but it had to be used to some extent, as the supply of private parcels was not yet coming through from England to the new address, and food brought from Crefeld did not quite last out the interval. The daily ration, for which we paid one mark fifty pfennigs, comprised the following:

Breakfast: black coffee, made, I believe, from acorns.

Dinner: soup, containing cabbage, black peas, mangel-wurzel, occasional pieces of potato, and once or twice a week tiny shreds of meat.

Supper: thin soup, more like pig's wash than anything else.

In addition to this, we were allowed to purchase two pounds of war-bread a week at sixty pfennigs. It was nasty sour stuff, and had violent effects on the stomach. The colour of the crust was brown, but inside it was khaki, and so putty-like that a ball of it rolled and flung against the wall stuck there.

Our private food was cooked in ovens dug into the sand of the camp. I never became expert as some did, 'but Bobbie' was a wonderful chef. Condensed milk, a little flour, and some Eno's Fruit Salts for raising purposes, was all he needed to make cakes fit for the King; and I have known him create an omelette large enough for six hungry people out of only three eggs and a little flour. Fuel was obtained on our walks, which were the one really pleasant feature of Schwarmstedt. The country round was wild but beautiful. There were woods in which to lie talking while tea was boiled on a stick fire; gorse and heather to smell; and streams to bathe in as long as we remained unseen. It was possible to wander for miles amid the red heather and the golden gorse without seeing a house, or a human being within shade of the dappled pine-woods, which dotted darkly green the countryside.

To these pleasant walks I attribute the general good health of Schwarmstedt prisoners, in spite of bad camp conditions; and the fact is that (strange as it may seem) I felt much better there than I had done at Crefeld, which was a far better prison.

One day a swarm of bees came into the *lager* and affixed themselves to the pump handle. No one cared to go near them except Bobbie, who was wearing kilts, a fact which most people would regard as an additional reason for avoiding close acquaintance with bees. But not so 'Bobbie' he revelled in them, and walked proudly about the camp with clusters hanging from him, sworn at by all he approached, and followed, though not too closely, by a timid but envious German guard, exclaiming at intervals, 'Meine schwarm! Meine Schwarm!'

The funniest things which happened at Schwarmstedt generally took place in connection with escaping, which was the chief feature of its history, and must have a chapter to itself. That it was not a difficult camp to 'break' was quickly discovered when three officers left suddenly within thirty-six hours of arrival, leaving the wire cut behind them. It was imagined by the Germans that this escape must have been effected during the night, and an order came out that no windows were to be opened between the hours of 6 p.m. and 6 a.m. Later on, as the escapes continued, and particularly as the glass got accidentally broken, this rule was suffered to lapse.

In answer to those who think it strange that camps should differ so greatly as Schwarmstedt, Crefeld, and Gutersloh, since Germany is, generally speaking, run on a single system, I must explain that in the matter of prison *lagers* that is certainly not so, for the Camp Commandant is independent of all Government departments, and responsible only to the Corps Commander, and through him to the Kaiser. The result is what might be expected. The camps differ according to the character of the Commandant, and particularly according to the Corps Commander in whose Division the camp is. Schwarmstedt, Ströhen, and Holzminden, probably the three worst camps in Germany, were all in the Hanover district, that is in the 10th Army Corps, commanded by Von H., who simply loathed the British: for what precise reason I don't know, but it was said because he had got into disgrace on the Somme by losing to them two German divisions.

I will conclude this chapter with a tale apropos of letters which is amusingly indicative of German snobbery.

After the letter strafe was removed, everyone was naturally very anxious to get news quickly through to England, reassuring friends of his safety after the long interval without correspondence. But the Germans did all they could to cause delay, and it was found that a letter written by any ordinary officer took about three months getting home. Then came the brilliant idea to one of us that perhaps the correspondence of an officer not ordinary, addressed to people whose rank was similarly unusual might receive more prompt attention. This wise man proceeded to re-write his letters, addressing them to the Duchess of Brighton, and putting his proper home address underneath. Could these letters, he asked the interpreter, be forwarded at once to England? The interpreter looked at the envelopes.

'Ah! the Duchess of Brighton, she is your mother, yes?'

'Certainly,' said the officer.

'I will at once see what I can do, mein Herr.' And in a very short time that officer's letters had arrived safely to his mother in spite of all the warnings of his friends that the English postal authorities would probably give them to Miss Connie Ediss.[1]

---

1 [Publisher's note] Connie Eddis (1871-1934) was a famous music hall star and 'gaiety comedienne' she appeared in the West End and on Broadway. She was born and raised in Brighton and by the 1920s, specialised in matronly roles; hence the joke that she might receive post addressed to the Duchess of Brighton.

13

SCHWARMSTEDT:
SOME ESCAPES

THE SOIL OF SCHWARMSTEDT was sandy, with peat about a foot down. By digging two feet one came to water. Obviously, therefore, it was unsuited for tunnelling. Nevertheless one or two tunnels were attempted, and I am sorry to say that the last one ended disastrously in two of my friends getting shot. 'Mossy,' who had been collared by the Boches at Crefeld a few days after our departure, was one of the victims, but he was not shot dead, as was poor M. A very shallow tunnel, hardly better than a rabbit-hole, had been driven from beneath the floor of a camp building to come out a few yards the 'right' side of the barbed wire. It was all that was possible under the circumstances, and all that was necessary.

The Huns got wind of the attempt and were waiting for them. Poor M. was shot without challenge or chance of life at five yards' range, and 'Mossy' got an arm badly smashed. Nobody whined about it (it would have been the last thing they would have wished; they had taken their risk and paid for it), but I cannot bring myself to imagine any British soldier deliberately killing a defenceless man in such circumstances. He might have shot him running, or said, 'Get back, and think yourself lucky with five months' gaol '—that was the penalty at the time—but since it is the duty of all soldiers to escape if they can, he would hardly have murdered him for making the attempt. Wolf was the name of the Hun who did it—a name which we took in case of any future chance of justice—and a wolf he must have been, with a wolf's heart and a wolf's brain, to shoot a defenceless man without challenge, in cold blood.

The Commandant allowed M. a military funeral, which took place in a small churchyard about six miles away. His particular friends, the members of his room, and a per-centage of other prisoners, were allowed to attend, and stood by the graveside when the German soldiers fired a salute of three rounds which echoed back from the over-shadowing woods. There, with sunlight, branch-filtered, falling across the brown earth which covered him, we left poor M. when the echoes had fallen to silence and only the sough of the trees could be heard. He was one of the gentlest and bravest souls I ever knew.

Most of the German sentries disapproved of Wolf, and were in fact kind and credulous men, as is proved by the following amusing occurrence. One day P. and H. dressed themselves in the clothes of French orderlies, of whom there were a few at Schwarmstedt, and looked so exceedingly comic that we had to roar with laughter. They marched solemnly to an empty sentry-box which was in the camp, laid it flat, placed their escaping kit inside, and carried it to the camp entrance. Unfortunately, they met the Boche sergeant-major.

'What are you doing?' said he.

'We are moving this old sentry-box outside the wire.'

'But why?'

'Commandant's orders.'

As they had no guard in charge of them the sergeant-major was suspicious. 'That is not true,' said he; 'you are Englanders.'

'But no, monsieur.'

'Yes, I have my suspicions. I will cause an inquiry to be made.'

Off he went to look at the list of men on duty that day, and the details of their work. When he returned later on with a guard, he was surprised and even hurt to discover that they had both vanished, taking their kit, but leaving the sentry-box to be moved back to its proper place.

Other attempts, equally barefaced, were successful. N., having stolen a German uniform, and M., being suitably disguised by an artist friend, one afternoon went to the gate, unlocked it with a home-made key, and walked out before the eyes of the whole camp.

Nor were they recaptured for a fortnight, by which time they had got nearly to the border.

The key they used was made of camp money melted down and poured into a mould; an impression of the lock had been taken with shaving-soap, and the rest of the business was done with a file and a candle, as previously described. Many such keys were made at Schwarmstedt, and after we had been there a month or two I think we were pretty well able to unlock any room in the whole camp.

Officers who had obtained maps of the country through bribery, or in some other way, lent them round for friends to copy. Thus it was that I managed to get a very good one. Thin paper, such as found in Huntley and Palmer's biscuit-tins, was generally used for tracing, and answered the purpose well. My compass was also home-made, one of the famous 'Black' manufacture, born out of a magnet, a needle, and an old watch-case. It was really laughable how, until they grew wiser with experience, the Germans actually allowed us to purchase magnets, not to speak of rucksacks and civilian hats, at the canteen; but the rucksacks were bought up so quickly that they became suspicious and would get no more in. They even tried to collar back those which they had sold, but without much success. Therefore, to carry my supply of food I cut up and sewed into a knapsack the old valise in which my clothes had been sent out to me from England. When finished it was large enough to carry food for twenty-one days, at the end of which time I certainly expected to be caught or over. Saving up food for the journey was a matter of some time and difficulty at Schwarmstedt, but it proceeded surely, although rather slowly, as parcels came along from England, and as one was able to slip occasional unopened tins into one's pocket when visiting the parcel office. Meanwhile, those who were fortunate enough to have a store ready tried various methods of escaping.

As we had been allowed to bring only one box with us from Crefeld, we all naturally brought the biggest we had. But it was obvious that boxes of that size could not be k'ept in rooms already overcrowded with the beds of fifteen or sixteen officers —even when the beds were double-decked (*vide* Mr. Bernard's drawing, p. 166)—so the German authorities ordered that they should be removed from the camp to a store-shed outside the wire. Certain officers, bent on emulating St. Paul, got into their boxes (as a matter of fact they were large wicker baskets), and arranged that English orderlies should carry them across to the store-shed, from which they would be able to escape during the night. All went well at first. By two o'clock the baskets were outside the gate, and moving merrily towards the shed. Then suddenly the German officer called a halt, and decided that as the soldiers were needed for other work the baskets should stay where they were until five o'clock. The day was very hot. After a time one of the occupants got cramp and awful squeakings and scratchings came from his basket. 'Cover it up with a lonely tune,' was our immediate motto, and by whistling, talking, and shouting, near the gate, we did our best; but the sentry was obviously suspicious, for he looked hard at the box. Fortunately he did not stab it with his bayonet; nor could he open any of them, because they were locked, all the keys being carried by one officer in another basket, who was expected to cut himself out and liberate his companions. At last the boxes were taken to the shed, but whether the sentry had mentioned his suspicions, or whether, as is also alleged, one of the escapers showed himself at the store-room window, it presently happened that at about eight o'clock a German officer followed by a guard went straight to the place where they were, and captured them

DOUBLE-DECKED BEDS

all. We saw them marched off to cells, where they were to do five months' solitary confinement, which was the ridiculously harsh penalty for an attempt to escape until it was reduced to a fortnight by mutual arrangement between the two governments in July, 1917.

A great dog was kept by the Germans to track down prisoners who escaped, but like most other Germans at Schwarmstedt, he was open to corruption, and on discovering that the English officers could give him better and more plentiful food than his proper masters, he promptly became great friends with them. So much so that finally, when one of the officers escaped, he took the dog along with him. Whether he made him carry his pack or not I am unable to say, but rumour has it that he was unable to persuade the dog to leave him even after he had made an attempt upon its life by endeavouring to drown it in a river. It is not easy to hold the head of a big dog under water against his will, and if he insists upon following you after you have plainly showed such disinclination for his company, what more is there for a poor prisoner to do? It was not long before several other officers who possessed wire-cutters escaped by using them, and two more succeeded in climbing over the wire in a dark corner of the camp.

As a result of this, extra sentries were put on, and larger lamps hung up. Therefore, though none of these men got over (most were recaptured quite near the Holland frontier), their failure was of service to their country, since it takes at least six men to provide an extra sentry-post, men who might be fighting, or at least replacing on farms and elsewhere other German fighting men.

The following note smuggled out of prison is of interest as the true diary of an escaping officer, and as showing the way in which experience was pooled in camp for the common good, so each failure might contribute towards somebody's success.

'My dear M.,

1. Climbing with a cross-fence is easy, and G. did it on the straight.

'2. Food: Sugar, biscuits, choc, Horlicks, and Quakers to soak in water, excellent. Much meat when tired dangerous. Water-bottle essential.

'3. Route: Consult Jacky's map and little flying man's. Jacky's especially for Weser-Ems and its surroundings.

'4. Our route: 400 yards north, then west with a little south, but not crossing Schwarmstedt road or trolley-line. Boggy, and two or three big shallow drains, but feasible this weather; a mile or so of water-meadows. Then south-west through forest of pine, and heath. Several kilos until road with small village on ridge. Cross-road and single rail to edge of pine-wood, cross grassy waste (curlews and plovers). South-west to river Aller where flowing north. Unfordable. Find boat opposite tongue of wood. Leave it wrong side. Strike up to ridge and cross rail in wood. Follow road through village to Schwarmstedt. Schwarmstedt watched. Nearly caught. Cross double rail, and lie up in wood. (End of second night.) South-west cross single rail. One kilo west, Schwarmstedt, to river. Follow river up to bridge on road leading from Hope to?. Stolzen village immediately on left bank. (Station Hope is on

Saltau to Hanover line, one station on Hanover side of Schwarmstedt.) Cross bridge through Stolzen village, turn left and straight along road to Niestadt. Lie up in pine-wood right of road. (End of fourth night.) Continue down road till scared by bicycle patrol in village, turn off to south-west through woods some miles; then stopped by bog and driven on to rail about three kilos north of Niestadt. Lie up in wood close to rail. (End of fifth night.) Cross embanked road and get through bit of heath and pine on to a track running through crops due south to level crossing (watched); leave rail on left and strike south-west along Wunstof road. Past north Wunstof and due west through huge private wood (oak). Leave wood and go south-west three or four kilos. Lie up. (End of sixth night.) South-west over road until reach Weser-Ems canal. Follow canal west four or five kilos until Stadthagen to Windheim (?) road crosses it. Then north-west (to avoid Minden) along this road. Lie up. (End of seventh night.) Continue north-west until Windheim. Through village and down by cart-tracks through water-meadows to river Weser. Find boat outside factory, and opposite another factory, at edge of tongue of wood. Leave boat on wrong side and lie up two to three kilos west of river in country of small farms and heath and pine-woods. (End of eighth night.) Follow tracks eight to ten kilos due west, until strike road with signpost saying "Friedwald, 5 kilos" behind us, last eight kilos through forest and waste. Then south-west by south along roads and camp in view of Wichenget hills. (End of ninth night.) South-west one to two kilos to canal, and due west along canal. Camp five to six kilos west of railway, running north from Lubbeke. (End of tenth night.) West along canal, making detour to avoid rail-bridges (first single line, then double line, two bridges).

N.B., Railway-bridges built thus:

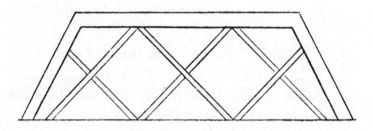

Road-bridges thus:

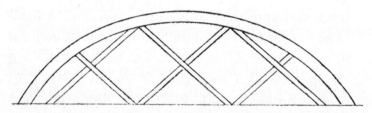

Camp about fifteen kilos west of rail in pine-woods north of canal. (End of eleventh night.) Along canal (passing three Ruskies) until two kilos west of rail running north to Wilhelmshaven. Lie up in big wood on hill south of canal. (End of twelfth night.) Detour round railway-bridge and along canal. Here very heavy sandy going. Canal runs through big sandy waste, part bog. Lie up close to canal south of Recke just east of small rail-bridge. (End of thirteenth night.) Start along canal, passing under a railway-bridge; run bang into

Hilfsdienstwache and four men fishing. Taken to small *lager* in Recke village, then to bigger *lager* two kilos north of Recke. Altogether five camps round Recke, one of which at Minteren. Eight prisoners (various) had been taken in that neighbourhood that week before us.

'All accounts, French and German agreed that:

'1. Between Norshoom and Bentheim (roughly) the guards had been strengthened last year owing to the flow of fugitives.

'2. All bridges from Recke west, including those over the Ems, were guarded.

'3. The Ems must be swum.

'4. Hardly any now go through there.

'Nothing was said to show that there was a sentry on the frontier every so many yards, but roads? bridges, and likely points were watched.

'Return journey: Recke rail to Ieverversburg, passing south of canal into hilly country of woods and small farms, with big woods on crest round Warsen. Ieverversburg to Osnabruck. Osnabruck to Nohen (hilly and woody), Nohen to Minden, Hanover, Schwarmstedt, and off at Hademsdorf station, north of Schwarmstedt, to which our trolley-line runs down.

'Trolley-line follows a dry line of country. Leave rail, through woods, then about one to two kilos of spongy meadows, then this heath. No sign of posts between 9 and 10 p.m. Between Schwarmstedt and Hademsdorf the railway crosses the Aller. Did not see watcher.

'Conclusions: On five occasions we passed right by a man unchallenged, saying either "Guten abend" or nothing. Once we were stopped, but got off by a little German and by having an ugly-looking stick. When we ran into anyone it was nearly always before midnight, and it was very dangerous to leave lying-up positions before 11 p.m. During the day we were several times lying within twenty yards of workers or passersby, and it pays to have a bit of loose heather ready to scatter over self and belongings. Rye at this moment makes the very best cover, though bad if discovered, no doubt. Walk up furrow between it and another corncrop, or between two plants of rye, turn in and walk quietly, keeping impediments high, then turn right or left and lie down. But it's fearfully hot midday, and water is essential. Damp woods—*e.g.*, alder, spruce, oak—have so many mosquitoes as to interfere with sleep and rob you of vitality. Young pines, heather, and juniper the best possible combination. Never fail to get water to take into hiding, and drink plentifully also at night. Seed spuds are all right raw (always found close to houses). Everything in a mackintosh is a good idea. We only had one wet night, good weather helps enormously, and especially north star.

'Another time I should never pass through a village till after midnight, and before 3.15 a.m. Fifty kilos from the frontier I should leave all roads and villages and use tracks. I should put into my map the name of every village; it helps so with the signposts. I should make for the Dutch re-entrant north of the Ems Vecht canal, and on the lines given I should reckon twenty nights inclusive, allowing a course of 200 kilos. Our best night we did twenty to twenty-two, the canal tow-path was easily the best going, and deserted until Recke.

'Twenty nights means a lot of food. I could have just done twenty to twenty-one on what I took, but at first I ate painfully little. Now, after four days' rest, I am, however, much better than when I started. I was weakest the third and fourth nights out. One has no spirit at the end, but one's legs will keep trudging well on a level surface. Men on bicycles are dangerous, and often, I fancy, telephone ahead instead of stopping one. Civilian kit would be a great help. Wear a hat—a "Gor'-blimy" is better than nothing.

'As to routes, I am not sure I wouldn't go the same until three to four kilos west of Recke. Then turn due north, ten kilos. Then north-west and into re-entrant. On the other hand I might try the trolley-line and Hademsdorf rail-bridge for speed. Then, avoiding stations, to Stolzen bridge, thence Drakenberg; try to boat the Weser near there, and take a line north of the big swamp that lies east and north-east of Recke, and so avoid the canal.

'The lieutenant here says west or south-west from this camp is impossible! A straight west line and good going like the canal is very tempting, but on the big heaths and reclaimed land the tracks run beautifully straight. Take change of socks, three big handkerchiefs, spare shorts, plenty of cord, and cut sticks. I shall probably get out to you temporarily in a few days. Love to the whole room. Keep this in cache.'

14

SCHWARMSTEDT:
SOME ESCAPES (continued)

The baggage-room at Schwarmstedt was, as I have said, outside the wire. We were allowed to visit it on occasions, and were guarded by a sentry who did not always count to see if the same number as went out returned with him. My first plan for escape was to go across and conceal myself in the baggage-room, getting away by jumping out of the window to a telegraph-pole, which would give me a slide of about twenty feet to the ground.

It was fortunate that on the day that I went across to attempt it, somebody noticed that the bottom of the telegraph pole had been recently twined round and round with barbed wire for about eight feet, a circumstance which would have made my slide down extremely unpleasant. Under these circumstances I concealed my equipment and waited for a better opportunity, which finally came when we were on the train and leaving Schwarmstedt for Holzminden—but that is another story.

About this time another officer was unfortunate in being discovered in the dust-trolley after it had been taken outside the wire. This truck ran on a light railway, and was filled and pushed in and out of the camp by our own orderlies under charge of a German guard. Usually it was not emptied until the following morning, and remained standing all night at a little distance from the camp. It happened, however, on this particular occasion that two hungry German soldiers came along, and seeing the loaded trolley standing there, determined to see if there was anything fit for food left in any of the old tins. To their great surprise, on tipping over the trolley, they discovered a dirty and bruised British officer.

In the summer of 1917 heath-fires were fairly frequent at Schwarmstedt. Flames swept down on the camp on several occasions, and as it would have burnt like tinder, all the orderlies and such German guards as were not on duty were turned out to divert the course of the fire by digging trenches, and beating away the approaching flames with green branches of trees.

It was a beautiful sight. Heavy smoke would tower up in the distance and a running wave of red fire be seen to sweep over the moor; a pine-tree suddenly outlined and painted in flame would stand up yellow against the sky, and the next moment be left behind a blackened ruin. Gradually the drifting smoke enveloped the camp, and before long neither guards nor prisoners were able to see more than a few yards in front of them. I forget whether it was during a fire, a thunderstorm, or a dust-storm, that Captains Fox and Caunter made their escape. An account of that remarkable journey to the frontier is given in a little book written by the latter entitled 'Thirteen Days,' which was the very short space of time they took in doing it. They were the first and last officers to get over from Schwarmstedt, although scores of others got out. Often there would be several officers out together, and sometimes they had been gone for a day or two before their absence was discovered by the Germans. Their beds at night were fitted with dummies, and their places taken on *Appel* by people already counted slipping round the back and being counted again.

Periodically the Germans made rigorous searches to find the hiding-places of maps, compasses, food, and escape kit generally, and these searches were often very diverting. It was the children's game of hide-and-seek played by grown-ups, and the Germans being in all respects so very much more 'growed-up' than the British, the advantage was naturally with the latter, because they enjoyed it, whereas the Huns didn't—indeed, at first they seemed to know nothing whatever about the game, and maps sportingly pinned to the backs of pictures, or on the underneath of tables, escaped scot-free. But laboriously and by degrees our hosts improved, and attained finally a certain proficiency, although, since they regarded the whole business merely as 'dienst,' they were naturally unable to throw themselves into it with the proper childish enthusiasm; and any new variation in the game always had them beaten. In this prison diversion the big dog was allowed to take part, and one day covered

YOU HAVE DER TINS—YES? NO?

himself with glory by unearthing a small store of hidden tins beneath the floor of a hut. This triumph pleased the Germans vastly, and was taken in very good part by the English officers, who immediately opened books and sweep-stakes as to the number of such hiding-places the dog would discover, and in what space of time. Cries of 'Good dog!' and 'Seek, seek!' gave him encouragement, and when at last he did discover a second and last store, a perfect howl of applause went up from all present. The Huns were puzzled by this behaviour, but as there was really nothing in it for which they could send us to prison, they contented themselves with sticking out their chests and scowling. At Ströhen, the sister camp to Schwarm-stedt, whither the rest of the Crefeld people had gone, an even funnier thing took place. Special detectives had been brought from Berlin, and a truly rigorous search was conducted by them, one of whom very soon bore pinned to his coat tails the inscription: 'You know my methods, Watson!' Several caches were discovered, and the experts seemed pleased; but the true point of the joke was that when they came to depart, they found that their pockets had been picked.

I think it would have been hard to discover everything that was hidden at Schwarmstedt without pulling the whole place to pieces. Floorboards, windowsills, walls, all had their secrets, not to mention any of the special stunts evolved for concealing forbidden articles in the personal belongings of prisoners—*e.g.,* handles of tennis-racquets. Sometimes the Germans did make a good haul, however, and then their difficulty was to keep it. The story of W.'s pack is a case in point. W.'s pack, containing all his escap-

ing kit and the hoarded food of months, had the misfortune to be discovered in its hiding-place by the Huns.
The German officer in charge of the search was not a bad
fellow, but arrogant and without humour save of the sour
kind which befits a Prussian. Delighted with his capture,
he went at once to the senior of the barrack in which the
pack was found, and prepared to gloat. An aged sentry
carried the pack, following him; and behind the aged
sentry went softly the owner of the pack, undiscovered as
yet, since it had not been opened. He was accompanied by
certain of his friends.

GERMAN OFFICER: 'A-ha, mein Herr, you see I have a
beautiful pack!'

BARRACK OFFICER: 'Indeed!'

G. O.: 'The owner, he was ready just to go, yes. And
you, mein Herr, when [smiling] are you leaving us?'

B. O.: 'Oh, next month, I think.'

G. O.: 'Ah, then I will show it to you. You will see what
to take with you.'

B.O.: 'That is very good of you, Herr Lieutenant.'

G. O.: 'Hans!'

AGED SENTRY: 'Yaw, Herr Hauptmann.'

He drops the pack to stand rigidly to attention after
the German manner.

G. O.: 'The pack, bring it here to me!'

Alas for Hans! that little bit of German discipline had
undone him. The pack was gone, vanished into air. W.
could do the hundred in about even time, and he was in
gym. shoes. A circle of friends closed round as he disap-

peared, and Hans saw nothing. He looked down first to the side where the pack had been. He looked to the other side. Then he looked behind him. He scratched his head. 'It is gone, Herr Hauptmann,' he murmured.

'Gone!' cried the Prussian officer, beating himself on the forehead and bringing out the most unusual oath I have ever heard, 'Mister God-Christ! These English!' Certainly an appeal to the Almighty was the only thing left him. The pack was two rooms away being pulled to pieces as fast as fingers could do it, and the contents being distributed hastily in hiding-places over all the hut. To retrieve it was beyond the bounds of human possibility.

15

ON THE COMRADESHIP OF
MEN AND BOOKS

THE FOLLOWING LECTURE WAS given at Schwarmstedt in 1917, and I include it in this record of prison life because I am getting rather tired of the Germans, and because I believe it shows amongst other things a good deal of the mentality of prisoners of war. People who don't like it can skip it, but I would rather that they did not buy the book.

One of the most amusing parts of a quaintly humorous book I happened recently to read concerned itself with the description of a very exclusive club. So exclusive was this club that it consisted only of the founder, the secretary, and the treasurer, and these were all the same man. To him meals were every day served solemnly in the club dining-room, and from time to time names were put up for membership by him in the capacity of secretary, and later on blackballed when he assumed the cloak of founder and the majority. It is perhaps hardly necessary for me to say that the club was an English one, with its headquarters situate in Oxford.

To-night I am speaking to an audience of Englishmen (I beg pardon—Britons!) on the comradeship of men and books, and the first thing I want to say is that there is in one sense—the sense in which I speak of them—very little difference between the two. Viewed as comrades, the things we expect to give them and the things we expect in return are in both cases almost identical.

But there is between them a broader and a closer relationship than this. Reflect for a moment on the general nature of art, and you will see what I mean.

Behind the book is the man.

Into every book is put consciously or unconsciously essence of the author.

The position of that person who inherits a fine library and never opens a book of it is identical with that of the club founder to whom I have referred; a man who regarded fellow-men with aversion, and never troubled to read a single volume of that large magnificent library of living literature which was his heritage, and which is the heritage of each one of us.

If every book is in essence a man, so is every man a book—humorous, noble, fantastic, dirty, as the case may be. And in the library of humanity there is no censor.

The man who will enjoy neither the one nor the other of these puts himself voluntarily into a viler prison than any this country affords. He lives, unhappy mortal, within himself.

Now there is no reason to generalize over our state when I can speak directly.

There are two possible prisons overshadowing our present existence. The one is of barbed wire, sentries, and roll-calls. The other is of green mould.

The first is one we may or may not (as Fortune wills) be able to escape. The second all may escape. How, is a question which, relating to the first, I may not discuss at the moment without involving you all in a charge of mutiny; moreover, you have your own theories on the subject, and quite possibly they are better than mine. Therefore let us pass to consideration of the second—escape from the prison of green mould.

Now we are all mouldy, more or less. We cannot help it, and it is a miracle we are not even mouldier. Without question there is no mould so thick, so gaudily green, as the mould which germinates in the minds of men who are prisoners of war. Months-stale cake and the mouldiness of Gorgon-zola cheese is nothing to this! I ought to know. It was thick enough over me when I wrote this poem to relieve my feelings, and to describe the state of men upon whom shadow of captivity has fallen with all its devitalizing darkness of mind and atrophy of sense: a state comparable to premature burial, if it supplied a single thrill worthy of that horrific experience. That it does not is its essential dreadfulness.

Here the memory of old adventure clashes with the present stagnation in a laughter more bitter than tears: more desperate, less refreshing.

PRISONERS.

Comrades of risk and rigour long ago,
Ye who did battle under Honour's name,
Hoped—living or shot down—a meed of fame,
And wooed bright Danger for one thrilling kiss;
Laugh, O laugh well, that we have come to this!

Laugh, O laugh loud! all ye who long ago
Adventure sought in gallant company.
Safe in stagnation, laugh! laugh heartily!
While on this filthiest backwater of Time's flow
Drift we and rot till something set us free.

Laugh like old men with senses atrophied,
Heeding no Present, to the Future dead,
Nodding quite foolish by the warm fireside,
And seeing no flame, but only in the red
And flickering embers pictures of the Past—
Life like a cinder fading black at last!

That is the prison feeling.

All get it at times. Some (poor wretches!) have it all the time. That is 'green mould.' The companion poem indicates a way of escape.

SOLITARY CONFINEMENT.

No mortal comes to visit me to-day,
Only the gay and early-rising sun,
Who strolled in nonchalantly just to say,
'Good-morrow, and despair not, foolish one!'
But like the tune which comforted King Saul
Comes to my brain that golden madrigal,
Anon the playful wind arises, swells
Into vague music, and departing leaves

A sense of bare blue heights and tinkling bells,
Audible silences which sound achieves
Through music, mountain streams and tinted heather,
And drowsy flocks drifting in golden weather.
Lastly, as to my bed I turn for rest,
Comes Lady Moon herself on silver feet
To sit with one white arm across my breast,
Talking of elves, and haunts where they do meet.
No mortal comes to see me, yet I say,
Oh, I have had fine visitors to-day!

That is escape. I do not suggest it is the only-way. Indeed, I think it a rather personal means, depending as it does on a certain temperament and mood interested in common things—ordinary sunshine, a wind, clouds, and common moonlight entering a room.

To become comrade of the sun, a friend to the breeze, or the moon's lover, is escape real enough— adventurous indeed!

But it is not a common ideal. It is not open to all, nor to any at all time.

The comradeship of men and books is more normal and much more easily attained. Deservedly it is a more popular way of escape.

Men, whether alive and veiled in the flesh, or dead and revealed in books, are 'the proper study of mankind.'

Now as prisoners it might well have been imagined that comrades of men and of books would be but few. This is certainly what I expected when I was captured.

My eyes, already gazing back a little wistfully on the free, varied fellowship of the ranks, were prepared to discover in an officers' camp a number of beings from

Sandhurst, Woolwich, and one or other of the universities, all belonging to one class, utterly typical, utterly conventional, utterly uninteresting.

What they did discover was a large mixed community of Russians, French, Belgians, Welsh, English, Scotch, Irish (North and South), Canadians, South Africans, Australians, and New Zealanders—to say nothing of Germans, whose ways are a joy for ever.

In a disused lunatic asylum I found more good men than I shall ever again meet.

What need to go round the world? The ends of the earth had contrived to come in to me!

Here were Regular soldiers of all nationalities, lawyers, priests, doctors, undergraduates, farmers, schoolmasters, artists, members of Parliament, and business men: men who had been everywhere and done everything, men who had been everywhere and done nothing, men who had done everything and been (apparently) nowhere; a fascinating crowd! Not even the varied ranks of a British regiment could compete with it.

Now there are many ways of classifying men—and they are all bad.

It is easy and futile to label men 'old Regulars,' 'New Army,' 'black troops,'[1] etc. It is simple to say 'farmer, poet, doctor'—as simple as counting plum-stones to the tune of 'Tinker, tailor, soldier, sailor,' and equally childish. The fact remains that they are all men, and therefore all different.

I have known babes of the 'New Army' more professional than any Regular. I have seen Regulars as irregular

---

[1] Black troops = Colonials. Photographs of some Canadian officers were thus labelled in a German paper, and the name was immediatelly adopted for camp use.

as the poets themselves. Even the most typical of his class, let one get beneath the mask, one may find utterly various and wonderful—as wonderful in weakness as in strength, in folly as in nobility.

In the trenches, one knows, there was little time for deliberate talk, and none at all for well-recollected impressions of things. But here in captivity there is simply nothing else to do. Therefore I have always been grateful to the Germans who sent me to a large mixed camp instead of a small 'all English' one. It may have been done with the mistaken notion that we should all quarrel, but still I am grateful.

To be interested in human nature as it stood, rather than as it might be supposed to be, was an experience exceedingly fascinating to many a young officer, and certainly to me.

And a community of men—nearly a thousand—drawn from the ends of the world, and necessarily of widely varied and highly dramatic experience, was fine material for study.

Often I have planned to get a number of such friends to write me merely the account of their capture. What fascinating reading it would make! But this was never done, since I found it easier and more interesting to get them to talk. In the unrestrained contact of prisondom one is able to get to know men more easily and more thoroughly than through five years spent in each of their separate countries—which would (in this case) be the work of a lifetime.

Absorption of such multifarious personalities is also carried on through the written articles published in our prison papers, through lectures, through contact in games and in work, and, best of all, through frank interminable talks from morning to twilight carried on while walking round and round the wire, and continued later in bed before drifting to sleep. So I found in this close community of men—so diverse in temperament and attributes—a small State imposing so prodigally tests of tact and character that the result was a world in miniature— a world, it is true, woefully deficient in what is sometimes called man's better half.

As to women, the current philosophy of the State has found expression in the remark of a Frenchman who was walking round with me on a sunny morning, while a rather pretty girl contemplated us from beyond the wire. 'It is not useful' (*i.e.,* no use), said he, 'to get excited.' I agreed.

I will not further describe the details of what was, I believe, an ideal prison camp—in so far as that is a practical possibility. Some of you had experience of Gütersloh, and the rest probably underwent rather similar experiences before you came to this place.[2] The point is, that to no one of all of us who was the least interested in mankind can have come the comradeship of all those men other than as a revelation.

To more than one of us undoubtedly had come the suspicion before war that England, held fast in the grip of her industrial system, was already upon the path of decadence. Experience of the British Tommy taught us to think differently.

The finest weapon ever placed in the hand of democracy is the New Army. It is also the soundest and most handy basis upon which to build a firm understanding.

---

2 Schwarmstedt.

When those young employers of labour, who have done such magnificent work as officers, return to England after the war to take up the threads, or rather the reins, of their former occupation; when trouble arises and the temptation to call names— 'lazy scoundrels,' 'cads,' 'ignorant agitators, etc.—let them remember that the vast body of these 'ungrateful wretches' are the same men who went to make up the platoons they were so proud of and so rightly proud. The men on their part should remember how many of these 'hateful and greedy capitalists' were once loved and trusted captains. Further, let them seek explanation of the change (which is, I fear, inevitable) in the fact that these men were previously organized—content and enthusiastic—in the pursuit of an aim common to all, and let them ask themselves where that aim is, if anything has arisen to replace it, what common ideal now exists to be served—in short, if we are as fully organized for peace as we were for war, as enthusiastic for Life as we were for Death.

The solution of the labour difficulty will doubtless lie in a common ideal. Perhaps the politicians will supply it.

Excuse the digression. I was saying that many men who had lost faith in the destiny of England had the personal fortune to regain that faith during the war, with what unspeakable happiness! To those of them who were also captured there came on the top of this, to confirm it, a close companionship, under exacting circumstances, with more fine men than would ever again be found drawn into a little wired-in space from the four corners of the world.

This is not flattery. It is merely emphasis of the one bright spot of our common captivity.

The prisoner of war who returns home knowing no more of human nature—its fascinating diversity, its contraction from big to little and back again, its cravings, its prejudices, its unexpected generosity, its unexpected meanness, its unexhausted, inexhaustible entertainment— has very certainly neglected his opportunities.

There are two things worth reading: men and books. What about women? They are, generally speaking, written in cipher: and somebody else has the key. But in the Bible of humanity they are certainly the last Book—the Book of Revelation. But it is an impracticable question in present circumstances : and therefore I say, 'There are only two things worth studying: men and books.' We possess both. We possess such leisure to study them as men seldom get, and such as we (please God!) shall never get again.

But what object is served by the study of one's fellows? That depends on the way you regard them. To a villain they are worth studying that he may exploit their weaknesses. A philosopher may study them from curiosity, a human being from mere warmth of heart. A Christian will certainly do so out of brotherly interest, and with the same affectionate regard which he is accustomed to give his right hand, his stomach, or any other really important member.

It is this feeling of membership, this sense of corporate existence, that is the keynote of what I believe is most considerable in modern literature.

Now people are always anxious to divide books under two headings, 'Classic' and 'Modern,' and the terms popularly imply books written by well-known men who are dead, and books written by men, generally not so well known, who are living. These latter are supposed to be 'trash' until the author has died, and elders are often heard advising younger people to waste no time on 'modern stuff' until they have read *all* the classics—to do which is manifestly the work of a lifetime.

Now, it is my belief that they ought to be read side by side; but if only one sort is to be enjoyed, then it is clear that it is not 'the classics' which should be preferred by a man whose responsibilities and opportunities of living lie in the present.

To say that life does not change is, in this sense, merely false.

It is obvious that life as it came to Dr. Samuel Johnson is in many respects wholly different to life as it comes to you and me.

True, its primal mysteries remain steadfast. But it is not until one has read a good deal of modern literature that one comes to realization of that truth, and so into comradeship with the great dead.

I cannot help thinking of books as if they were men—and, indeed, books are flowers of a man's mind, and exhale his essential odour.

This is not to say that to talk to a man is more profitable than to read his books. It is a great advantage to be able to do both—a wonderful help—especially in the case of the lesser artists, not necessarily lesser men. But even with the very greatest it is a help. That is the value of biography. 'The Devil was the first Whig' would be nonsense in the mouth of any but Sam Johnson. 'The path of excess leads to the palace of wisdom' is a saying which, in the mouth of Blake, means something quite different and something far more wise than it would have on the lips of Wilde, who might easily have said it.

No questions of conduct influence the matter; it is merely a different spirit which informs the words and gives them a different meaning.

> 'Beauty is truth, truth beauty—that is all
> Ye know on earth, and all ye need to know.'

Is no significance added to this great and almost hackneyed saying, when you read the following in one of Keats' private letters?—'I am certain of nothing but of the holiness of the heart's affections, and the truth of imagination. What the imagination seizes as beauty must be truth. . . . The imagination may be compared to Adam's dream; he awoke and found it truth.'

Take a few of the other great sayings of life.

'Fellowship is life, lack of fellowship is hell.'

'There is no wealth but life.'

'What shall it profit a man if he gain the whole world and lose his own soul?"

'Love is the fulfilling of the law.'

These words found inscribed on some lonely rock would have been great, but do you think that, detached from the personalities of Morris, Ruskin, and Jesus Christ, they would have had the same weight, or even meant the same thing?

They would not.

The reason why a man's book is more important than his talk is that which causes libel to be treated in English law as a more serious offence than slander.

It is not the flippant child of any mere impulse allowed carelessly to roam, nor a Folly escaped to gambol in the sun behind the back of Wisdom.

It is the voluntary and considered utterance of a man saying, 'This is what I mean, or did sincerely mean at one time of my life.'

And to heighten the force of his utterance, and strengthen its appeal, art supplies him with form, passion with rhythm, and music with fit words and rhyme.

Carlyle has pointed out that when men speak passionately—moved, for example, by indignation, love, or fear—their speech becomes definitely rhythmic. Rhyme is a fitful enchantment, pleasing the ear, and befriending Memory.

But what, in general, sets the written and deliberate word above the casual phrases of any heart-to-heart talk—be it never so sincere or impassioned—is form.

Now form is not, as is sometimes suggested, a cast-iron mould designed to hold the matter of a novel, a play, or a poem, and labelled accordingly, but it is, none the less, a very real and very wonderful thing.

So a naked boy or girl may fall into some unconscious attitude which seems literally to lift it above humanity. One would wish it struck dead and turned to stone, so to preserve unbroken through the ages that gracious beauty.

Such is the miracle of form, I conceive, and so I have symbolized it in the following poem:

> Flower-like and shy
> You stand, sweet mortal, at the river's brim:
> With what unconscious grace
> Your limbs to some strange law surrendering
> Which lifts you clear of our humanity.

> Now would I sacrifice
> Your breathing, warmth, and all the strange romance
> Of living to a moment. Ere you break
> The greater thing than you, I would my eyes
> Were basilisk to turn you into stone!
> So should you be the world's inheritance:
> And souls of unborn men should draw their breath
> From mortal you, immortalized in death.

Style is said to be the marriage of matter to manner.

Form consists in striking them dead in the hour of consummation, that so they may be made immortal.

It is probably this transformation (as of men into gods) which has caused a certain section of writers to regard literature as something outside themselves to be attained to, rather than as something inside themselves to be expressed: and to suppose that the business of an artist lies in the filling in of art-forms, and not in the making of them.

Now, having considered separately men and books, their relation one to another, and the distinction evident between them, we may go on to examine the rules which should govern our choice of them as friends.

But first of all there is the business of introduction. This service is usually done, with regard to books, by our recognized literary chaperones—the critics. Critics are of two classes.

There are those whose aim is to make other men's work the raw material of a new creation—a theory put forward in Wilde's Essay 'The Critic as Artist.' (In this sense biography is often a kind of criticism.)

And there are those (experts in taste) whose work is the sampling and classifying of other men's books, so that, as a result of their reports and the time spent in preparing them, we may save our own time and money, and learn easily what is worth reading. In choosing books we must always depend a great deal on the critics.

We simply haven't the time, money, or inclination to go experimenting among the millions of books—good, bad, and indifferent—which are produced yearly.

It is a wise rule to read a book before you buy it; and when this is impossible (through the fallibility of libraries), to make sure that the man who reads it for you (i.e., the critic) shares in the main your idea of what is a good and what a bad book. Having that assurance, you can afford to trust him.

Occasionally, since critics are not more divine than other men, you will be deceived, but that is in the course of nature, and neither affects the necessity of trusting nor the wisdom of knowing him. 'Test your critic' is a golden rule. Trust him—afterwards.

I speak of buying books as a necessity. Libraries, like reviews, are not an end, but a means. They enable you to judge a book by testing it.

Books worth calling books should be 'read, marked, learned, and inwardly digested.' These things are a literal and absolute necessity.

And the same is true of all great art. So William Watson writes:

> 'Have I not seen the starry throngs
> Dance; and the soul of April break in bud?

Have I not taken Schubert's songs
Into my brain and blood?"

It is to take these things into your brain and blood that
you read.

Fine books should become part of you like beef and
beer, and through a similar process of digestion. Artistic
appreciation means nothing else but that.

Shall we prate of keeping untouched our individuality
when we are being influenced, yes, and *altered*, every day
and every moment of life?

One's skin is changed every seven years. One's soul is
changed every day of the week, and every moment of the day.

There is no slightest sensation or idea crossing man's life
which fails in its fateful chemistry. Not merely one's deeds,
but one's inactivity; not merely one's company, but one's
solitude; not merely one's perceptions, but one's blindness,
help mould the changeful thing we name oneself.

Clearly, the choice is not between changing, or
remaining the same; but between being moved greatly and
in fine directions, or meanly in the byways of mediocrity.
This is an essential reflection in choosing comrades of men
or books.

Perhaps it is even more important with regard to books
than to men, since they are our free choice, but, in general,
one's human companions are not.

It is hard to over-estimate the privilege which, at price
of a couple of drinks, gives entrance to the mind of Shakespeare, and for the cost of a good gun allows fellowship
with the world's greatest, most fascinating men.

And how accessible are these friends! Flow they will
talk to you!—with what tenderness and tact, with what

humour and wisdom, if you will but listen!

I am altogether against the abominable habit of using books as a drug. To shut myself off from life and dwell in a fool's paradise is a thing for which I have, in the words of the soldier, neither time nor inclination.

But the great books are always true to life, more real than the outward show we sometimes call life, more practical than any of our 'modern business men.'

It was practical advice Byron gave to Greece before he went on to the very practical work of dying for her:

> 'Trust not for freedom to the Franks—
> They have a king who buys and sells.
> In native swords and native ranks,
> The only hope of courage dwells;
> But Turkish force and Latin fraud
> Would break your shield, however broad.'

The poet was more practical than the politicians.

So, in the conception of what most matters in the making of a city, the poet Whitman is much more practical than all the town councillors, expert in planning and improving.

> 'Where the city of the faithfullest friends stands,
> Where the city of the cleanliness of the sexes stands,
> Where the city of the healthiest fathers stands,
> Where the city of the best-bodied mothers stands—
> There the great city stands.'

And again: 'How the floridness of the materials of cities shrivels before a man's or woman's look!'

London and Liverpool are perhaps not such great cities judged by that test!

It is the mark of all big men that their great practical sayings (founded upon eternal principles, not on passing expediency) do not wear out with time, but are applicable to the Future and the Present also.

Burke is speaking to the Government of 1775, but he is speaking also to the Government of To-day, when he says: '. . . My hold of the Colonies is in the close affection which grows from common names, from kindred blood, from similar privileges, and equal protection. These are ties which, though light as air, are as strong as links of iron. . . . As long as you have the wisdom to keep the sovereign authority of this country as the sanctuary of liberty, the sacred temple consecrated to our common faith, wherever the chosen race and sons of England worship freedom, they will turn their faces towards you. The more they multiply, the more friends you will have; the more ardently they love liberty, the more perfect will be their obedience. Slavery they can have anywhere. It is a weed that grows on every soil. They may have it from Spain, they may have it from Prussia. . . . Magnanimity in politics is not seldom the truest wisdom ; and a great empire and little minds go ill together.

'Our ancestors have turned a savage wilderness into a glorious empire; and have made the most extensive and the only honourable conquests, not by destroying, but by promoting the wealth, the number, the happiness, of the human race.'

Perhaps 'the black troops' will tell us whether that speech (nigh 150 years old) is out of date to-day.

But the time has come to recapitulate, and so draw to a close. The point of my words is simply this, that (again to employ the magnificent phrase) 'fellowship is life, and lack of fellowship is hell.'

With comrades of men and books, nobody need live in hell—even in a German prison camp. The reasons for studying the two are not different.

There are funny books we read for entertainment; there are also funny men. There are informed books, and there are also encyclopaedic human beings to whom we resort to satisfy the thirst for knowing things.

But the best thing we may discover in either of them is fellowship with a fine, lovable personality. This is possibly the most homely aspect of that which the Church calls 'the communion of saints.' There is no sweeter human joy.

I suppose that it is usually a particular and personal realization of one or other of the few great primal facts of life which first drives men to become comrades of men and books, as indeed to think at all.

A man one day makes the astounding discovery that he must die, or his mother, or somebody else that he loves very much. Or a breath of the beauty of fleeting things blows suddenly into his life, disturbing his content. Or the misery of a million fellow-beings is stuck in him like a dagger. Or Love exposes the inadequacy of human experience.

In this way or another comes upon him 'the burden of the mystery.' Like that old pagan who sat long ago with the apostles of a new religion—firelight brightening the walls, and outside the darkness' of the wide night—he sees life as a sparrow flying into the great hall, and knowing for a moment the warmth and firelight ere it flies out into the storm.

'Such is the life of a man: and if these can tell us more, I hold we should gladly listen to what they say.' That is the beginning of all true reading whether of men or books.

Life precedes literature, as the cause. It follows it, as the test. Thorough appreciation of a great book is only the result and reward of a lifetime's experience.

But it is possible to regard this prison life as a retreat (an enforced one), wherein we may attain at leisure a perspective of life and literature which will send us home completer men than we were when we came.

And that is our duty to the country we serve.

16

STRÖHEN

'They charmed her with smiles and soap.'

THE PRISONER INHABITANTS OF Crefeld who did not come to Schwarmstedt were sent to Ströhen, and in this chapter will be given an account of that lager, supplied to me by a friend, which reveals life there to have been quite as comic, if not more so, as that in our own camp.

> *'DEAR POET,*
> *'Here is the rough draft of a few Ströhen episodes. I am leaving you to supply the literary style, etc.'*

But I hope the 'Little Man' will excuse me for printing the story just as he wrote it. His letter was exactly what I wanted, and no amount of literary style laid on with a trowel or with a shovel will add a jot to its humour and interest.

'This camp was a sister-camp to Schwarmstedt, but in addition to all the bad conditions of the latter, such as bad sanitation, bad food, leaking huts, lice and flea ridden beds, we ran up against some Boche officials who did their level best to make things more impossible even than they were. There was no means of exercise here, but no walks were allowed for a long time, and then only if we consented to have our photos taken. Cigarettes and potatoes from England were confiscated; and all windows had to be shut at night, although the weather was extremely hot and our overcrowded rooms unbearable at night. Having no ventilation, we broke all the windows; but the Boches refused to have them mended when winter came, so got their own back that way. These and numerous other acts of petty *schweinerei* made life unbearable, and we decided to adopt strong measures. At first we tried orthodox methods such as complaints to the Dutch Embassy and the *Kriegministerium*; but letters never got any farther than the Commandant's office, so we took matters into our own hands. I don't suppose anyone who was at Ströhen will ever forget some of the priceless *Appels* we had under our 1st Prussian Hauptmann; how he would try to make us salute, click our heels and stand to attention; how we used to come on to *Appel* later and later each day, and clad in any old ragtime garments, slouch into our places, hands in pockets, and stand there ready to make ourselves a nuisance. One morning he thought he would like to see what an English officer looked like, so carefully inspected each squad, pointing out little irregularities in our dress and showing us how to salute, etc.—with the result that about half-way round, some took off their hats to him when he came, others stepped out and tried to shake him by the hand, or bowed in a ludicrous manner amid screams of laughter from the whole square. Finally the climax came when one room of seven or eight all 'sized themselves off,' and bowed like a machine on his arrival. This was too much for Prussian discipline, and he gave it up with a shrug of the shoulders, as if to say, "You're hopeless."

'Of course we paid for all this, and there weren't many who didn't do their three days' "cells" at one time or another. During June and half July, 125 of us visited the Jug for some petty offence, but this method of laughing at and harassing him gradually commenced to pay—as it generally does with bullies—until they eventually gave us a sensible Commandant Hauptmann, who treated us with consideration, and got proper respect and a certain amount of discipline in return.

'One of our chief sources of amusement was; "Porky," a G. under-officer who closely resembled a pig and who was simply made to be ragged. At first he tried the old G. game of shouting and screaming at us if things weren't going as he thought they should, but it didn't pay! A great dodge was to make it as difficult as possible for him to count us in our beds when it was his turn on duty in the evening, and many an imaginary rat was seen and chased by the inmates of a room mid scenes of indescribable confusion, while "Porky" was hopelessly trying to count. "Porky" was a great asset at Ströhen.

'But the best means of annoying the Boches lay in our attempts to escape. Ströhen was only about 140 kilometres from the border, and during the eight months we were there there were over 120 attempts to get out— nearly 50 of which succeeded, and 11 of those who got out actually got over the frontier. Tunnels were tried in almost every hut, but the sandy soil generally proved our undoing by falling in, and we usually struck water after digging a few feet. What a scene there was one morning when two tunnels from one hut' fell in,' and crowds of excited and angry Germans dug into them to the cheers and laughter of dozens of the English, who had done all their hard work for nothing!

'The first to get away were the Adjutant, Martin, and an English orderly, Riley, by cutting the wire one dark night; but they were caught a few days later.

'Then came a whole series of attempts. Lt. Couchman got out as an orderly feeding the Boche pigs outside, followed two days later by Capt. Anthony by the same method. Ellis and Brean got out dressed as Boches; Blunn and Robertson cut the wire in broad daylight, and six were away without the B. knowing it for two days. Dummies were put in their beds at night, and their places on *Appels* were ingeniously taken by others who fooled the Boches this way. When we could keep up the pretence no longer it was left to "Porky" to find, one fine night, that six were missing, when apparently all had been present on the evening *Appel* a few hours before. Poor "Porky"! That was an unhappy night for him. Unfortunately all six were recaptured.

'About this time we had to put up with our worst treatment, for the Boches were not yet tamed as they later got to be, and their 'blood and iron' policy was being tried on us: they had got thorough wind up over these attempts to get away, and orders were given to all the sentries to shoot on the least provocation. It was during this time that Knight was bayoneted inside the camp for some trifling offence, and later on Lt. Downs got stuck too—luckily neither fatally.

'Knight, about a month later, after leaving hospital, made what was probably one of the cleverest escapes of any from Germany, and succeeded in getting over to Holland too. There was a bathroom outside the wire, supplied with hot showers under which we were allowed to wash ourselves once a week. In this room was a whitewashed brick buttress, standing a few feet away from the wall. Knight, by an extraordinarily clever bit of work, had slips of cardboard painted white, fitting into each other, so as to resemble the buttress. He fixed this up one morning during his "bath," and got inside, making it appear as if flush with the wall. He was missing on *Appel*, but although the Boches searched everywhere they never found him, and at night he got clean away through a trap-door in the bathroom floor which had been cut previously. Just after this four more (Harrison, Insall, V.C., Templar, and ——) tried the bathroom "stunt," by getting through the trap-door and lying under the floor of the bathroom all day. This again was successful, and the former three got to Holland just after Knight. Meanwhile numerous other efforts had been made, quite the funniest of which was when some sportsmen thought to break the main gate with a battering ram, dash through before the sentries outside could take aim, and then take their chance. Unfortunately the "ram" hit the gate-post instead of the gate-lock, so they dropped the 'ram' and fled just as the sentry fired. But there was a humorous ending to this, for the Boche Commandant, who lived just outside the main gate, and who was a doddering, knock-kneed, blustering old Prussian, would have it that this was not an attempt to escape, but one on his life! So henceforth he never appeared in the camp except with a guard armed with loaded rifles and fixed bayonets!

'Niemeyer, afterwards Commandant at Holzminden, arrived about this time as our 2nd Hauptmann, and his first morning *Appel* was not a happy one! For his under-officers reported "five absent." They were all under the bathroom floor waiting for dark to get away like Insall, Harrison, etc. Niemeyer kept the whole crowd standing there nearly two hours while the camp was thoroughly searched. He himself sent for a chair and smoked a fat cigar; his under-officers started cigarettes too, but any of the English who lit up were promptly sent to Jug. Major Toogood, the S.B.O., quickly summed him up, and sent the English Adjutant to tell him that he wished to have nothing further to do with him till he could behave like a gentleman. What a hope! But that was the only way to treat Niemeyer. The five were eventually discovered and the *Appel* dismissed—by a common G. soldier at N.'s order.

'The Germans could not understand how we got our food for the 'journey' if anyone escaped, since all tins were locked up and could only be taken out at certain times, when they were opened by the Boches and the contents looked into; so they were always springing surprise searches on us, to try and discover unopened tins which we had smuggled out. (Anyone caught with these of course got Jug.) Niemeyer, however, issued an order for us to deliver up by a specified time all unopened tins, and if we obeyed promised that the offenders should not be punished. A long table was placed outside one of the huts with a sentry to guard it, and a big haul was expected. The result was humorous, to say the least of it, for at the appointed hour the stolid German sentry was jealously guarding 1 small tin of Oxo, 1 tiny unopened tin of mustard, and another of Bovril—all looking quite pathetic in their loneliness, and surrounded by a crowd of sarcastic officers! Niemeyer was furious, ordered us all to our huts, and threatened some with his revolver.

'Shortly afterwards he left, to become Commandant at Holzminden, where he had more scope to show his powers for bullying. But he hadn't got much change out of us at Ströhen.

'Our 3rd Hauptmann was one of the best Germans I have met. He didn't agree with "hating" prisoners, like so many; was quite reasonable in his treatment of us: and, what is more, had a sense of humour. On one occasion an officer had escaped and his place had been "faked" on *Appel* by another. The luckless "Porky" was nonplussed as usual, but had his suspicions, so reported to the Hauptmann that he thought one was absent but that someone else was taking his place. The H.'s answer, "Oh, what does it matter! One comes and one goes," shows how badly tied up they were to look after us.

"A regular fusillade occurred one night when Lyon, Marshall, Wingfield, and Robinson all escaped by cutting the wire; but all got recaptured except Wingfield, who got safely over. Another clever escape was that of Fitzgerald and Harding, who noticed that every evening two of our English orderlies (who lived in a separate wired-off hut away from the officers) were allowed outside the wire to fill up from the pump two big jugs of water for the night. F. and H. dressed as orderlies, got into their hut in the afternoon, and with their kit and packs in the empty jugs walked past the sentry as was usual and started to pump the water; as soon as the sentry's back was turned, however, they pulled out their kit, dropped the jugs and ran. Both got over to Holland, but Fitzgerald was killed shortly afterwards in Italy. Following this, Capt. Somerville and Lt. Collier got out by bribery, and Somerville got across. His was a funny case, for he had been in Jug, and had only just come out when he got the opportunity; luckily his kit was all ready packed in his room, so he simply walked out of the Jug into his room, got hold of his kit, and then straight out of the camp!

'Towards the end of the autumn, 1917, the Boche sentries at Ströhen were getting particularly fed up. They had very long hours on duty, extremely bad food, and they absolutely got hell if negligence of any kind could be proved against them, especially when an officer escaped. We were always flaunting in their eyes our parcels which came from England (this to them must have been the unkindest cut of all), and they hated and loathed most of their own under-officers: consequently, a little judicious "palm-oil" in the shape of a small tin of meat or a bar of soap (things never seen by them) would obtain you nearly anything they could give, except your release. In no other camp can I remember anything like the eating-out-of-your-hand stage to which we had reduced the Ströhen sentries by the end of seven months' hard fighting.

'It was possibly this fact, combined with the number of escapes made, which induced the Germans to send us all away early in 1918 rather than let us have the summer there, with its further opportunities for escape.

'Just before the end the Boches sprang a big search on us to try and find how and where we had got our compasses, maps, etc., for escaping. One morning we were all shut in the dining-room after morning *Appel*, and a whole fleet of cars with private detectives from Berlin drove up, and proceeded to search everyone's belongings and person with great zest. But some of us were expert thieves by this time, and quite a few of them went away with less than they came.

'Nor must one forget the episode of the "dentist's assistant." She was a girl!—the first we had seen inside a camp for a long while—and used to come once a week with the camp dentist. Poor wench! I suppose she thought she was quite popular with the English, so many bars of soap did she get and small tins of meat, etc. But the English officers wanted something in return and they got it. At first it was only small bottles of Boche brandy; but later she was bribed to bring in compasses and maps, so before long everyone was a walking Encyclopaedia as to the geography of the country between Ströhen and the frontier. Her end was tragic, for both she and the dentist were suspected by the German authorities with supplying us with means of escape, and thrown into prison. Both got long sentences, and the lady died shortly after—which was, perhaps, as it should be.'

Note: It is clear, from the last sentence, that 'The Little Man,' who suffered rather severely at the hands of the Hun, keeps yet that grim attitude of mind towards him (or her) which so much amused those who knew his cherub looks and ways in captivity.— F.W.H.

17

SOME OCCUPATIONS AND CHARACTERS AT SCHWARMSTEDT

ALTHOUGH THE CHIEF EXCITEMENTS of Schwarmstedt and of Ströhen were undoubtedly of German origin, taking the form of searches, strafes, escapes, and recaptures, our spare time was filled with other more peaceful interests. Part of the day was of course occupied in waiting for parcels, drawing tins out of the tin-office, cooking food, washing clothes, and such affairs of camp routine. But after these had been done there still remained time on hand, and as the learning of foreign languages had for the most part stopped with the departure of our Allies, various other employments were taken up. Some specialized in camp requisites—*e.g.*, 'Old Pin,' who made keys; and 'Black North,' that good old soul who devoted every moment not occupied in a discussion of Irish politics to the production of compasses. (It was a matter of much regret that we had no gun-running to give him.) Others used their spare time in reading books which they borrowed from friends or found in the camp library, which had by this time grown to be quite good.

Tauchnitz editions could also be bought through the canteen, and in this way I came to read George Moore's 'Ave, Salve, *atque* Vale,'[1] surely the best 'bed book' since Boswell's 'Life of Johnson.' My reading in captivity was very varied, and included volumes that I should probably never have found time to read had I not been taken prisoner. For this I am grateful, since the list includes Saintsbury's 'History of English Prosody,' Tolstoy's 'War and Peace,' Hardy's 'Dynasts,' A. E.'s 'National Being,' and many other such valuable books.

Twice a week at Schwarmstedt a party of us met to read and discuss the lesser known plays of Shakespeare. The debate which followed the reading was generally a very amusing one, for our party comprised men of four or five nationalities, and included many professions. There was a medical student, an Oxford don, a publisher, a professor of philosophy, a portrait-painter, an architect, and four Regular soldiers beside myself. There was a dulcitone in the camp belonging to one of the prisoners, and it sounded very pretty accompanying the songs at the end of 'Love's Labour's Lost.' A piano was out of the question at Schwarmstedt, so the dulcitone was used for all concerts, and was a godsend both there and at Holzminden, until in the latter camp it was possible to hire a piano from Hanover. Camp concerts contributed very greatly to

1 [Publisher's note] This is a refernce to Irish writer George Moore's (1852-1933) *Hail and Farewell* 'Ave,' 'Salve' and 'Vale' trilogy.

general amusement; and to the stock of topical songs so popular among prisoners in Germany, they also gave us a collection of queer ditties from overseas.

"Have you heard of Lyd-i-a Pinkum, and her love . . . for the hu-man race? How she sells (she sells, she sells) her won-der-ful com-pound, and the pa - - - - pers pub-lish her face?

'Casey Jones' was another resident of Canada, and by way of being a celebrity; but you must please get your colonial friends to tell you about him.

The Schwarmstedt rooms held, as I have said, from sixteen to thirteen officers, and so were very well adapted for the exchange of ideas, and the spinning of yarns between the various occupants. Not only this, but the walls were so thin that you got the overflow of talk from rooms on either side of your own. Many a queer story and many a piquant phrase was heard in the hour before we dropped off to sleep. There were some magnificent liars. Nobody, least of all himself, believed that 'Nobby' had held up the German army at Mons with a field cooker disguised as a cannon; nevertheless, such was the artistry of the tale, that

217

he was always able to compel 'that voluntary suspension of unbelief which constitutes artistic faith.'

But the best of the tales were true—obviously true. They had come from the four corners of the earth, and so had the men who told them. 'What a set!' as Matthew Arnold would have said, with a meaning very different from mine. I have talked of the study of books during captivity, but the study of men should have been the chief interest of prisoners, for what opportunities they had! Certainly the study of my fellow-prisoners was the chiefest of my interests while I was at Schwarmstedt. Dull, clever, good, or thoroughly wicked, these men finally sealed my philosophy of life. Goodness comes into the world like a blinding flash; and like lightning it vanishes, or seems to; but it comes to all. There are no heroes and no hero-ines—at least, there are none like those we find in books; but every man is a hero sometimes, and every woman is a heroine. Nor is life a piebald thing; nor is it a grey thing; but it is shot through with shifting colour like the flitting wing of a hornet, and so quickly it changes. How dare we think goodness commonplace? How dare we give it permanently to a few? The glory of God is reflected with a fitful splendour on a million diverse natures. All reveal it some time, and in those moments must we not merely love, but worship them. The worst people I have ever met have contrived to make me an optimist after the best had almost succeeded in making me a pessimist. There may or there may not be blinded and damned souls working willingly for the devil. I have never met them. I have never seen a man without some goodness in him. But to explain what I mean by goodness, I will quote a sonnet on the subject which I wrote while I was a prisoner at Schwarm-stedt.

> Think not that anything more strong can be
> Than simple goodness!   But consider well
> The nature of the thing; how in a hell
> Of blazing wickedness and misery
> It shines more fierce than fierce iniquity.
> Oh, heed you not those lying mouths which tell
> God's zeal of burning love more terrible
> To lie in pools of passive piety!
> For goodness is a passion of the soul
> More fierce than earthly passion, and its peace
> Is pinnacled on violence. Desire
> There burns in blossom of white ecstasies.
> Mighty like thunder hear God's message roll,
> 'Whoso is near to Me is near the fire'[2]*

How multiform is life, how fine, how pathetic, how impossible to judge! G. and another youth went round the Horn in a windjammer. Both were apprentices, and both, as it happened, public-school boys. One day in the privacy of their cabin G. made what he thought a rather good joke in the shape of a quotation from Homer. Then a great voice came suddenly through the wall behind which sat the old sail maker. 'That is incorrect,' it cried, and then proceeded to roll off line after line of 'The Odyssey.' The sail maker had been a Swedish professor. Some woman had come into his life and spoilt it. He had taken to drink, lost his post at the university, and every succeeding post he obtained after it, drifting finally into making sails

---

2 Sayings of Jesus

on a windjammer. In such capacity he had travelled the world, and visited nearly every known harbour, but the only thing he could tell you about any of them—and this he could tell with unfailing certainty—was the name and position of the nearest pub. Thither he went when he left the ship with his money; there he stayed until that money was gone, and he was thrown into the road, or until the ship's captain sent men to fetch him because they were due out. So he will go on till he dies.

That is but one of the countless tales I heard. There were men who had shot with Selous, and with John Glynn, the Sir Henry of 'King Solomon's Mines,' and who could yarn to you about Africa quite as well as Rider Haggard. There was the Canadian V.C. (as a matter of fact he was no more Canadian than I am) who was the hero of one of the best-known books of the late Jack London. There was the Irishman, a delightful chap but quite incorrigible, who came, as he put it, of a 'piebald family,' one genera-tion being black and the next white, figuratively speaking, and who had chanced to fall on the dark patch, which was perhaps the reason of his predilection for noir at roulette. Three times, he said, had he been a rich man, and each time had he lost his all attempting to double what he had. Many and various had been his occupations since deserting Sandhurst at an early age, owing to a difference with the authorities touching 'the freedom of the individual' but to fighting he had always come back, as testified long rows of ribbons which he seldom donned, picked up in every part of the Empire. Between times he had been miner (and, of course, strike leader) in Africa, steward on board ship, farmer, gold prospector, and waiter in a restaurant.

He fought in the Boer War, and joined up again in 1914, working his way from private to sergeant-major in East Africa; which done, he started again as a private in France. On St. Patrick's Eve he was promoted to be lance-corporal, and on the following day he was very naturally reduced. The whiskey came out in long loaves of bread shaped each to contain a bottle. After that he was given a commission. He joined another regiment, and with them in one day, and I believe within three weeks of entering his battalion, he won the D.S.O., the Croix de Guerre, and promotion on the field from Second Lieutenant to Captain. The King was over at the time and personally congratulated him, a pleasure which was somewhat marred for the recipient by the suspicion that he might possibly be hardly sober enough to meet His Majesty. However, everything went off quite well. The next week off he went up the line and out on to patrol, where he was captured in a way very similar to that in which I was taken. What his end will be neither he nor anybody else knows, but I am sure it will be the reverse of dull; so good luck to him!

I wish I had time to speak of the many other interesting characters I met at Schwarmstedt and elsewhere in Germany: the Scot who thanked God that he was able to " R-r-r-read Shakespeare-re in its or-r-original tongue," and who got so mixed and excited when you asked him to name the best book ever written by Sir Walter Scott, generally ending up (and quite rightly) in giving about six; 'Bobbie,' another Scot, parcel-office expert, friend of bees and of children, who told the most magnificent ghost stories, talked (logically) of 'porridges,' and a corp as distinct from two or more 'corpses,' cooked like a French

chef, and coined the word 'insinuendo'; 'Tommie,' business manager of a London theatre, who put on a simply
killing production of the 'Whip' at Ströhen, on a raised
platform in a hut, and who acted a whole play by himself,
taking the part of villain, hero, and heroine, with conspicuous success, even when it was necessary for them to be
all 'on' at the same time; 'Out,' surely the most English of
all Englanders, who, when yelled at in Holzminden prison
by Niemeyer, the Camp Commandant, replied, as who
but an Englishman possibly could, 'All right, don't shout
at me, you bloody foreigner!' and went gaily to prison.
Ponder the word 'foreigner.'

*　　*　　*　　*

To these and to many, many others, English, Canadian,
Irish, French, Scottish, Welsh, Russian, Australian, South
African, and cosmopolitan, I shout 'Good luck!' at the
close of this chapter. Good-luck, boys! I shall never see
you again, most of you, but I shall never forget you; and
you have given me more, far more than I can ever thank
you for.

19

SCHWARMSTEDT
TO HOLZMINDEN:
TRAIN-JUMPING

ONE EVENING AT SCHWARMSTEDT after dinner, dear old L. came up to me and said, 'Would you like a suit of civilian clothes?'

Like it? It was the very thing I had wanted (vainly) for months. I gasped, and said, 'Yes, please!'

The suit was British, one of two sent him by his mother and smuggled out of the parcel office. How, I don't know, but I have heard it said that a tin of dripping was the price of a man's honour and a woman's virtue in that part of the country. I think it must have been dripping!

Thus it came about that my escape kit was completed about three weeks before we were moved away from Schwarmstedt.

For several days before our departure the Huns were very busy searching the camp for *verboten* articles in order to prevent escapes on the journey; and to conceal my civilian clothes I resorted to the very simple expedient of wearing them (under a Burberry) when they searched my boxes, and putting them in my boxes when they searched me. Knowing the ways of the Hun, I was almost certain that this barefaced plan would be successful, and it was. The sentries were, to use the German phrase, 'earnest men,' and their very earnestness prevented them from being bright. They concentrated. They didn't half search my box, and they didn't half search me: they did both thoroughly. And having done so, they felt perfectly satisfied that everything must be all right. I very nearly gave the show away by laughing: it was so ridiculous to watch the funny old things going slowly and carefully through my boxes for the clothes that I was wearing less than a yard away.

The next morning we were marched down to the station to entrain for Holzminden. In a wood where we halted close to the railway-line an officer made a bolt for it through the trees, and rifles went off right and left, although half of the men could not possibly have had anything to aim at. Having fallen into a ditch, the officer was recaptured, and the Germans showed no particular ill-will except one breathless old man, who had dropped a large hunch of bread and lard (his day's rations) during the chase, and was unable to find it again.

We gave him a tin of meat (which cheered him up at once), for it was necessary that the sentries should have something more to do than watch us: and nothing appealed to them like eating.

When we entrained, one sentry was stationed in each carriage, and sat in a corner seat near the door; the other door was locked. Each carriage held, besides the sentry, five or six officers. The train was a corridor, and a lavatory lay between our particular compartment and the next—a fact which I mention because it had considerable bearing on my subsequent escape.

I took off the knapsack in which I had packed food for a three weeks' journey, and placed it in the corridor outside the lavatory door. My map and compass were in the pockets of the civilian suit which I was wearing under a Burberry. The problem was to get myself and my equipment off the train without being seen. There was plenty of time, for it was inadvisable to jump until dusk, both for sake of getting concealment, and because the train was carrying me in the right direction.

For the first hour or two we were watched very carefully and every moment, but as time wore on the guards became more slack. One after another each man in our carriage made a point of visiting the lavatory, and remaining there or outside in the corridor for an increasing space of time, and as they always returned the old sentry became less and less suspicious, and at last quite used to having one short in the carriage.

My first plan was to jump out through the lavatory window, but I found that it was too small.

Moreover, it was on the sentry-side of the train, and so my jump would certainly be seen by scores of armed guards in other carriages, one of whom would probably shoot straight.

The window which was in the corridor was on the convenient side of the train, but it, also, was too small for me, though it was wide enough for my knapsack.

There only remained the window in my own carriage, which was both large enough and on the right side of the train. But there was the sentry.

The sentry in our carriage was a kindly old thing, but very weary. He had been up most of the night. He closed his eyes occasionally and blew little spit-bubbles from his lips. But he would not go to sleep. Once or twice we almost believed that he was 'off,' but always he would open a watery blue eye at an unexpected moment. It was very trying. We gave him food. He ate it. We gave him wine. He drank it. But he would not go to sleep. He just continued to blow bubbles.

Finally I decided that it was during the bubble-blowing or not at all that I should have to go.

Five seconds was about all I could afford to spend doing the vanishing trick, and I could not rely on that, for at any time his blue eye might open.

The window was down—we had fought hard for that during the first hour—and there was an arm-strap near the window. By putting one foot on the seat, and if the arm-strap was sufficiently strong to bear the weight of a body, it was, I argued, quite possible to be out of the carriage in one moment by diving through the window. The arm-strap would save me from falling head-first on to the line; and by grasping the outside rail with the other hand I could lower myself silently and quickly on to the step by withdrawing my feet from the carriage. I should be less likely to get shot this way, since my feet would be the only part left inside the train after the first spring.

The knapsack I could not take with me, but that could be pushed through the corridor-window by a friend as soon as I had jumped from the step, and so we should reach the ground about the same time. As things turned out, we certainly did, for I got it in the back!

I could not jump while the train was doing more than twenty miles an hour, or I should break my neck; nor must I jump too near a station, or I should be seen; so the proper place was on an uphill gradient in open country. If, on top of this, I could get a wood for cover, conditions would be ideal.

It was unlikely that I should have to face a train-load of bullets, because the sentries were all sitting the other side to guard the door which was unlocked, but even supposing some few did get across and fire, it was very unlikely that they would hit me, for not only was I pretty certain to be a moving target, but they would be moving marksmen.

While I was thinking out these chances I heard with horror that we were due to arrive in about half an hour. It was not nearly dusk and dusk was an important link in the chain of my calculations— but then, I seem fated to have to do things in daylight which are generally done at night!

Having been captured in daylight, it seemed (thought I) a sort of poetic justice that I should also escape in day-light—so 'here goes!'

Knowing my plan, and that I purposed carrying it out at once, several of my companions stood up in the car-riage on pretext of reaching things from the rack, and so screened me from the sentry, who was not then blowing bubbles. As I pushed off from the seat on which he was sitting I could hear someone directing his attention to the beauty of some stunted hills on the other side of the line. I dived. To withdraw my feet took only a moment, and there I was outside the carriage on the step, watching the ground whiz by underneath. It seemed to be going by very fast; but I had been lucky in the place, for we were doing a bend, and my carriage was then on the outside of the circle, so that no one looking out of the windows in front or in rear of the train could see me.

Then I jumped. The ground seemed suddenly tilted up towards me, and I came down an awful bump with the pack in the middle of my back, and my throat across the opposite rails.

I had jumped forward, but as a marble escapes from the bag which a boy swings, had been thrown outwards from the curving train. For a moment we lay there, pack and man, flat in the trackway, while the train clanked past a few yards behind; then I realized where I was and why. I got up and ran quickly for cover, leaving the pack where it was.

We were on an embankment. I threw myself over the edge of it and lay down while the train dragged its huge length past. I saw the German interpreter go by, leaning out of the window, a cigarette in his mouth. When the last carriage had passed, I got up and went to get my knapsack. It had split open in the fall, and many things, which included a towel, several tins of meat, and some very large hard Canadian biscuits, lay strewn over the railway-track.

I was hastily picking these things up when I heard shouting, and saw a stream of people running towards me from the half-reaped fields below the embankment on that side—reapers and farm-hands, male and female, headed by crowds of children and a dog.

I did not wait to collect any more of my belongings, but shouldered my pack and set off down the opposite slope, reflecting that if English labourers had seen a man jump off a train they would not have made all this fuss because it was *verboten*, but have thought him rather a sport for 'doing' the railway company.

'Damn them!' Why must they come chasing after me! Since I was in civilian clothes, they could not possibly know that I was anything else than one of their own countrymen. Why couldn't they mind their own business? Alas! that is not the German habit.

They had seen me jump from the train. To jump from a train was *verboten*. There must be something wrong. It was the duty of all to discover what it was, and have the offender punished.

I marched on as fast as I could towards a wood which lay the far side of a village near by the railway. Run, I dare not, since it would only attract suspicion, and because more things would fall out of my pack, which I had not had time to fasten up again at the top. Nobody attempted to stop me, and by walking fast I hoped to get through the village before the crowd; but it was round me before I had done so. I kept straight on, ignoring the shouts and menaces; still nobody attempted to stop me. I decided that if once I could get outside the village I would make a dash for it, and get cover in the wood till nightfall.

But I was not allowed to reach the open.

In a place where two roads met before branching right and left out of the village, I was collared by a youth, trembling with excitement. I put on my best scowl, and attempted to shake him off, but he held on, shouting. The crowd surged round, and I felt there was nothing for it but to give up.

Had I been a fluent speaker of German I might yet have got off, for I was in civilian attire, and, save that I had been seen jumping off a train, there was nothing against me; but being unable to give any good explanation of myself, I was arrested as a civilian spy, and taken to the police-station. Then I found out that I was suspected of having tried to blow up a tunnel.

This I did not like the sound of at all, for the Germans have a short way with spies; therefore I thought it well to explain quickly that I was a British officer. They could verify my statement, said I, by telephoning to Holzminden. This was done, and as by that time the officers had been counted and I had been missed, the message soon came through that my statement was correct, and that I was to be brought immediately in to the prison.

While waiting at the station with my guard to catch the next train on to Holzminden, I was amused to see several of the large hard biscuits which I had left on the line lying on a table in the station-master's room. They had been brought there by those who found them under the impression that they were slabs of dynamite, and hence the rumour that I had come to blow up the tunnel!

I was able to destroy my maps on the journey down, and to get rid of my compass, which things (being *verboten*) would mean imprisonment additional to the fortnight's confinement given for simple escape; but contrary to my expectations I was not searched when I arrived at the *lager*.

I passed my old guard as I went in and winked at him, but he did not respond in any way to my salutation. The door slammed behind me, the key turned in the lock, and I lay down to endure a second spell of solitary confinement, and to write an acrostic on the word DAMN!

19

HOLZMINDEN: SOLITARY (?) CONFINEMENT

W**HEN I CAME OUT AT** the end of a month (for it was the German way of keeping their agreement to let you lie in prison for a fortnight before trial, and then to sentence you to do again the fortnight you had already done!), people asked me what my solitary confinement had been like, and I replied, 'Not so bad! I might have added, 'Not so solitary, either!' for the fact was that during the first month at Holzminden so many officers escaped and got retaken that there was no room for them in the prison except by putting two in a cell.

And so it came about that within ten days after I had begun to languish 'alone in durance vile,' I was given a companion.

He was a fellow I liked—in fact, the only thing wrong with him was that he had diarrhoea, and the Germans would not allow us out of the cell except at certain hours, and threatened to shoot me when I opened the window.

To be finally interred in Germany was a thing I had no wish should happen to me after all I had been through, so I shut the window before the sentry had finished counting, 'Ein, zwei, drei!'

It is better to breathe poor air than not to breathe at all.

My friends very kindly smuggled books down to me through the orderly who helped in the cells, and from him I got all the camp news, which was very amusing. 'Three more out last night, sir. The old Commandant is hopping mad!' was the gist of his talk, and it was good enough!

I had many interesting talks with L., who was an Irishman, and therefore knew his history as no Englishman ever does. I showed him how to write ballades, rondeaux, and triolets, and lent him Tolstoy's 'War and Peace' (surely the greatest novel in the world) volume by volume as I finished with it. He gave me in return cigarettes, an appropriate gift in the circumstances, and we got on together extremely well. After 'War and Peace,' it was extremely interesting to read Thomas Hardy's 'Dynasts' as soon as I got out, and to obtain an English view of the Napoleonic drama in a work equally colossal. But the poetry that I wrote in cells was very bad. The truth is that I was just beginning to get mouldy, the outward proof of which was that I grew a beard and looked like Judas Iscariot. I had been a prisoner not much more than a year, and my temperament is not naturally a mouldy one; but captivity is an insidious evil which saps one's vitality and eats away one's spirit. I have come to the conclusion that to give a man 'live years' may be necessary, but it is damnable cruelty. Whether a man highly strung feels it more than a duller and more animal type, or less, I cannot tell, but with a little more than two years' experience of it, I can say with certainty that it is by far the worst thing that ever happened to me, and a thing from which I shall possibly never recover. It is not the physical hardship, it is the purposelessness of it, and the awful monotony, that sickens the heart. And I only did two years, and I had books, and I had the finest friends man could wish to share it. I mention all this now because this was the first time that I had begun to feel mouldy, and because up to that time I had always despised those who gave way to the disease. But some had done three years when I had only done one, and how was I to know that mouldiness accumulated at compound interest! Therefore I ask their pardon, not for anything I may have said concerning the foulness of the complaint, but for daring to judge them at all when they were afflicted by it. The books that I read, the arguments that I had, and the bad verse that I wrote during this month in cells, and at other times during captivity, served to exercise my brain; but nothing could prevent the creeping paralysis of prisondom from gradually overtaking me, and the time came to me as to other men when I was too hopeless even to fight against it. Fortunately my cell windows were transparent, and I could see the road and the live people on it, and animals, and growing things, and laughing children. I saw them as the Lady of Shalott must have seen the processions of life pass her river islet, and in my heart already I was crying, 'I am half sick of shadows.' I have no doubt that this state was partly caused by lack of exercise—but enough of such things!

At the end of a month I came out, and found that Hol

'THREE MORE OUT.'

zminden was a thoroughly bad camp, and that the Commandant, Niemeyer, was the evil spirit of it. Some of the prisoners had already met him at Ströhen, where he had been second-in-command for a short time, and knew him for what he was—a cad, a boaster, and a bully of the worst type. He had lived in America, and was commonly known as 'Milwaukee Bill.' He talked broken American under the impression that it was English. 'I guess you know,' his commonest expression, became a catch-phrase with all who knew him. His bluster of manner and speech was not difficult to mimic, and an amusing incident happened at Ströhen, where one of the English officers became so proficient at doing so that his roar deceived not only prisoners but guards. Officers would hastily hide the maps they were copying, and sentries would spring to attention as B. came shouting through the barracks. One day after an escape Niemeyer, passionate with rage, was striding through the camp flourishing a pistol, and shouting, 'I guess you know I will shoot, schweinhund! You think dat I do not know nothing, but I know damn all,' when his impersonator, shouting equally loudly, came suddenly round a corner, and they met face to face. But before the astonished Hun could recover himself sufficiently to do anything unpleasant, the officer had vanished. For the rest of that evening the real Boche had the stage to himself.

His twin brother, the Commandant of Clausthal, was as like him as, say, two peas may be to each other—in fact, nobody could tell them apart; not that anybody at all wanted to—and a funny thing happened to him also in the impersonation line. For one of the officers there, imitating his appearance and manner, as well as his voice, and wearing a German uniform, walked straight out of the camp, pausing only to curse the sentry who had opened the gate for being slack. Then he waved his stick Niemeyer-wise in the direction of the friends who were watching him, spat on the ground, and disappeared. It was several days before they recaptured him.

Had it not been for Niemeyer, Holzminden might have been quite a good camp. The buildings were of substantial stone and mortar, not leaky hutments of wood; the rooms were clean and pleasant; the surrounding country was beautiful, though bleak in winter—but what good was that to us since we could not go for walks? A studied insult on the parole-card, and Von H.'s lying statement that British parole had been broken at Ströhen and Schwarmstedt, determined us to sacrifice our right of exercise outside the camp till the card was altered and the lie withdrawn. Both these things were done finally, but for six months the small monotonous walk round and round prison was our only form of ramble. Personally I never had a walk at Holzminden, for it happened that when the card had been corrected and we were allowed walks, after a delay of six months, I was sent away to another camp the day before my turn came.

Several police-dogs were kept by the Germans at Holzminden, and there was a fairly good bathroom with showers of hot and cold water. The connection between the two will be explained by the following notice, signed by Niemeyer: 'When a more suitable place in the camp can be found for the dogs, officers may have baths on Tuesdays and Fridays.' The loathsome state of the floor when we went for a hot shower inclined most of us to bathe in the open under a pump, a proceeding which the Germans did not forbid, although in this case the camp was at the edge of Holzminden village, and a public road ran by just outside the wire. Probably the fact that we were laughed at by passers-by appealed to Niemeyer as a reason for allowing it; but it was very unpleasantly cold when snow was on the ground, in spite of all Bobbie's pretences to the contrary. He used to go out and bathe coram-populo every morning, for was he not a Scot? and 'The Scots they are a hardy race,' etc.

Standing in queues was always a prominent feature of prison life, and always a nuisance; but at Holzminden it was not merely a prominent feature and a nuisance, it was the whole ugly face and a damned nuisance. You stood in queues for parcels, you stood in queues to draw out what had come in the parcels, and again to cook it at one of the open-air stoves. You stood in queues for letters. You stood in queues for cells, and to take food to those who were in the cells. You stood in queues for baths. You stood in queues to be robbed at the canteen. You stood in queues for firewood, which they sold at an exorbitant price when you were unable to steal it from them, as you had a perfect right to do, since they should have provided reasonable warmth free. You stood in queues for your bread-card and for your wine-card, and again when you bought either of these most detestable mixtures, and again to be inoculated with whatever they decided to pump into your system, and again when you wanted to report sick and be excused from attending as a result of standing in any of these other queues, but especially the bread and wine ones.

If a man had had to stand in them all, his whole day-would have been taken up with waiting about in the cold; but by sharing the work, and getting, *e.g.*, your friend's letters when you got your own, it was possible to escape with about four hours each *per diem*.

All this was Niemeyer's doing. At every other camp letters were brought round every morning by one of the officers, who called for them at the censor's office. Here, the Germans themselves gave them out after censoring, and for some reason always tore up the envelopes first. The result was that 'Darling Jack' frequently got a letter intended for some other person, and the kisses for 'Sweet William' went to another flower. It was very embarrassing, for often one had got half-way through the letter before discovering it was meant for another man. Again, it was customary elsewhere to allow an English officer and several orderlies to help in the parcel office and in the tin-room, so that the distribution could be done quickly and efficiently, but Niemeyer forbade this, and as the parcel office was grossly understaffed, and the Germans there sometimes unable to read the names on the packages, parcels accumulated in piles which even systematic theft could hardly reduce to any manageable proportions.

Under anyone but Niemeyer we might have had walks, and a playing field; games, and baths after games; and so kept ourselves fit and hard, but he made such things quite impossible. Also he disallowed our little entertainments, concerts, and so forth, which we gave in the dining-rooms, where planks on trestles did for a stage and the dulcitone replaced a piano—and this merely because he felt annoyed that somebody had got away. On such occasions he would order all the officers into their barracks, and forbid them to open the windows or to look out of them. People who showed themselves were shot at, and I shall not forget the splintering and smashing of glass which went on the day when Bobbie rigged up a dummy figure at one of the windows, and worked it up and down with a string; the rest of us, crawling about on our hands and knees, were laughing until we could hardly move, but Bobbie was just absorbed and proud, like a child with a new toy.

Bobbie's cooking I have already praised, but not sufficiently. His 'ste-ews' saved us all in those icy days. Never before did I realize the extent to which food is not merely sustaining, but warming, and that even if it is itself cold. But Bobbie's 'ste-ews' were very far from being cold, and how so frozen and feeble a man sat down to them, he rose up warm and refreshed.

The small room we were in (eight of us, and all particular friends) was at the top of the house. As R. the P.T. engineer was in it, there is no need to say that it was soon as full of moving panels, planks which lifted, and sills which slid, as any medieval castle. It was simply honeycombed with hiding-places, and half the escaping kit in the barrack was stored there, if only the Huns had known. Even in appearance it was an extraordinary room, for 'Mossy,' whose diary you have read, had covered the plain walls with chalk drawings of prehistoric animals which were enough to frighten you if you had had a bottle of Boche wine. Spiders, being very special pets of his (he kept a large box of them), were also realistically depicted hanging here and there from the ceiling, gigantic fellows, and just ready to drop on your head. Over my bed he had drawn a pool of water, and amid the rushes floated some fine white ducks, which have a history.

One night (it was soon after I had come out of solitary confinement) everybody was drifting off to sleep when there came sudden peals of laughter from my bed. Sponges were thrown, and boots, and voices demanded what the devil was the matter; to which I replied, 'I was just thinking what an extraordinarily funny thing a duck is!'

And the next morning, to make clear my meaning, and to explain the secret beauty and humour of that bird no less than its relationship and significance to the heavens above and to hell underneath, I wrote the following poem:

DUCKS
(To F.M., who drew them in Holzminden Prison.)

From troubles of the world
I turn to ducks—
Beautiful, comical things,
Sleeping and curled,
Their heads beneath white wings,
By water cool;
Or finding curious things
To eat, in various mucks
Beneath the pool.
Tails uppermost, or waddling
Sailor-like on the shores
Of ponds, or paddling
Left, right-! with fan-like feet,
Which are for steady oars
When they white galleys float,
Each bird a boat,
Rippling at will the sweet
Wide water-ways.

Solitary Confinement

When night is fallen you creep
Upstairs, but drakes and dillies
Nest with pale water-stars,
Moonbeams, and shadow-bars,
And water-lilies:
Fearful too much to sleep,
For they've no locks
To click against the teeth
Of weasel and fox.
And warm beneath
Are eggs of cloudy green
Whence hungry rats and lean
Would stealthily suck
New life, but for the mien,
The bold, ferocious mien,
Of the mother-duck.

Yes, ducks are valiant things
On nests of twigs and straws;
And ducks are soothy things,
And lovely on the lake
When that the sunlight draws
Thereon their pictures dim,
In colours cool.
And when beneath the pool
They dabble, and when they swim
And make their rippling rings,
Oh, ducks are beautiful things!

But ducks are comical things—
As comical as you. Quack!
They waddle round—they do;
They eat all sorts of things,
And then they quack.
By barn and stable and stack
They wander at their will,

And if you go too near
They look at you through black,
Small, topaz-tinted eyes,
And wish you ill.
Triangular and clear
They leave their curious track
In mud at the water's edge,
And then amid the sedge
And slime they gabble and peer,
Saying, "Quack!" "Quack!"

When God had finished the stars and whirl of coloured suns,
He turned His mind from big things to fashion little ones.
Beautiful tiny things, like daisies, He made; and then
He made the comical ones, in case the minds of men
Should stiffen and become
Dull, humourless, and glum,
And so forgetful of their Maker be
As to take even themselves quite seriously.

Caterpillars and cats are lively, excellent puns;
All God's jokes are good—even the practical ones!
And as for the duck, I think God must have smiled a bit,
Seeing those bright eyes blink, on the day He fashioned it:
And He's probably laughing still, at the sound that came
    out of its bill.

20

SOME HOLZMINDEN ESCAPES

I STAYED AT HOLZMINDEN for six months, and I suppose things happened during that time, but they were unpleasant things, and I am not one of those with whom hate is a productive passion—in fact, I am a very poor hater.

To write about it, I have to be fond of a thing, or at least amused (I am not hard to amuse); and as I found very little in my stay at Holzminden to like, or to be amused at, I will not do more than relate a few escapes before quitting the damnable place for ever.

Were I not writing a book on captivity, I doubt if I should care even to mention this camp, except incidentally and for the sake of a few fine incidents and friends closely associated with it.

But these few escapes seem funny and plucky enough to record.

First of all, there is the Capon affair, of which it has been written and sung in strange rhyme (at a Holzminden concert) how:

> 'Capon swore a feud
> 'Gainst the fierce Niemeyer,'

and how, sadly to relate, all his brave plans fell with his planks to the ground.

The original scheme evolved by Capon for escape was to break down some long planks meant for shelves in the dining-room, and to push these suddenly out of a second-story window, so that the far ends rested on the top of the wire. Down these slanting runners he, pack-complete, would slide on a small home-made sledge, over the head of the sentry (oblivious or astonished, as the case might be), and into the road. A wall upon which the barbed-wire rested would afford cover from immediate shots, and by the time the sentries had run round it or climbed over, Capon would have got a good start in the race for freedom.

The first thing I knew of Capon was that he had given a very good lecture on the stars (his civilian work was, I believe, at the Greenwich observatory); and the next (it was not so many hours later), that he was seeing them, having fallen, sledge, runners, bag and all, into the well between the barrack and the wall, almost on top of the startled German beneath.

The fault lay with the runners, for as the song relates—

> 'None could keep them back,
> Though strong men did tug hard,
> So the blooming show
> Was absolutely done in."

Then (as the song proceeds),

> 'The frightened guard
> Shrilly blew his whistle,
> Then the great Niemeyer
> Bravely waved his pistol,
> And he did resolve
> To extirpate the vipers,
> All the men of Mons,
> All the boys of Wipers.'

And since the planks had been abstracted from one of the dining-rooms, Niemeyer soliloquizes thus:

> 'Fat is dis dey do?
> Dare dey cock der beavers!
> I vill teach dem—zo,
> Fat is good behaviours:
> I a sight will have
> For mein gaze to gloat on:
> I will notice give
> Dining-room's VERBOTEN.'

But Niemeyer, in shutting up the dining-rooms, had reckoned without the morning liver of 'Broncho,' who had spent long years in tropical climates. All Broncho's plates were shut inside the dining-room, and it wasn't till he wanted them for breakfast that he found it out. Growing a trifle more livid, he seized a stool and battered down the door. He would have battered down Niemeyer himself in such a mood, or the Kaiser himself, for that matter, any morning before 10 a.m.

'When the great Niemeyer
Came along and saw it,'

according to the song, the sight so overcame him that he
took a table-knife and committed suicide by striking it
through his gizzard.

'Camp Commander dead;
Got to get another;
Wonder will it be
The devil, or his brother!'

But the real conclusion was far less dramatic, and far less
desirable. Niemeyer confined all the officers in camp
to barracks (this although the inhabitants of the other
building could not possibly have had anything to do with
Capon's escape, nor with the breaking down of the doors),
and then, frightened at the pandemonium which resulted,
and fearing a riot, he climbed down off his tall horse and
cancelled the order—thus furnishing another argument
to support the fallacious but generally accepted platitude
that bullies are always cowards.

Neither the escape which I am about to relate, nor the
famous Holzminden tunnel, had been completed when I
left the camp in the early spring of 1918, but the principal
characters were all well known to me, and this account
of Holzminden would be very incomplete without some
reference to them.

'Fluffy,' a fellow of my old school, was a fine little
sport, and the chief female impersonator in our plays and
sketches at Holzminden, though I don't think he much

liked the job. Still, somebody had to do it, and he did it very well.

As a sidelight on prison psychology, let me here give in parenthesis an interesting extract from the diary of another female impersonator in Germany.

'The attitude of officers towards other officers dressed as women in plays, etc., was very peculiar. E.g., at the mardi gras festival, in a large mixed camp, I was in female attire, representing Egypt in an Empire tableau, and noticed with surprise how attentive officers were in keeping me supplied with refreshments, and also that (quite unconsciously) their manners completely changed when speaking to me. They were most careful in avoiding the usual camp language, and almost fastidious in their choice of adjectives. They insisted on giving up their seats to me, and it was quite pathetic to see the efforts made to engage my female interest in subjects no sane prisoner of war (if any of us are sane) would consider. How pretty the room looked! And the costumes so picturesque, weren't they? Perhaps a glass of lemonade . . . I had to pull them back into reality by swearing vigorously, and so far had they fallen under the illusion of my femininity that I fear I shocked them by doing so.'

But it was not merely the prisoners who fell under the sex illusion in the case of 'Fluffy,' for one day, dressed as a German girl typist, and having gained entrance to the staff quarters, he walked quietly out of the camp. It was very hard luck that the officer escaping with him, although perfectly disguised in German uniform, was recognized by a guard, so that they both got caught, for up to that time not a soul had suspected him.

The famous tunnelling company had been started while I was in cells, and when I came out had a waiting list about a mile long, so I was disappointed to find my chances gone when I reappeared in the camp. Their sap started from behind a sort of barricade, and though there were two German sentries posted outside it, work was carried on so quietly that they never suspected anything. The tunnel passed out of a cellar, under concrete flooring, to the farther side of a stone wall surrounding the camp, and opened up in a field of corn on the other side of the roadway. Nine months was the time taken to make it, and its length then was about sixty yards. The escaping officers had only just room to crawl through, and some of them, hampered with kit, took nearly an hour to do it. Several of the tunnellers were moved to another camp, or sent to Holland, before the sap was completed; and poor old Bobbie was one of them. It was the third time the same thing had happened to him. In the P.T. at Gütersloh, and again in the tunnelling scheme at Crefeld, his tunnel was nearly finished when we were suddenly moved. Still, it was a good thing to get out of the country, and if one couldn't get out in the best way possible, repatriation was second-best, and a true godsend to old prisoners. Bobbie would never have gone mad, he thought too little of himself; but certainly repatriation has saved the reason of hundreds.

It was in July, and on the 23rd day of the month, that the tunnel at Holzminden was at last ready for use. Two days before Niemeyer, boasting of camp arrangements, had said:

'Well, gentlemen, I guess you know if you want to escape you must give me a couple of days' notice!' Notice was not given, but two days later, almost to the hour, twenty-nine officers crawled out through the sap, and though nineteen of them were retaken in various parts of Germany, ten got right away into England, a record for any camp in Germany during the war. The fugitives included two Lieutenant-Colonels, and the German authorities offered £250 for each prisoner brought back. As soon as the members of the party were out, they very wisely separated, travelling in little groups, or alone, for the rest of the journey. Several of them, to avoid suspicion, started off in a direction directly opposite to the frontier; and curiously enough it was some of these who were first to 'get over.' A fortnight was about the average time taken to reach the border, and during that period the men tramped 180 miles or thereabouts. Naturally most of them travelled only at night, but a few, I believe, risked daylight marching; and one or two, who spoke German fluently, and had supplied themselves with forged passports, saved their legs and took the train.

It took Niemeyer and his staff about two hours to find the tunnel on the following day, and he then ordered it to be opened up. This work would take his soldiers several hours to carry out, said he, so it would be impossible to censor any parcels. The officers were therefore deprived of their food during that time, and had to live on German rations. This resulted in an additional queue. At meal-times the officers would stand in a long line with dishes and plates in their hands, and as they passed by one German would fling a few potatoes into the dish, while another thrust his dirty hand into a great cauldron to deposit a piece of fish upon the plate. Niemeyer, thoroughly pleased, stood by to taunt his victims, saying, 'Ach, it is not so goot as Piccadilly, zo?'

I hear that on the morning following the escape, when his *Feldwebel* reported 'Twenty-nine missing, Herr Captain,' Niemeyer was so full of evil rage that he almost lost his reason. He simply raved. Calling out the guards, he commanded them to fire on any British officer who dared as much as to look out of the windows. After that, he ordered a parade on the barrack square; and several senior officers who appeared in shoes instead of boots were sent immediately to cells. As a reprisal, on the following morning everybody came on parade without either hat or tunic. Niemeyer, furious with rage, ordered the sentries to charge, but as they hated him more than they did the British, the thing was a ridiculous farce. One officer had lost a leg, and so could not disappear into barracks so swiftly as the others. Him the sentries collared. He was put into cells and kept there for three weeks.

The success of the tunnel was a tremendous blow to Niemeyer's pride, and completely killed his prestige in the army corps. He was never quite the same blustering bully afterwards, and finally, hated alike by Germans and British, became a mere laughing-stock. After the Armistice he was (I am told) relegated to cells by the Workers' and Soldiers' Council, which, if true, is surely one of the best bits of work it ever did.

Of all Camp Commandants I have met, Niemeyer was the worst. Von Groeben of Gutersloh I have not mentioned before. He ran his camp very successfully by keeping out of it. Like the Scottish minister, he was 'inveesible for six days of the week, and eencomprehensible on the seventh,' or whatever other day he showed himself. We heard him roaring at his guards, as is customary among all Prussians; but for the rest, he might as well have lived in Berlin, and probably did so. With his 'twofold shout,' "Achtung!' he resembled Wordsworth's cuckoo; and was, as far as we were concerned, " but a wandering voice." The Crefeld man was courteous, kindly, and drink-coloured. The dad-doky old Commander of Schwarmstedt never really lived at all except as a picturesque caricature of himself in 1870. There was certainly no harm in him. He had a bad camp and knew it, and he did what he could in his marionette way to remedy the resultant unpleasantness. His situation was the reverse of Niemeyer's, for the latter had a camp which was potentially good, but went out of his way to spoil it. Hellminden, as it was generally called, was of Niemeyer's own making.

And now we will take leave of this camp and its Commandant. If readers want to know what he looked like they can read the newspaper descriptions (there are plenty of them); or still better, they can study the picture of him done for this book by my friend C. E. B. Bernard. As for me, I am out of sympathy with the subject. Everybody hated him, including the Germans, with the exception of one officer, who with more kindliness than I expected to find confided to me one day: 'He is not zo bad, not zo . . . but he drugs, yes.' Perhaps there was some truth in that. But I am not going to describe the foolish brute, anyway.

'MILWAUKEE BILL'

22

BAD-COLBERG

I N THE END OF February a party of us was sent from Holzminden to Bad-Colberg, and with us went a letter to the Commandant, warning him that we were all bad characters.

Niemeyer had chosen the party, and all of us, except two, I believe, had been sentenced for escaping; one man no fewer than twelve times, and of him more later—for it was at Bad-Colberg that he was murdered.

Fortunately Niemeyer had passed over most of the tunnellers.

Bad-Colberg, in Saxe-Meiningen, is, as its name implies, a sanatorium built over some thermal springs. The village is quite small, not more than about eighty houses, and it is five miles from the nearest railway station. It is situated in a valley set among low hills covered with considerable stretches of pine-woods.

As might have been expected in the circumstances, our

reception there by the Germans was not very cordial; but the camp itself was a good one, and many officers were there whom we had not seen since old Gütersloh-Crefeld days. They had been sent to Colberg from Ströhen, when it was broken up about the same time as Schwarmstedt, and we were delighted to meet them once more.

Bad-Colberg camp comprises the Kursaal, and a 'villa' about 100 yards west of it, connected with it by a wired-in path. The villa was quite a large building, with a garden in which four wooden huts were erected to accommodate the overflow of prisoners. Into these huts we went when we arrived, and after the rigorous personal search which was performed upon us in the baths. Some time afterwards, when some of the officers had left the camp to be repatriated, we were moved across to the main building. It was electric-lighted throughout, and things generally were more comfortable there than any camp I had been in since Gutersloh. The baths were quite luxurious. Officers slept three to eight in a bedroom, according to the size of the rooms, which were for the most part steam-heated, though a few, including the one I shared with W. and the 'Little Man,' had coke-stoves. Walks were granted freely, and the surrounding country was occasionally something better than picturesque, and abounded in wild-flowers and rare butterflies.

But as Holzminden has shown, it is possible for a bad man to spoil the best camp, and a stupid man is almost as bad as a bad one. Kröner, the Commandant of Bad-Colberg, was a stupid man: in fact, he was a credulous and obstinate old fool, the more dangerous because he was weak, as obstinate persons usually are, and entirely under the thumb and intellect of his Adjutant, Captain Beetz, whom I believe to be the worst man in Germany. He (Beetz) was certainly responsible for the deaths of poor M. and W., though, try as we would (and we tried very hard), it was impossible to obtain and produce a sufficient stock of evidence to get him tried for murder. But of that later.

The Germans, since they are so deadly earnest, have legs better adapted for being pulled than any other people in the world, and are in this respect a very natural prey for the Irish, of which curious people we had a good sprinkling in the camp, both Nationalists and Ulstermen, delightful fellows all. The Commandant was a German of Germans. Now, since the English cannot understand the Irish, and since for that matter the Irish cannot understand themselves, it was small wonder that the stupid Kröner should quite fail to do so. Yet the 'leg-pull' to which he fell a victim was so 'kolossal,' to use his favourite word, and so barefaced, that everyone (including, I think, every one of the Irish) was a little breathless at its success. Undoubtedly the perpetrators were aided by Kröner's conviction that all Irishmen were really rebels pressed into the service of England; undoubtedly (speaking German with a brogue) they cooed like sucking-doves, concealing the serpent guile within them, when they requested to be allowed to celebrate St. Patrick's Day, because it was a great Irish feast and anniversary of the bloody Battle of the Boyne, when proud England was beaten to her craven knees by the sword of Erin. Whether Malachi the Brave came into their story or not, I don't know, but anyway the result was that, under its lying eloquence, the Commandant of Bad-Colberg not only allowed the feast of St. Patrick to be magnificently kept, but, lest its celebration should fall below a style befitting the importance of so great a victory over England, gave permission for barrels of oysters and crates of wine (hock, burgundy, and champagne) to be brought into the camp, and facilities to purchase such other incitements to rejoicing as might be deemed in any way desirable.

On the reverse side of the printed programme of music and events now before me for a reminder of that improbable day, March 17, 1918, are these words, which are all that could conceivably be needed to complete the full flavour of the joke: 'The Irish officers at Bad-Colberg request the pleasure of Mr. F. W. Harvey's company at lunch, 1.30 p.m., and at a smoking-concert in the theatre at 7 p.m.' Such was the perfidy of the sons of Erin—to request the pleasure of the company of those whose defeat they had gathered together to celebrate; and if anything else is required to demonstrate their utter baseness, it is that at the bottom of this programme? and in letters equally large as 'ERIN-GO-BRAGH,' is printed the following inscription: 'GOD SAVE THE KING!'

I have heard it contended with some skill, and demonstrated with convincing evidence such as Bernard Shaw, that the Irish have no sense of humour, but only a very great store of wit; and certainly there is a great deal of difference between these two things, for wit is" mainly intellectual, but humour of the immortal spirit. Of course, a man may have both (I believe Sydney Smith had, and very certainly had Shakespeare), but that does not alter the fundamental difference, nor the fact that, of the two, humour is the much more desirable gift of God.

There are people who would measure the amount of a man's humour by the amount of laughing he does. They should keep a hyena. Others treat it as if it were a set of false teeth, to be kept in the mouth all day and laid aside when there are no more chestnuts to chew; but humour is mainly silent, and can never be laid aside. One sees it in people's eyes, but chiefly in their conduct towards life. I believe that its dominating note is courage (and who are more courageous than the Irish?). It is a Christian thing (and Ireland is almost the last Christian country left), founded upon faith, hope, and charity, those three cardinal virtues of Christianity. Its courage derives out of a sense of the final invincibility of the soul, and comes out of a deep, though often unconscious, belief, as well as from a certain abstraction from worldly affairs which is not far off contempt for them. This misfortune, these insults, are unpleasant, annoying to the mind and to the body (and what a funny old thing the body is!); but how grotesquely laughable they must be to the soul!—such is the unconscious reasoning of humour in human life. Humour is wonderfully sane; it is a cooling medicine for all the fevers of life. Humour is a passionate, laughing impulse of the soul which saves men from committing suicide by preventing them from ever despairing. A man might commit suicide very wittily, it might well be the wittiest thing he ever did; but he could not do it humorously. He might be unkind very wittily; but not humorously. Wit is a diversion; humour an employment. Wit is an after-dinner element; humour a world element. Wit flashes out occasionally, but best in prosperity. Humour shines always, but most clearly in adversity. Wit is the laughter of a full man, but humour is the laughter of a man who is probably starving. Oh yes, there is a great deal of difference between the two! But now that I have written concerning them what I wanted to say, and have got it read, I will leave my reader to decide for himself whether the Irish have or have not a sense of humour, for it is no business of mine.

On the day after the feast of St. Patrick, we got up early and walked about nine miles to Mass. It was a trying business and needed a stern effort of will, but the country was very lovely in the morning light, and the shade of the pine-woods like a cool hand laid upon brows which certainly needed it. Afterwards, out of remembrance of my own country, so different from this, and from Ireland, but so equally beautiful in approaching Spring, I wrote a poem under the title:

GLOUCESTERSHIRE FROM ABROAD.

On Dinny Hill the daffodil
Has crowned the year's returning,
The water cool in Placket Pool
Is ruffled up and burning
In little wings of fluttering fire:
And all the heart of my desire
Is now to be in Gloucestershire.

The river flows, the blossom blows
In orchards by the river:
O now to stand in that, my land,
And watch the withies shiver!
The yearning eyes of my desire
Are blinded by a twinkling fire
Of turning leaves in Gloucestershire.

Bad-Colberg

The shadows fleet o'er springing wheat
Which like green water washes
The red old earth of Minsterworth,
And ripples in such flashes
As by their little harmless fire
Light the great stack of my desire
This day to be in Gloucestershire

Kröner was not the only unconsciously funny German at Colberg. Some of the sentries were surpassingly amusing. I have mentioned the butterflies which abounded in that part of the country. Well, it happened that there were several very keen entomologists in the camp, of whom 'The Little Man' was one. These enthusiasts, later joined by others who knew nothing of the science of entomology, but who saw in the bug-hunting business a chance of roaming freely about the country (and of these was that fat little man, 'Mac'), had obtained permission to go out accompanied by a guard to pursue the rarities which were to be found in the vicinity of the camp. I think they flattered Kröner into the belief that he was in some subtle way responsible for their abundance, for although he never actually said so, his whole manner suggested that he had an interest in them akin to the Almighty's, and could produce even greater numbers of yet rarer specimens if only he cared to do it. (It is true that I have sometimes noticed a similar manner in English landowners talking of their estates.) This proprietary attitude towards the butterflies was notice-able also in the guards, but very particularly in the old fellow who accompanied Mac. He carried the killing bottle, and was positively angry when the butterflies which Mac was chasing refused to come and be transformed into 'specimens' for the glory of their country. It was gross breach of discipline on the part of a German insect, and he resented it in a delightful and characteristic expression of feeling, which the following tale relates.

Imagine Mac (that nice fat little man) panting in pursuit of a beautiful swallow-tail. Behind him, carrying the bottle, galumphs the perspiring Hun. Mac makes a slash with his net, but misses his footing and falls headlong into a prickly bush. The guard rushes up; the butterfly hovers exasperatingly near, fluttering yet above the bush. Mac, picking thorns out of himself, looks up to see his old sentry standing impotent, but furious with rage, shaking a fat fist at the lovely swallow-tail now fluttering away upon its innocent airy course, and shouting 'Schweinhund!'

Mac casually mentioned the whole affair to me when he came home, but was not greatly amused by it. As for me, I felt that something ought to be done in immediate celebration, and for want of a better thing I shaved off the beard which had been my badge of mould since I grew it at Holzminden. The story had made me feel five years younger; but if what my friends said is true, I amply repaid the debt, for the removal of the beard (so all averred) took off twenty-five.

22

ANOTHER LECTURE

BAD-COLBERG CAMP WAS IN many ways another Gütersloh. There was a very good tennis-court, and besides games, walks, concerts, and theatrical entertainments, they ran a good prison paper, called the Morning Walk, because it was pinned up on the walls of the pump-room and read by people who were walking round. They also gave lectures and held classes of all sorts.

Here is a paper which was read at Bad-Colberg to some very earnest young officers by another equally earnest, though less young, fellow-prisoner. I believe that none of us had at that time heard anything about the League of Nations, so it is very interesting to see how the thought which was in the heads of thousands of others throughout Europe found its expression among prisoners quite cut off from the outer world.

WAR ITS CAUSES AND REMEDY

To offer elaborate proof of the fact that war is in itself, and from all sane standpoints, a cruel, stupid, ineffectual, wasteful, and thoroughly evil thing, is insulting to the intelligence of all men who are not mentally deranged or morally perverted. Yet inasmuch as writers of this kind have in the past—and especially in the years preceding 1914— been the singers of its glory; inasmuch as some of these writers were men of great pretension and influence, though of small importance; and inasmuch as a thorough appreciation of the true character of war must be the first step towards its remedy, it has seemed worth while to devote a little time to the matter. If a man with scarlet fever thinks himself a hero and admires the spots, he is less likely to be cured than if he knows himself to be suffering from a disease. War is the scarlet fever of the world, and the world will not be cured until it realizes its disease and seeks a remedy.

To gentlemen like yourselves, fresh from the study of economics, it is surely unnecessary to do more than outline the economic disadvantages of war. War is economically evil because—

1. It reduces to an absolute standstill the production of all articles of value above the minimum required for the sustenance of those engaged in the war.

2. It misdirects the self-denial (*i.e.*, capital) of past generations, and stops the accumulation of present capital.

3. It destroys 'the labourer.'

4. It misdirects invention from positive and constructive channels into negative and destructive channels.

5. It impedes exchange. Economically its total effect

is, therefore, not less than absolutely disastrous. I do not apologize for these somewhat bald statements, both because I am addressing students in economy and also because such statements can, if necessary, be elaborated in the general discussion which follows the reading of this paper. Subsequent generalizations must be excused on the same grounds; otherwise the paper would be unduly long.

Politically it sometimes brings emancipation to small communities of whom the belligerents are afraid, and whom they wish temporarily to propitiate; but its effect in general is to hang up useful measures of reform, to place power in other hands than the State's, and to fetter national and individual freedom. The few gain, the many lose.

Socially it disorganizes society and destroys the citizen which goes to make it. It is not merely a return to the Dark Ages, it is worse than that, for, by selecting the best citizens for annihilation, it makes for the survival of the unfittest. Take the present war: the first men to be used were all volunteers, and of these the best were first selected. The best of the remainder were then conscripted, also in the order of their fitness. The remnant will be our future bridegrooms and legislators. But, it may be objected, will not the young men who have served return home fitter than they were before? Well, putting aside those who have been killed, those who have been maimed, and others shattered in health, they probably will; but one would hesitate to advise one's dearest enemy to join a class of physical culture the result of which was to kill, or maim, say, ten per cent! And one would hesitate to advise any country to sink six millions a day in such a sanatorium. War as a health restorer is an idea which will not hold water—there are so many better and cheaper. The societies which take poor children from the cities into the fields and sunshine have done more for national fitness than the longest of our bloody wars, and have done it much more cheaply.

Judicially—that is, as a means of settling the disputes of nations—it is simply ridiculous. It is everything that justice should not be; slow beyond words, costly beyond dreams, and (since the wrong party is as likely as not to win) totally ineffectual. It is founded upon a principle abhorrent to all civilized law, the principle that 'might shall be right.'

Morally it is indefensible; but so much nonsense has been talked, taught, and preached on this point that it will be well to go into the matter a little more fully. 'War, the beneficent mother of virtues,' is a famous phrase that is familiar in the cars of most of us. Beneficent mother! Hunger, wounds, and hate are her children. She is garlanded with the stinking weeds of death. At her bloody skirts cling the pretty dancing joys of arson, pillage, and rape. Picturesque in her train is the lamb of servility led by 'Folly in Power,' and dancing before her go her darling triplets whose names are 'Famine, Fear, and Ferocity.'

But does not war bring to light many acts of heroism, endurance, and self-sacrifice? It does. So does the sinking of a great liner. So does a serious railway accident. So does an explosion in a coalmine. So does any great fire in a theatre. On that argument let us do away with compasses, let us forbid sobriety in engine-drivers, let us repeal the mining Acts, and do away with fire-curtains, and have such ennobling disasters at least once a month. It will be cheaper, and if it kills the heroes which it produces it will do so less frequently than war. Or, as an alternative to any of these things, let us sweep away the sentimental lies of the moral supporters of war and get back to cold fact. Analysis of our subject, and recapitulation of headings, shall bring to a conclusion this preliminary portion of our paper.

If one man kills another in dispute he is called a murderer. The act is labelled as crime by the State and sin by the Church. Such deeds are suppressed by the whole community. They discourage such conduct by education, moral influences, and grave penalty. Now if a million men kill a million men, what happens? They are called soldiers. The act is labelled 'service' by the State, and receives the Church's blessing.

To suppress such deeds there is no machinery. That which is considered wrong in the individual is considered right in the nation. What is a nation? It is a collection of individuals.

Is murder carried out by a nation less ferocious in its execution than that which is done by a single man? The reverse is the truth. Backed by every scientific discovery and ingenious device, it is in effect more protracted and cruel a device of murder than any yet devised by a single brain.

Is collective murder less disastrous than murder by the individual? On the contrary it is incalculably more disastrous. Is the successful State ever in the position of an undetected murderer who has become the possessor of his victim's goods? No, in this case the victim's goods have generally been destroyed in the process, or bartered away for weapons.

Merely from a business point of view, therefore, the murder is not nearly so successful. Moreover, the process of collective murder is so long that, owing to productive energy having become destructive, the whole world is impoverished.

Thus, from a material point of view war is collective loss. Morally it is collective murder. Judicially it is ridiculous. Socially it is disastrous.

Politically it is retrogressive. Economically it is an unmixed evil. *Why, then, is it ever engaged in?*

The first and best reason why a nation goes to war is because it has been attacked by another nation.

This reason (being the best) is the one which belligerent nations most wish to claim, and they will go to almost any lengths in order to prove their case.

Yet even this best of reasons is not necessarily a good one. To admit this would be to admit that the defendant in a lawsuit should always have judgment given in his favour. But it may happen with nations as with men that the defendant has injured the plaintiff and is in the wrong. In this case the only right course, as well as the only wise one, is to settle the matter out of court rather than to fight it to a finish. The lawyer will advise this if he is an honest man, and the client will agree if he is a sensible man. In the event—cynical persons will say the probability—of the lawyer not being an honest man, and of his acting in a manner contrary to his client's interest, he should be replaced by one who is.

Now, substitute 'politician' for 'lawyer,' and 'nation' for

'client,' and you have a parallel which, in these days, is the more perfect because 'politician' and 'lawyer' are practically synonymous. The glaring difference is simply that the politician, who is paid by the nation exactly as the lawyer is paid by the. individual, is, nevertheless, allowed powers and privileges which the most lenient client would gasp to hear suggested.

Imagine a man permitting his lawyer the power of pledging him in honour and possessions, and even life itself, to a cause or alliance the result of which maybe the loss of all three, but which, whether he approve it or not, is to be kept a secret. This thing—unthinkable to the individual—is permitted by all modern nations under the name of 'Secret Diplomacy.'

Whether 'Secret Diplomacy' is a thing capable of remedy is a matter which will be discussed in a later portion of this paper. It is here sufficient to place it amongst the causes of war, since by that agency a nation pledges itself to fight in a cause, and under conditions, kept secret, and therefore not approved or authorized by the people pledged. They must 'pay the piper' though they may not 'call the tune.'

Apropos of the present war, here is an extract from a book on its diplomacy, written by an American at a time when America was neutral.[1] 'The whole tangle of recent diplomacy has been immensely complicated by secrecy. Very few of the men who are now fighting so desperately throughout the length and breadth of Europe realized during these years of tension' (he is speaking of the years 1906-1914) 'how little they knew of what their Governments—and often inner circles of their Governments—

---

[1]. *The Diplomacy of The Great War*, by Arthur Bullard

were doing in their name. . . .' And when at last war broke out, three members of the British Cabinet resigned— committed political suicide in the face of a popular war— because they were *horrified* and *surprised* to discover where Sir Edward Grey and the inner circle of the ministry had brought the nation. And if Cabinet members did not know what the Secretary of State for Foreign Affairs was doing, it is evident that the people at large were led—perhaps wisely, but certainly blindly—like sheep to the slaughter.' That the case was not different in this country is evident by the newspaper agitation for 'open diplomacy,' which occasionally breaks out in spite of strong official control, and which recent events—the Clemenceau-Czernin revelations—have again made audible. Such are the facts which need not be elaborated. 'Secret Diplomacy' will reappear in the speculative portion of this paper which concerns itself with the remedies for war.

That large armaments are in themselves a cause of war is a truth which has long been recognized, and in 1911 an attempt was made to reduce armies to the status of police for the maintenance of law and order, and to substitute for war a court of international arbitration. The proposal was put forward by President Taft, U.S.A., and I was present when Sir Edward Grey replied in the House of Commons. 'Bleeding to death in times of peace' was the phrase which he used to describe the state of European nations then spending vast sums of money on increased armaments. The way to reform was, he said, then blocked by one great European Power—which he would not name, but which had absolutely refused to countenance such a scheme.

We are not at present dealing with remedies. It is

needful only to state that a great army or a great navy, created and kept up at enormous expense, is made for one end. It is made to be used: The temptation to use it is always present. Unused it is wasted. And sooner or later, when 'bluff' has extracted the last ounce of gain, it will go into action.

How a machine can influence and at last overmaster its creator is a theme admirably treated by Mr. Jacks in his second volume of essays 'From the Human End,' a book which I would advise every man to read.

It would be superficial to suppose the matter ended there. There are wheels within wheels, causes behind causes. What, then, is the cause of large armaments? Taking once more the case of unaggressive nations, and recognizing the principle that 'self-preservation is the first law of life,' the cause is mistrust of one or more neighbouring nations. 'Fear,' says John Galsworthy (I quote from memory), is the Dark Angel of man's life which inspires ninety per cent, of his cruelties.' And Ignorance is its mother. Man fears the unknown. Nations, like children, dread the dark. Nourishers of that fear which causes war are all things which raise barriers between nations.

Reference has already been made to 'Secret Diplomacy,' but there are a thousand other secrecies, and every one of these go to prevent that frank understanding of aims, ideals, and needs which would do so much to obviate war.

Let us now turn to the aggressor. 'Unprovoked assault' is a thing which is not frequent between men or nations, but we will suppose it. We will suppose that for no reasons other than those of pride, envy, hatred, lust, greed, and the love of ferocity, a Government which is wholly and thoroughly bad has declared war on another Government. Now, I say without hesitation that, though a Cabinet of twenty, and perhaps even a Parliament of three hundred, might be one and all evil men, dead to all dictates of conscience, yet it is utterly impossible in human nature for a whole nation to be so. It is insanity to suggest that nations of, say, sixty millions are ready to go to war, sacrifice their sons, their possessions, life itself, in order to gratify such lusts. When, therefore, such a thing as 'unprovoked war' occurs—if it ever does—it is made possible only by wholesale deception of a people living politically in darkness. It is made not by the nation, but by the Government, and it follows that such a Government must be secret in execution, undemocratic in design, and unrepresentative in character.

'I have seen knaves and fools—many of both—' writes Stevenson, 'and they all get paid in the end; but the fools first.' Nations foolish enough to allow themselves to be ruled in such a manner are likewise 'paid in the end'— with war; and the cause of all such wars is the *permitting* of any Government not directly responsible to the people and under their control. It is in their power to remove this cause of war, and few who have experienced the penalty will again forget to do so.

When a people—as distinct from a Government— goes to war, it is to satisfy some national need, aim, or ambition not to be assuaged but by victory. If the need is real, the aim just, the ambition right, then they are justified in going to war, since there is no other mode of arbitration. Whether it is wise, whether they will win, is another matter. They can at least die for their cause.

If they choose to do so who can blame them? But what, in such a case, can be said for their enemies? Wisdom (since they may not win) and Justice (since they are opposing a legitimate cause) both cry out against them. If they are mere tools to their Government they may not hear. But if they are a free people, able to see and hear, why should they fight? The answer is that just and unjust causes of war have never been taught to them. Patriotism is not to fight for one's country, right or wrong; it is being able to decide when your country is wrong or right.

What, then, are the legitimate causes which should urge a self-respecting nation to fight? To tabulate these would go far to end war. Humanity is on the whole good. Nations are on the whole just. Few would fly in the face of conscience—to say nothing of public opinion—by opposing those causes.

The first and foremost is undoubtedly the need for expansion. When man has populated and developed a certain portion of the earth, it is absolutely necessary for him to be allowed ground elsewhere. It is not as though there were no more room. Over-population of the earth has never yet been a cause of war. But, even if the world were as well populated as a small island in the South Seas, the matter could be quickly and eugenically settled without war after the manner of many so-called primitive tribes.

Note that this vital need of expansion is not at all synonymous with the 'need' of *expanding an Empire*. It is founded on the principle that the earth is man's, and not the property of any particular people. The Imperialist who collects lands as a boy collects birds' eggs—not for sustenance but to add to his collection—is the worst enemy of peace. Sooner or later he always comes up against a starving man who wants food, and who means to get it or die in the attempt.

Whether nationality is or is not a cause of war is a question which has been discussed many times since the days of Tolstoy. I do not think it need be. Nationality is to a people what individuality is to a person—his chief interest. and charm. It is important to remember that we are all the same, sons of one human and Divine heredity. It is equally important to remember that we are all different. By being so, we bring so much the more wonder, interest, and knowledge to the common stock; and with nations as well as with men it takes all sorts to make a world worth living in. Nationality only becomes an evil when it is forced upon others; which is to say that it is only evil when it destroys nationality. 'Deutschland über alles' is a motto as intolerable as 'Jones über alles.' It means the suppression of all the Smiths and the Robinsons among the nations. Yet Jones in himself may be a very good fellow, proficient in certain crafts unknown to the others, and of the greatest use to them. We cannot afford to lose him either. Tolstoy's dream of world-brotherhood can only come through national brotherhood.

We learn that man loves God because He has first loved man. He loves man because he has first loved a small circle of people related to him. A man will come to love of the world-State only through first loving his own particular State. The terms 'legitimate national aspirations,' 'national destiny,' and so forth, as they are used by politicians, have in truth been the excuse for many wars, but they have no connection with nationality. They are the texts from Scripture which, as Shakespeare remarks, v may be quoted by the devil to further his own purposes.

To believe in nationality is nothing against believing also in arbitration and, for that matter, in federation. 'Birds of a feather' will 'flock together'; and to suppose, for instance, a federation of the English-speaking, or Anglo-Saxon, races is not to suppose that England would cease to be England, or America essentially the United States and 'God's Own Country.' As this subject comes rather under the heading of the Remedies we will pass on, pausing only to restate the case thus: If the idea of nationality could be stamped out and substituted by that of a world-State, wars, as known, would certainly cease: but wars might equally well cease if they were looked upon *throughout the world* as a detestable and self-inflicted curse, and humanity might still retain its 'individuality' by means of nations.

There is no better first step towards doing away with an evil than for everybody together and at the same time to want to do away with it. It is surprising how difficulties vanish in such a case. It follows that persons whose influence is against this must be considered as causes of its continuance.

The first two persons to come under this category are: (1) 'Our Great Leaders,' and (2) 'Our Great Platitude-Mongers.' Not infrequently the terms are synonymous. 'Our Great Leaders!' I never see that phrase applied to a politician by some foolish journalist without a desire to rip up the newspaper. If politicians are anything at all they are the men appointed by us and paid by us to represent in Parliament the whole body of the people and carry their wishes into effect. That it is customary to call them 'Our Great Leaders' and not 'Our Great Servants' is typical of the state of mind of a people who permit 'secret diplomacy' and 'secret funds' (those who have read the book by Hilaire Belloc and Cecil Chesterton entitled 'The Party System' will understand the significance of the latter), men who gaily give over the liberty gained by their fathers by the efforts of hundreds of years into the hands of men theoretically responsible but practically uncontrolled.

As to Platitude-Mongers—there are two classes of people in the world. God made them to worry one another, and perhaps to instruct one another in the virtue of Charity. There are those who are content, for various reasons, to voice platitudes and to think the thoughts of others; and there are those who are not so contented, but who are determined, for various reasons, to worry things out to the best of their ability, and to speak as they find. This one set of people having made up their minds, and the other people having no minds to make up, they decide to quarrel whenever they meet. We can imagine the conversation being opened by any such well-worn platitude as 'The best way to insure peace is to prepare for war' (in that case it is hardly necessary to follow the subsequent discussion); 'War is an unfortunate but necessary evil'; or 'While human nature remains human nature war will never be abolished.' It may be worth while to take a slice out of the conversation naturally following these latter statements.

'War is an unfortunate but necessary evil.'
'Is it necessary?'

'Sometimes it is.'

'Why?'

'You may be unjustly attacked.'

'Then couldn't the other side refuse to fight?'

'Yes, but they don't.'

'No, because they don't know that it is an unjust war. Wouldn't education solve that problem?'

'Sir, war is a punishment for sin. The vicar said so in his sermon last week. I thought it very sound.'

'Yes, it is God's punishment for sin. But what sin? Is it necessary that we should commit it? A few years ago cholera was considered a visitation of God for sin. And so it was. A few people, Charles Kingsley among them, came along and said 'the sin of bad drains.' People had never heard of such a thing. They laughed. But so it turned out. And the event is typical. Man is constantly discovering that he has to blame himself for events which he has always been accustomed to attribute to God. It is a quaint idea to attribute evil to God and call it a visitation.'

'Sir, God's ways are inscrutable. "He moves in a mysterious way His wonders to perform."'

'So, sir, does the devil—ably assisted by man; and I will swear he is the author of all such calamities} including war.'

'Young man, you are blasphemous and insufferable.' (*Curtain.*)

*　　*　　*　　*

'While human nature remains human nature war will never be abolished.'

'But is not human nature always changing as a result of experience?'

'Human nature never changes.'

'That, sir, is a supposition highly unflattering to yourself, for it puts you on a level with the latest discovery in yonder burial barrow.'

'Be as insolent as you please, young fellow, but there will always be quarrels.'

'True, aren't we quarrelling now? But I do not take a club and hit you on the head as I might have done a million years ago. And if you had done me an injury—which you have not—I should not do so, since there are law-courts.'

'Ah! That is where I have you. Between nations there are no law-courts. War is the only means of settlement, and as such it is inevitable.'

'Then why not substitute a court of arbitration similar to that appealed to in such cases by individuals?'

'It is impossible. Arbitration is bosh—a Utopian dream.'

'That, sir, is a statement which your Grand-father-Platitude-Monger-to-the-nth degree told to mine when he suggested that there might be a better way of settling personal differences than that of hitting your adversary on the head with a club.'

'If it is possible why has it not been done? Do you, young man, claim to be so much wiser than your fathers as to succeed where they have failed through thousands of years?'

'Sir, all progress in the history of the world is the result of man doing things which were 'impossible.' That is man's work in the world. It was impossible for man to settle his differences other than with a club. It was impossible for him to kill his enemy from afar off. It was impossible for him to travel at sixty miles an hour. It was impossible for him to fly. As to succeeding where my fathers have failed, that is what I am here for.'

'You are a conceited young pup. Your fathers were better men than you will ever be.'

'That I do not care to dispute, for they had their problems and solved them, which their fathers— who had solved other problems—had failed to do. As for being a conceited young pup, perhaps I am. But your humility is a more damnable thing than my conceit, for it is nothing more than self-satisfied laziness and lack of imagination.'

The Platitude-Monger might continue to argue for a long time, but sufficient has been said to show his method and to lead us directly into the third portion of our subject— namely, the remedies, many of which have been foreshadowed.

The Remedies.

It goes almost without saying that there is no immediate magic available for the cure of war. Life is no fairy story, and beneficent changes do not come to us by the wave of a wand, but by a whole series of effort. Little by little the thing which seemed scr wonderful to the dreamer of it becomes more and more obvious as a possibility; and when the people at the pinnacle of their fathers' efforts do what their ancestors dreamed, they do it as a matter of course. The thing has become a matter of common sense.

So it will be with war. The first step towards doing away with it was taken long ago, when dreamers first saw its possibility. Our endeavour to find a practical remedy is only a continuation of their work, the completion of which is possibly for our sons, possibly for men who will be born in another century. Our duty is to bring the end nearer.

Study of the causes of war is a signpost which will guide us in keeping direction. But the first and most important condition of travel, without which one will not move at all, is a sincere and ardent desire that the end should be reached. To this state of mind we of the twentieth century are specially incited by two things: (1) recent experience, (2) the fact that future wars will be even more terrible and probably also larger.

The popularity of such a recruiting phrase as the 'war to end war' shows that the most ardent volunteers were at heart conscientious objectors. They fought not because they liked fighting, but because they hated it. They fought that their sons should not have to fight.

This universal conviction as to the utter undesirability of war is a great thing. It is the energy to walk forward. Without it there would be no hope of arriving, and the fact that it is more widespread throughout the world to-day than ever before gives us a unique opportunity of moving forward in the right direction. This age may not and prob-ably will not solve the problem of war, but at least it has better opportunities and keener incitements to do so than any other in the history of the world.

I have referred to the causes as signposts; speaking more accurately, they are danger-signals. They do not point out the right way to go except by implication: except by pointing out the right way not to go. The right way to go is a matter of speculation.

The best, and by far the most popular, speculative remedy for war is that which is known as International Arbitration: and it is not purely speculative, since it is founded upon an analogy. The extending of principles from the individual to the community is a modern tendency which has manifested itself of late to such an extent that it is perhaps the most notable feature of to-day's literature.

Arbitration is possible between individuals, and the tendency of the age is to ask, 'Why is it impossible between nations?' It is a question which is being asked with increasing emphasis throughout the world to-day: and it is a question to which there is no answer, for the plain truth is that it is not impossible. (That it has not been done is another matter.) The idea requires small elucidation. I will put the case as I always think of it myself, and as I first thought of it when I was a law-student, compelled to defend an honourable profession against the attacks of irreverent acquaintances. 'You may curse law as much as you please,' I would shout back. 'You may say—only I shall deny it— that injustice results more often than justice; that wrong, when represented by a clever counsel, will always triumph over right—a thing which occasionally does happen when laymen are foolish enough to conduct their own cases; you may say that law is slow and inhuman, and lawyers costly and unscrupulous. I will not argue such points, I will simply say, 'Imagine both law and lawyers abolished. What have you got then?' 'Heaven!'

'That is perhaps witty, but it is not true. The right answer is not Heaven, but the other place—or something very like it to any civilized man. You have the Age of Savagery. No longer will you possess any way of settling your differences but by beating your opponent with a club, or piercing him with a spear. You, Jones, are a big man; you are also hot-tempered and rather stupid' (struggle with Jones); 'it might suit you, but sooner or later you would meet your master, and the case would go against you however tight you might happen to be. You, Smith, are a miserable weakling' (short struggle with Smith). 'The fact that you are less hot-tempered than Jones would not protect you. You too would perish.'

The argument was a bantering schoolboy's, but nevertheless it was, I think, a sound one. Perhaps, as Wilde asserts, 'Men become older but not wiser,' and I among them. Certainly I think to-day on that matter as I thought then; only to-day, following the spirit of my time, I am tempted to carry the idea a little farther—to push it, in fact, to its logical conclusion; to extend the principle from the individual to the community.

What, when all is said and done, is war but that same old savage, stupid mode of settling differences which was abolished and replaced by law in the case of the individual? The reason why it was not abolished and replaced by International Law Courts long ago is that there exists between nations of the world barriers which have long since been broken down between individuals. To-day some of those barriers are crumbling, yet I do not say it will be easy to break them down.

These barriers or differences are not always realized as being so great and so powerful as they really are.

Take the difference of language. Even among the minority—the tiny minority—of well-educated people—and our politicians are not all drawn from that class—many speak but one living language and few more than two or three. Internationally the remainder of the nation is, for all practical purposes, dumb. It is not difficult to imagine how almost impossible it would be for men who had not yet invented speech to live amicably together. The inventions of the telephone, the telegram, and daily newspapers are now crumbling this barrier. Travel also makes for understanding. But the nation is not yet in so fortunate and so favourable a position as the individual. Again, men quarrel or agree with a known person, and generally while in company with him. Nations, from one side of the world to the other, quarrel and agree with total strangers, and it is a fact that the agreement is in such circumstances frequently as disastrous as the quarrel. Temperament, and in a narrow sense nationality, are likewise in their nature barriers, and there are others which it is unnecessary to mention. Nevertheless it is true that all such racial barriers crumble, and already have done so to a degree, under influences of wider education, travel, and scientific discovery, which open up communication and exchange of values both material and mental. That such barriers will in this generation be razed to the ground is a thing which the youngest of young dreamers can hardly hope to see. That does not rid us of our responsibility to posterity who shall see it. Unless we wish to identify ourselves with the person— probably a politician—who demanded, 'What, I ask you, has posterity ever done for us?' (and I venture to say even if we *are* of that state of mind) the duty that lies plainly before us is to assist the crumbling, and to drag down anything which goes to support those barriers or build them. The dark angel of Fear and his mother, whose name is Ignorance—these are they whose hands pile up barriers and support them with the props of Secret Diplomacy, vast armament, democracy subservient to 'Great Leaders' and 'Great Platitudinists,' and that perverted patriotism whose crest is a bloody sword and whose motto is 'My country, right or wrong.' These sinister powers will not be disarmed at a blow, but it is our hope and firm belief that Man, whose destiny has been to achieve the impossible, to harness to his chariot unharmed of their beating hooves the great forces of Nature, and to throw scornfully aside all things sinister and insulting to the divinity that is within him, will not at the last fail to achieve between nations what his forefathers achieved between individuals.

International arbitration will come; that is as sure as it is that there is a war on now, or that the sun will rise to-morrow. It may not come in our generation, but it is nearer than it has ever been in the world's history, and perhaps it is nearer than any one of us imagines. We have more opportunity and more inducement than ever had our fathers, and I repeat that when men want a thing, want it intensely, and want it altogether, Satan and all the host of hell are insufficient to prevent its ultimate attainment.

*   *   *   *

I have endeavoured in the ridiculous space of half an hour—which is all the time at our disposal—to make an outline round my subject. The task of filling in this outline and of altering it where necessary must be left to others, yourselves included.

Personally I have nothing more to do but to thank Chichester for writing out my thoughts so that I could read them, and you for your attention to a paper necessarily inadequate. It is not altogether my fault. The difficulty of finding references in a prisoner camp is aptly illustrated by the fact that with the one exception of Ballard's book, all I was able to discover on the subject of open diplomacy, except within my own mind, was this cutting, taken, if you please, from the *Continental Times*. It is a fragment from the writings of Walter Bagehot, the celebrated Victorian essayist, and this is what he says:

'I am disposed to deny entirely that there can be any treaty for which adequate reasons cannot be given to the English people, which the English people ought to make. A great deal of the reticence of diplomacy had, I think history shows, much better be spoken out.'

In conclusion, the points I put before you to debate and consider are these:

(1) That war is an unnecessary evil which it is the duty of all civilized men to prevent for the sake of those who come after.

(2) That practical steps in this direction are—

(a) Steps leading towards sound Democratic Control.

(b) Open Diplomacy.

(c) Reduction of Armaments. (This, of course, must be carried out by all concerned, and at the same time.)

(d) Wider Education (which shall not count as unimportant the teaching of sound patriotism and the just rights of nationality.)

(e) A readiness to unite in Federation with other nations closely allied in ideal, and so take the first step towards a world-agreement and peace.

(f) Fair and free discussion of the (perfectly possible) aim of all such measures—*i.e.*, International Arbitration.

* * * *

The meeting will not have been in vain if every one of the above suggested points is discredited.

My aim, and I believe the aim of all subsequent readers in this course, is to promote interest in a problem rather than to give you any cut-and-dried scheme.

From any honest thought and sincere desire to abolish evil, good will result, and its particular form is immaterial.

23

A TRAGEDY, AND BAD TIMES AT BAD-COLBERG

IT WAS THE ESCAPING which showed up Beetz and Kröner in their true characters; the one as an unscrupulous bloody-minded Hun, the other as a weak fool.

The trouble started when it was discovered that somebody out of our building had been attempting to cut the wire. A search resulted in the discovery of several escape kits, owned apparently by no one (for naturally they remained unclaimed when the Germans found them).

The Commandant was furious, and ordered all the officers in the three suspected rooms to report themselves at the interpreter's office every hour of the day until further notice. This was clearly a flagrant case of collective punishment which the German and British Governments had agreed should not be inflicted. The result of it would be that the officers who had to report themselves would thereby be deprived of walks; not to mention the obvious disadvantage of having to stop doing whatever they might be doing, and run off to the interpreter's office every hour of the day. We therefore decided that we would not go.

Finding his order had been ignored, the Commandant sent for us the following day, and we lined up against the wall in his office.

'Why have you refused to report?" was the question he asked each one, passing down the line; and the answer was taken down in writing. Some said one thing and some said another, defending their refusal to obey; but I was at the end of the line and had had time to think things out a bit. It was clear to me that his object (which was, no doubt, suggested to him by Beetz) was now to obtain from each officer a signed admission of disobedience, which was the unforgivable sin in Germany. However good one's case might be, that case would avail nothing at court-martial in the face of such an admission. I therefore made up my mind that he should certainly not have one from me, and our conversation was as follows:

KRÖNER. 'And you, why have you refused to report?'
SELF. 'I have not refused to report."
KRÖNER (surprised). 'But you did not come!'
SELF (sweetly). 'No, I did not come.'
KRÖNER (angrily). 'Why did you not come? Why did you not come?'
SELF. 'Herr Commandant, I am a lawyer.' (Pause to let that sink in.) 'I have read much law, but never yet have I discovered any civilized people punishing prisoners without telling them what they were being punished for. I have not been told.'

BEETZ. 'He says that the Germans are not civilized.'

KRÖNER. 'Do you say that the German nation is not a civilized nation?' (Writer prepares to put down my answer—insult to the German nation being about as damning as disobedience.)

SELF. 'But no, Herr Commandant, that is precisely what I do not say. It is just because I know that your nation is so highly civilized that I could not bring myself to report. 'There is some mistake,' I said, 'so I will refrain out of respect to the German nation.'

KRÖNER. 'But there is no mistake; it was my order to you.'

SELF. 'Herr Commandant, I am very sorry to hear you say such a thing. I shall of course not make myself guilty of disobedience. But since collective punishment is forbidden, and since I am about to be punished for no offence, I will request you (as you know I have a right to do) to forward at once my complaints to the Dutch Ambassador, and to your own Kriegsministier. All these officers are witness that I have made the request.'

That was a nasty one for the old man; for not only had he failed to get me to admit disobedience, or even an intention to disobey, but he had to report to his own Government and to the Dutch Ambassador that he was about to punish me for no offence. As an alternative he could ignore my request, which had been witnessed by about twelve officers, and risk getting himself into trouble later on. Apparently he was not willing to do either of these things. He climbed down.

'Mr. Harvey,' he said, 'has not refused to report himself and so he need not report. I cancel in his case the order. The rest of you shall report, and shall also be tried by court-martial for disobedience.' (I knew it!) 'If you do not come, soldiers shall bring you. It is not a punishment, it is a camp precaution, and I have a right to make the whole camp report every hour of the day if I think fit.' This was quite true, but the point was that he had not made the whole camp report, and therefore this was not an *Appel* but a strafe—an argument which we put up at the court-martial, which I afterwards attended as witness for the defence. But the Germans did not require me to swear to my evidence after I had given it, which is their way of saying that they did not believe it. It was just as I had expected: disobedience admitted, a defence was hardly listened to, and certainly not considered by the judges. My friends, with the exception of M. and W. (who got each ten months), were sentenced to six months' imprisonment in a fortress.

But before they were taken away to do it, other things happened of much more tragic importance. M. and W. made a daring escape and were 'out' for several days before recapture. One morning—it was Whit-Sunday—we heard that a guard of eight soldiers from the camp had been detailed by the Adjutant to meet the two recaptured officers at a railway station about eight miles away, and to bring them back to the *lager*. About midday a queer rumour began to spread about the place—coming, it is said, from a sentry—that one of the officers had been wounded. That they were both of them un-wounded when recaptured and even so late as that morning, was clear, since they were to be marched eight miles.

At about three o'clock in the afternoon *both* of them were brought into the prison on stretchers—quite *dead*.

They had been shot in a wood at Heldburg, a short distance from the station, at which they were handed *over to the carefully chosen soldiers of Beetz*, to be brought back (?) to Bad-Colberg.

The story circulated by the German authorities was that they had tried to escape; but the Colberg officers said openly that they suspected that this was not the case, and asked for permission to examine the bodies. I myself (though holding no official position amongst the British) drafted the letter which went to the Commandant after the verbal request of the S.B.O. had been refused, and I made a special point of the fact that British officers, many of whom were soon to be repatriated to Holland, would depart with an impression, and express an opinion, very prejudicial to Germany, and the camp in general, if an examination of the bodies was refused. But the Hun authorities again absolutely refused. No doubt they had good reason, for an examination would have definitely settled such vitals questions as these:

(1) Whether they were shot from the back (as they would be if running away) or from the front (as they would be if lined up for execution).

(2) Whether they were wearing their packs (no sane men who were three hundred kilometres from the frontier would attempt to escape without them).

(3) Whether they were shot from a distance, or whether the muzzles of the rifles had been placed against them.

(4) Whether they showed signs of other ill-treatment.

(5) The number of times they had been shot.

(6) Whether they had been bayoneted.

That the guards picked for duty by Beetz were the most brutal and anti-English that could be found in the camp we had heard from a sentry that same morning. What their private instructions had been we could not discover, but we knew:

(1) That Beetz hated M. and W., and that they had not concealed their opinion of him.

(2) That he had told them that they would never escape again.

(3) That on an occasion when another officer attempted to escape by walking out of the camp while disguised in German uniform, Beetz was angry with the sentry who stopped him because he had not allowed him into the neutral-zone, from which he could not escape, and shot him there.

(4) That friendly sentries, talking of M. and W. and their many escapes, had said something which became significant in the light of subsequent events: 'Yes, they are two very brave men, but they will be shot.' We knew also that M. and W. had agreed with one another before escaping that if recaptured they would try no foolish stunts on the way home.

Now at the time at which they were shot it was broad daylight; they were presumably without their packs, unless purposely allowed to keep them as a temptation to escape; they had four armed guards each; they were seventy yards apart, so that there could have been no collaboration; it was a lonely spot; they were both shot dead, and neither merely wounded; Beetz was responsible for picking the party to fetch them.

These facts, each slight enough in itself, were, when massed together, of considerable significance, and made us morally sure that there had been foul play, but try as we would, we could get no farther than that. We could get no inspection of the bodies, and the rest of the evidence, though suspicious, proved nothing, for the friendly sentries would not give their names, nor put in writing nor repeat verbally anything they had previously admitted.

These two brave and unfortunate officers were men I knew very well, for one of them lived in the same room and the other next door. They were liked and admired by the whole camp, and their friends may be sure that their fellow-officers did all that was possible to clear up the mystery of their deaths. That they, could not do more was due to deliberate obstruction by the German authorities, for reasons which may be conjectured.

I have related this sinister and sombre occurrence for two main reasons: (1) To pay tribute to the bravery of two men who died in service for their country as surely as if they had fallen on the battlefields of France; (2) to brand for so long as this writing lives and as far as it penetrates through the world the names of Kröner and Beetz.

24

LAST DAYS AT BAD-COLBERG

M Y LAST DAYS AT COLBERG were occupied with various interests, but chiefly with being (by virtue of past legal training) 'prisoner's friend'— an employment kept entirely unofficial and secret, though the Germans certainly had their suspicions of what I was doing, as shown by a remark made at one of the courts-martial when Beetz snarled suddenly, 'And these lies have been carefully made up for you by Lt. Harvey, I suppose?'—a suggestion which was, of course, indignantly denied by the prisoner.

What, in fact, happened was this: the best line of defence to whatever questions had to be answered was thought out, written down, and learnt by heart. It was then translated into German. At trial the translated defence was handed to the judges. The prisoner did not require a German counsel. He had written out his defence. He had got it translated for the convenience of the court. He had no more to say. The court was naturally pleased at this saving of time, and to the chagrin of the camp authorities showed its first appreciation of such a frank and concise explanation by inflicting only three weeks' imprisonment upon an officer whom Beetz and Kröner had accused of burglary, being in possession of stolen goods, destruction of German property, and attempted escape.

The Germans asked some very curious questions at their courts-martial, and solemnly took down some very curious answers—*e.g.*, 'Where were you born?' Answer. Dixie."

Q. 'What was your mother's maiden name?"

A. 'Pinkham.'

Q. 'Christian name?'

A. 'Lydia.'[1]

Except in their often very unpleasant consequences these German courts-martial of British officers were a comic farce; and as for justice—!

I must not forget to mention another very plucky escape from Colberg which occurred about this time, and was in many ways amusing and spectacular. One bright summer day people at upper windows in the villa were amazed at the sight of two British officers in full escape kit proceeding to cut the wire almost under the nose of a sentry. As a matter of fact, the sentry was interested in a game of tennis and did not see them. They crawled out of the camp and began running. Then they were seen. One

---

1 [Publisher's note] Lydia Pinkham 'Lilly the Pink' whose Medicinal Compound was widely marketed to cure many ills, especially 'women's complaints.' A sanitized version of this popular song was recorded by The Scaffold in the 1960s: '*We'll drink a-drink a-drink to Lily the-pink the-pink the-pink . . .*' Over a million copies sold. Harvey provides a snippet and score on page 217.

shot rang out, then several shots, but the officers continued to run. There was a very curious and unpleasant thrill in watching the German nearest to us rest his rifle against a tree to get good support while he took aim and fired at our friends running up the hillside. One wanted so much to push out a magic invisible hand and jog his elbow. Finally the officers were cut off and recaptured by camp guards, and there was almost a riot when it was seen that one of these was beating X. with the butt of his rifle. The German orderly-room sergeant who had run out to watch the chase was so frightened by the attitude of officers round him that he drew his sword, nearly cutting off his own head. (Orderly-room clerks should not be allowed swords, it isn't safe for them.) A roar of laughter greeted this piece of frightfulness; the trembling man looked stupidly at the naked sword in his hand, and returned it with some difficulty to its scabbard. Another great clap of laughter followed him as he hastily returned to the shelter of his office. He had saved the situation.

A thing which particularly puzzled the German sentries at Bad-Colberg was that every evening the English officers (some of them quite senior) would play a game of rounders with the English orderlies—common soldiers! And when a General, who had recently been brought into the camp, joined in, and went walking about with bare legs, they gave it up altogether. General D. was a great asset to the camp, and his tact and firmness in dealing with the Huns, who were always impressed by military rank, caused an improvement in their behaviour towards us. Our grievances, including, of course, the shooting affair, were put into his hands to be dealt with in the best way possible. Details of all bad cases of injustice or ill-treatment were memorized by officers being sent to Holland on repatriation, and so taken through one by one to the British authorities, causing dignified protest on one side and insolent denial on the other. Theoretically I am against reprisals, but undoubtedly experience is in favour of them as the only protest which appeals to the German mind and obtains prompt remedy of abuses.

One might as well argue fair play with a tiger? or chivalry with a pig, as either with a Hun. There are exceptions, but I am speaking generally and of a policy rather than a people. This opinion is shared by all prisoners of war who have had anything more than a short and superficial experience of captivity. Pacifists may, if they are foolish enough, accuse me of nourishing hatred, but as a matter of fact I do not know what it is. Quite without malice but with all my strength I hit a nasty thing when I see it. To like nice things and nasty things at the same time is dishonest, and shows that you do not care a damn for either.

At last (it was somewhere about June 20), after I had done nearly two years of captivity, my name appeared on a list of officers to go to Holland. I was delighted, and so (I think) were some of the Germans. By this time I was heartily sick of them and their country. To get out of it seemed too good to be true. I felt that it was not to Holland but to Heaven that we were going.

On the day of departure we were subjected to a very rigorous personal search, and required to give up all camp money in our possession whether notes or otherwise; the reason for this being a trick played on Germany by repatriated Frenchmen in another camp. Our Allies, having taken away with them some of the paper which passed for money in that camp, proceeded to forge thousands of notes, which they sent concealed in parcels of food to their friends who remained in the camp they had left, where such paper had, of course, the purchasing value of money. There resulted an unheard-of boom in the canteen (money is no object when one has only to go up to a friend and say, 'Give me a thousand marks'), and the Germans, who made a profit on everything sold, must have thought that they were making a fine fortune, till they discovered at the end of several months that more money had been spent than was ever issued, and that a vast percentage of notes for which value had been given was absolutely worthless. Our search over, and nothing of importance found, we drove light-heartedly away to the station in a rickety one-horse char-a-banc. The guards who accompanied us were stolid, amiable men, and the driver a village 'character.' On our way to the station we passed through Parson's Wood (Pfaffenholtz), near Heldburg, and had pointed out to us by the driver the exact places where poor M. and W. had been shot. The two spots pointed out were certainly seventy yards apart.

Saddened with the memory of that tragedy, and gladdened at the thought of quitting the place of it for ever, we boarded the train and were soon being carried swiftly away on our road to freedom.

25

AACHEN

Now comes what was in many ways the greatest disappointment that befell us in captivity.
We arrived at Aachen (Aix la Chapelle) about
June 24, and expected to go over any time within a week.
Officers continued to come in from various other prison
camps for a few days, and we were pleased to meet quite
a number of old friends and to rejoice with them that we
met in such happy circumstances.

When we asked the Germans the date of our departure, they replied with the motto of every German canteen,
'*Morgen früh*' (to-morrow morning), and for several days
we believed them—but we did not go. The stock of
British food we had brought with us decreased and finally
ceased—still we did not go. German rations were enough
to keep us alive, but always hungry; it was simply refined
torture. Always when we inquired, it was the same tale:

'To-morrow morning'; and so it continued until 'Morgen
früh' became synonymous with 'never,' and both heart
and body grew sick with hope and food deferred.

On the walks which we were allowed to take on
parole we frequently saw woods and steeples which lay in
Holland, and on one occasion, when our guard lost his
way, suddenly found ourselves within twenty yards of the
frontier. And still we did not cross. The reason for delay
was, it is conjectured, trouble between the English and
German Governments over the sinking of the *Königen
Regentes*, which took place about that time—but possibly
there were other reasons.

Whether we were permitted by honour to escape in
such circumstances was a question debated frequently,
and with some heat; but since we were still guarded with
wire and sentries I fail to see that there could have been
any doubt in the matter, which was the more clear since a
special parole was exacted for walking out.

I therefore began preparations, by acquiring a civilian suit from a friendly naval officer. How he had got it
through I don't know, but there it was, and he was kind
enough to part with it. There was neither opportunity nor
necessity to save food, since in one night one would certainly be caught or over; nor were maps and compasses a
necessity, though desirable. The only problem was to get
unseen out of the large building (a technical school) in
which we had now been shut up for a month. Its front
was guarded by sentries, and the courtyard at the back
patrolled by guards at night and whenever we were allowed
there in the daytime. With a German uniform I believe it

would have been easy to walk out, but it was not possible to obtain one.

When I arrived at Aachen I had two leaky worn pairs of boots, and after a week or two I sent the better pair into town to be mended, and never saw them again. Still, I thought that the old pair I had would carry me through a night's marching, and at the worst I could go barefoot; the main point was to find some way out. E. was going with me, and at length we discovered through the kindness of an Australian sergeant a chance of escape which we thought worth trying. There was a room upstairs at the side of the house, which was filled with wounded soldiers waiting, like ourselves, to be repatriated. Below the window outside was a clump of bushes. Sentries passed them periodically patrolling the courtyard at night, but often stood chatting round the corner of the building. This the Australian sergeant told us, and gave as an opinion (which afterwards proved perfectly correct) that a man might descend undiscovered in the darkness from the window to the bushes, by means of sheets tied together, or a rope. Once in the bushes, it only remained to wait till the sentry's back was turned, and then to climb an eight-foot wall into the poorly lighted road which ran past the building, and was not much used after 11 p.m.

We managed to get hold of a suitable length of thick wire cable, and were only waiting while E. negotiated for a navy blue suit in the possession of another officer, when there suddenly arrived from a fortress, where he had been put for safety after many determined escapes, a Captain taken in the first few weeks of the war, who had hitherto refused repatriation because he hoped to escape. He had now told the Germans that he wished to exercise his right, and since his time was long overdue, was being taken straight over, only waiting a couple of nights at Aachen while necessary arrangements were made for his passing into Holland. Now it turned out that this officer had told the Germans that he was willing to be repatriated merely because he found escape impossible where he was, and hoped to get a good chance from a place so near the border as Aachen. Thus after four years of captivity he had come simply to escape, and he had two clear nights in which to manage it.

We had already had a month, and it looked as if we might well have another month. Therefore E., the new officer, and I talked the matter over, and decided that under the circumstances it was only right and fair that he should have the first and immediate chance of putting our scheme—or rather, the Australian sergeant's—to the test.

I am very glad to say that the following night he got out safely, and reaped a well-earned reward by 'getting over.'

But it was very unfortunate for us that under his weight the wire cable cut a deep groove in the window-sill, which, though immediately filled in with soap, dust-sprinkled, was discovered by the Germans. So our scheme went West.

Before we could discover another way of escape at all feasible, orders came that we were to be shifted to another camp. On the morning of departure E. and I endeavoured to creep out by way of the fowl-house, and thence over the wall; but the German *Feldwebel* discovered us downstairs, and we only escaped punishment by lying dexterously, and anointing him with 'palm oil.' This was, I believe, on

Aachen

August 16, and about an hour later, wearing still civilian clothes under our Burberrys, we boarded a train bound for Stralsund, an island camp in the Baltic.

26

STRALSUND

THE JOURNEY TO STRALSUND was long and wearisome. For some time our course ran parallel with the frontier, but though we kept a sharp lookout, the guards kept a watch equally good, and no chance of 'jumping' occurred.

I will say no more of it than that when we arrived (about midnight), after two days' travelling, and were ferried over to sleep in our new prison, we all felt desperately tired and mouldy.

'Mouldy,' did I say? My mouldiness was such that even to-day, as I look back and try (but not very hard) to describe the camp of Stralsund, my chief impression is one of wired-in green mould upon a sunset. Stralsund is within sight of Rugen (where Elizabeth wandered about), and its sunsets are very beautiful.

Once only during my stay there did I come out of my shell to sing at a camp concert, and then I narrowly escaped being sent to prison over a song I had made up about the condition of the bed-linen in one of the huts. It went to the tune of 'Cockles and Mussels'; and what the Germans principally objected to was the chorus of 'Alive, alive-O!' which, as I tried to explain to them, I had not written at all, but was part of an old Irish song.

Since my boots had by this time completely worn through, I now returned to lie on my bed and grow a beard, only rising to let the Germans count me at such times as they thought it advisable. I did not write a single letter all the time (which was unkind of me), but read a dictionary. It was all I could read; not that Stralsund was a very bad camp—as a matter of fact it was rather good, and the library above the average of camp libraries—but I was unspeakably mouldy. Still, I had sufficient guts to make a long list, which is, in fact, before me at this moment, of words which struck me as being unusual, such as 'quob' and 'yoicks'; or lovely, as 'violet.'

Words are, as Trench[1] pointed out, 'crystallized poetry,' and there is much to be said in favour of reading dictionaries. But that was a thing which I found out after I had done it, and I did it simply because I couldn't do anything else.

It was so easy to stop when one wanted to, and just dream. 'Wild thyme'—ah, let me see, 'wild thyme'; surely I had smelt that! It grew on May Hill. Again I saw that tree-tufted bubble float up upon a sulphur dawn. Hadn't I read it also?

> 'I know a bank whereon the wild thyme blows,
> Where ox-lips and the nodding violet grows.'

---

1 [Publisher's note] Richard Chenevix Trench (1807-86) Dean of Westminster, theologian, poet, philologist and author of *On The Study of Words* (1866), to which Harvey refers.

Old Shakespeare . . . yes . . . ah, what music! And so on, picture after picture, thrown upon the blank darkness of captivity by a 'Chambers's Dictionary.' Oh, there is no denying that I was in 'a state.'

Notwithstanding this, I wrote a fair number of poems at Stralsund, and their tone is not unduly pessimistic as judged by the following.

A MEMORY

Now joy is dead and hope o'ercast
I call a dream out of the past
And thus command him: "Slave, go bring
Out of my days, one day in Spring!

'And out of *that* a certain hour
Which glimmers through an April shower.
Let apple-blossom crown the day,
And heap the hedges white with may!'

'Tis done. In one great backward surge
Of Time the Past and Present merge:
For Time is not a drifting river,
A moment here, then past for ever—
And what is done in the heart's deep core
Is done not once, but for evermore.

Therefore, upon a little hill
Where once you stood, I see you still.
And in that moist and diamond weather
We two take shelter still together.
And still there tumble from the tops
Of emerald trees the teasing drops
To hang within your dusky hair,
And be for queenly jewels there.

*   *   *   *

So in my heart I kiss you still
Upon a rainy April hill.

THE TREASURY

I have such joy in my heart's coffer,
Little I care what Life may offer;

Little it matters if I lie
In dungeons, who possess the sky.

The sparkling morn, the starry night,
Are locked away for my delight.

But in my heart there hangs a key
To open them, called Memory.

How should I ever lack a friend
Who so have lovers without end?

How can I ever lose my home
Who bear it with me where I come?

My home is in my heart, and there
In dreadful days I do repair;

And I have broken off the seal
Of that Dream-box, whose dreams are real.

So rich am I, I do possess
Their overpowering loveliness;

And have such joy in my heart's coffer,
Little I care what Life may offer.

It is a strange thing, this power of poetry, to substitute life, or recreate it, when life has failed us. It is responsible for all the fine poetry which has come, surprising us for no reason, direct from the trenches.

27

TO HOLLAND

I N THIS BOOK ON prison life I have endeavoured to
avoid monotony—which is, of course, the chief feature of prison life. Art is not life, but selection. It is
not experience, but experience filtered through personality. This book took two years and more to live; it has taken
about two months to write: and it will take two days or
less to read. Readers who desire to know more than it tells
them about how it feels to be a prisoner need only read
it over again, and after that over and over again till they
are sick. Then, when they have thrown it on the floor in
disgust, let them remind themselves that this was precisely
what prisoners were not able to do, though many tried
hard and some paid their lives for the attempt. And not
only must they read everything I have written in this book
a thousand times (if anything so horrible as that can be
contemplated), but a thousand times also they must read

blank pages. It is the blank page which kills you in the end; even nonsense is better than that.

I continued to read blank pages and 'Chambers's Twentieth Century Dictionary' alternately for two months, and then (about October 20) I started off again to Holland, together with about half the party who should have gone over from Aachen four months previously. The other half, including E., was kept back, and these unfortunate officers remained at Stralsund until the Armistice and the Workers' and Soldiers' Council put an end to their weary captivity by sending them on a ship to Denmark.

I think it must have been rather funny just at the end, when the Commandant had been deposed and his place was taken by the local bookseller; but even under this new and enlightened regime an American officer was shot dead by a sentry for wandering about the island outside the wire—surely not a very serious crime after the signing of an Armistice!

It was nice to hear that T. had kicked the interpreter down a few steps before leaving. He was a very beastly little man, who got angry because we laughed at his silly lies. 'You laugh!' he screamed one day, 'but I tell you it is no laughing matter. It is a shame and a curse!'—which same became a proverb.

After another wearisome journey we arrived at Aachen for the second time, a thoroughly mouldy party, not really believing that we should ever be allowed over the border. But we crossed it a few days later, and, where the sleepers changed from iron to wood (the escaper's invariable assurance that he is 'over'), saw incredulously a crowd of Dutch children cheering us and blowing kisses. It was a very choky feeling that we had then, a lump in the throat which almost prevented our returning their pretty welcome; but soon we were all shouting back lustily to greetings which met us as the train rocked quietly through that low-lying land of bell-towers and canals. If we found later on that Holland and Heaven chiefly resembled one another in the fact that both were extraordinarily difficult to reach, we seemed certainly to be getting into Heaven the day we crossed over from Germany. Miss V. met us at Venlo, as she met so many who will remember her with gratitude; and the 'old Mullah' (who arrived terribly immaculate) dragged me out, beard and all, to be introduced, from the place where I was hiding because I feared she would ask me, "What do you think of Germany?'and knew that my reply would be too much in prison-camp parlance to be fit for any lady's ears. But she didn't ask me that, and I got through the interview without a slip; although one or two of my friends dropped heavy bricks. However, she was probably pretty accustomed to it by this time, after meeting so many train-loads of repatriated prisoners.

At Scheveningen station we were met by hundreds of friends, both officers and orderlies, pressing round and cheering us as we came off the train. I believe there was a reception somewhere, but am not sure, for I was immediately whirled off to The Hague by dear old R. There suddenly and with violence our swiftly running tram was boarded by two highly excited officers, O. and D.S., who had seen us from the roadway. Then altogether we stood up and sang 'The Old Bold Mate.' The Dutch passengers looked stolidly on without astonishment, being apparently used to this sort of thing. After that, we went to the

AGONY!

'House of Lords,' Hook's, and various other places of good repute, finishing up exhausted and happy about 1 a.m. The same morning my beard, that badge of mould, was taken away from me, and thrown with every bad memory upon a dust-heap.

The Armistice, which came about a month later, did not surprise us very much. For more than a year we had seen the German people gradually starving. Even the sentries would go round every day picking out dirty old tins from the rubbish-heap in the hope of finding a bit of meat or some dripping. After Armistice most of the early captures were sent home, but some officers (and I was one) were retained to help in the repatriation of prisoners then flocking over the border after having been turned loose in Germany. Amongst those who came over were some very bad cases of Hun brutality.

Germans and British repatriated in Holland were very wisely kept apart, the former round Rotterdam and the latter in the Hague district; but occasionally they met, and fights could not always be prevented.

One man, whose foot had been badly frostbitten in a Russian strafe camp, spent most of his time in Holland within prison walls because the first thing he did when released was to go round looking for a Hun, and, as soon as he had found him, knock him out. Our men were exceedingly smart in their dress, and were great favourites generally, especially with the Dutch ladies. Their bearing, and punctilious saluting, formed a great contrast to that of the German and Dutch soldiers, who were by this time somewhat affected by the wave of Bolshevik feeling sweeping Europe.

I was sent, together with five other officers and a number of orderlies, to distribute food and clothes at a central camp, which was fed from frontier stations as the men came through. Leeuwarden was the name of the place. Afterwards, when English prisoners had ceased to come over, I went with another officer to feed Italians and Portuguese at Harderwijk by the Zuider Zee.

I did not much like either of these places, and at Leeuwarden, where I got Spanish 'flu' and spent a bad Christmas and a lot of money, I wrote the following ballade:

BALLADE OF LEEUWARDEN.

Like as a mighty painter draws
    God drew the world, and even as he
Rubs out a line or two because
    'Twould mar the picture, so with sea
    God covered over carefully
Whenas He fashioned Eve's green garden
    And azure skies on Italy,
The loathsome city of Leeuwarden.

Beneath the water many a year
    'Twas hid (and wisely so) from view
Until at last an engineer
    (Undoubtedly a German Jew)
    Reclaimed it, and in such wise grew,
What time the sad sea slime did harden
    To something like an Irish stew,
The loathsome city of Leeuwarden.

A place of straying, staring cows,
    And staring cow-like human creatures;

To Holland

Built over-broad across the bows,
    Cow-like of mind with cow-like features,
The home of avaricious lechers
Who'd rob you of your last poor farden.
    A wicked town of no renown,
The loathsome city of Leeuwarden.

L'ENVOI

Prince, here is no one kind or matey;
    They steal your hat and don't beg pardon.
Not one is fair 'twixt eight and eighty,
    The devil be its proper warden,
The loathsome city of Leeuwarden!

In February of this year I was very glad indeed to be told that I might go back to old England. Home—that was what I hungered for. Holland might be a sight better than Germany, but it was hardly that.

28

THE LAST: HOME AGAIN

HOW DOES ENGLAND SEEM to a returned prisoner?
That is the last question within the scope of
this book, and I will attempt to answer it.

First, I know it myself, and have it as a unanimous
opinion by many other returned prisoners, that what is
most striking is the kindness and sympathy one meets.
(This has no bearing on the demobilized soldier question.)

It surprises us all very much. That it surprises us is
queer, but quite accountable: for good things are always
surprising. This is not cheap cynicism, but the reverse. In
the same way a poet is surprised by beauty. 'Too good to
be true!'—the motto of our mortality—is the feeling of all
men in contact with kindness.

But if such is the instinctive feeling of the ordinary
man, how much more so is it the feeling of the returned
prisoner, who for months and years has forgotten what it

is like! For the fine friendliness of prisoners one to another was but a gallant and ineffectual candle in the night of captivity, so heavy with hate or (at best) cold with callousness.

It is true that Vice and Virtue carry their atmosphere, and that it affects all who come in contact. One had only to fall into morbidity (and it was easy enough in prison) to fancy that one heard like waves beating in on all sides the many thousand thoughts of ill-will and hatred in all the German land around. And though one said that one 'didn't care a damn,' the heart was being starved, and vitality flickering down under that siege.

Morris was right when he said that fellowship was life and lack of fellowship death.[1] Kindness (whether of God or of men) is the common air of the human heart, which dies without it. When a man feels that there is no kindness either in heaven above or on the earth beneath, he will commit suicide, and well he may, for he is already damned and dead.

But I am not writing an essay on Kindness (though it is high time somebody did), but only explaining why returned prisoners of war were all surprised and touched by the general flavour of the welcome they received.

England itself, it seemed to me, was just the same: and the only surprising thing (of any importance) which I noticed on my way through it from the north to the

---

1 [Publisher's note] This is a quote from A Dream of John Ball (1888) by William Morris about the English peasants' revolt of 1381 and the rebel priest John Ball who helped organize and lead the rebellion—it describes a dream and time travel encounter between the medieval and modern worlds. a man dreams of meeting John Ball and discusses Balls optimism for the end of serfdom.

south-west, was in a Midland town, where I saw a servant-girl washing some steps, and wearing silk stockings.

Everything else (of any importance) I could, I think, have seen before war broke out.

It is wonderful to get home—home: in the grave beauty of night to lie wakeful, disturbed only by the delicious unrest and distress of the trees—kept awake, as by a lover, all night. It is happiness. There is the moonlight cold and quiet, and bars of darkness, within the room; and outside in the whiteness of moonshine my dear hills, so blue, phantom-fast, and shadowy—the hills that I shall see again (and so changed) at dawn.

But as I was sitting reading to my mother in her bedroom (for she was ill at the time), talking occasionally, or listening to the little lapping voices of the fire, I said to myself, thinking of all I had seen and experienced, 'This is the most wonderful thing that has ever happened to me!'

So life resumes its normal but curious course. One applies for demobilization. One applies for extra leave pending it. One returns to one's unit, about two hundred miles off. One comes back the following day quit of the Army. Subsequently one receives War Office communications asking if one wishes to be demobilized, and sending all sorts of funny forms. Waste-Paper Basket! Finally a certificate comes testifying that the circumstances of one's capture have been investigated, and that no blame attaches to one in the matter. Many thanks!

Meanwhile one is entertained by the mayor, and possibly by the vicar of the parish, and in bewildered happiness and effort to recognize all old friends one drifts here and there, receiving 'the glad eye' and 'the frozen face' from a number of perfect strangers.

*   *   *   *

Gradually 'the tumult and the shouting dies': one gets back into one's old stride. Then, with leisure at last to look at familiar things (now in their full blaze of summer beauty), the final realization comes in upon the soul of what is implied and effected by *Casualty Lists*; and the first mood is that of this 'Lament.'

> I am smelling the smell of the old brown river,
> And hearing the bumble of bees:
> Half-blind I stand with the shine and shiver
> Of waving willow-trees.
>
> These were a dream when that I wandered
> Beyond the seas afar;
> But now so much of life lies squandered,
> Less than a dream they are.
>
> Death, you have robbed the Earth of her glory!
> You have robbed the Sun of his fire!
> And because of my brothers' pitiful story
> My heart is robbed of Desire.
>
> Would I were there in the wind and weather
> Of your dark Flanders sky!
> Would we were sleeping there together,
> My brothers—you and I.
>
> A colour is on the rose, and the clinging
> Clematis, never before I saw: the colour of blood!
> And the singing
> Of birds may charm no more.

The Last: Home Again

Oh, would I were slumbering, sleeping blindly,
Beneath those wet-eyed stars,
With the heavens to shelter us bending kindly
Above—till the end of wars!

A second mood (in reaction from the mood of the
'Lament') comes later when

The purple plums lie scattered on the ground
Under the garden hedge, where Sun has etched
Outline of Prune and Damson tree, and sketched
Grasses in thin dark shadow. A sweet sound
Of windy whispering runs the garden round.

Lines of high-clambering rainbow-tinted peas,
With coloured butterflies that seem as if
Those flowers were taking wing, are here: and stiff
Still soldier-pea-sticks, heeding not the breeze
That shakes to merriment the Damson-trees,

So that they fling their fruit for very mirth
(Small dusky plums) around me, as I sit
Pondering with a wasted love and wit
The old Earth's sweetness, and that mortal worth
Buried beneath the beauty of the Earth:

Because the utter sweetness of this ground
Comes of a strength and sweetness hidden there—
The golden lads, and girls beyond compare
In beauty: and they speak in every sound
Of this old garden when the wind goes round.

And between these two moods we travel all the days of
our life.

Now at last I am back in my own country and in my own county. I don't care if I never leave either again, and so conclude this book of wandering with a last poem on

GLOUCESTERSHIRE

"They brew good beer at Haslemere." So let it be, but I,
Who never have been to Haslemere, would liefer lie
In a snug little tight little inn on the Cotswolds close to the sky.

I never walked into Sussex, but be all her praises true,
And do I never behold her downs beneath their sky of blue,
Nor the sea that batters on her downs, my heart won't break
in two,

If the devil steals my flask away, and my ash-stick splits in twain;
If the soles of my walking-boots wear through, and never at all
again
I move from where I am sitting, even then I'll not complain.

For I am come to Gloucestershire, which is my very home,
Tired out with wandering and sick of wars beyond the foam.
I have starved enough in foreign parts, and no more care to roam.

Quietly I will bide here in the place where I be,
Which knew my father and his grandfather, and my dead brothers
and me,
And bred us and fed us, and gave us pride of yeoman ancestry.

Men with sap of Earth in their blood, and the wisdom of weather
and wind,
Who ploughed the land to leave it better than they did find,
And lie stretched out down Westbury way, where the blossom is
so kind;

The Last: Home Again

And lie covered with petals from orchards that do shed
Their bloom to be a light white coverlet over the dead
Who ploughed the land in the daytime, and went well pleased
  to bed.

Appendix

The Comrades in Captivity

Researched by Roger Deeks, F.W. Harvey Society

COMRADES FROM GÜTERSLOH

EARLY IN *COMRADES IN CAPTIVITY* Will Harvey describes a few comrades in Gütersloh who were probably his closest friends and they are often referred to by their nicknames or just an initial throughout the book.

'R' *(PAGE 58)*

'R' was Captain Joseph Nelson Octavius Rogers of the 8th Battalion, Durham Light Infantry. He went to France on 20 April 1915.Rogers, born in North Shields, spent most of his life in County Durham and remained a Territorial officer after the war. He must have had a singular impact on Will Harvey who dedicated the very moving and powerful poem 'Iron and Coal' to him. Rogers was the son of a draper, and was born in 1890. He was a coal industry apprentice before the war and received his manager's certificate in January 1913. He used his skills to design and make bellows to ventilate the Gütersloh escape tunnel. Following his repatriation he became manager of Bourmoor and Silksworth collieries. He concluded his career as area production manager for the Mid-East division of the National Coal Board. The first verses of Harvey's poem reads:

> Iron are these great rails that fill
> A Durham truck,
> But not only these;
> For your steadfast will
> Is iron too,
> And your steady pluck,
> And the old horseshoe
> That hangs in your heart for luck.
>
> But in your soul
> To brighten it
> God has put coal,
> And fires are lit
> To warm your friends, yourself, and all
> Who have found their way in over the wall.

PUCK *(PAGE 129)*

'Puck' was Captain Ernest James Strover (1885-1962), an officer in the Indian Army serving in the 23rd Sikhs and 3rd Brahmans. He was stationed in Singapore before becoming one of the early aviators. He returned to England and gained an aviator's certificate from the Royal Aero Club, flying a Bristol Biplane over Salisbury Plain in October 1911. In September 1915 he was attached to the Royal Flying Corps (RFC). In 1919 after the end of the war on the Western Front he fought in Iraq.

'O' *(PAGE 59)*

'O' was Captain O.A. Owen, (1889-1961), of the 8th Battalion, Argyll and Sutherland Highlanders. He was the son of a Cheshire vicar who became a land agent before embarking on a military career in August 1912 when he was commissioned a second lieutenant. His battalion left for France in May 1915. *The Times* unofficially reported him suffering from gas poisoning and a prisoner on 12 June 1915. Will Harvey noted his near fatal accident in a tunnel collapse at Crefeld. Puck was an enthusiastic but unlucky escaper and consequently, in late 1917, he was sent to Fort Zorndorf, a secure camp where an exclusive group of escapers were kept, including some of the earliest captives and notorious escapers. Among his friends were Onslow, Horrocks and Hardy. He also spent some time in Schweidnitz camp, Silesia. He was interned in Holland and welcomed Will Harvey when he came over in October 1918.

ONY *(PAGE 59)*

'Ony' was Captain Eric Montague Onslow, (1891-1969), a Regular Army officer who joined the 2nd Battalion Royal Warwickshire Regiment. His grandfather was Lieutenant Colonel Arthur W. Onslow of the Indian Army and his father, who fought in Afghanistan in 1879, was Captain Gerald Charles Onslow of the Royal Engineers. He was part of the British Expeditionary Force reinforcements that landed in France on 4 October 1914. He was captured on 30 October 1914 and reported missing in *The Times* on 16 November 1914.

After meeting Will Harvey at Gütersloh, Ony apparently remained with him throughout many movements between camps. Hamilton Hervey in his book *Cage Birds* described an incident on Christmas Eve 1917 at Fort Zorndorf that involved Onslow. A Russian prisoner known as The Artist, threw a bottle that hit Onslow on the head as he passed one of the

Russian rooms. Onslow and his compatriots went to confront the Russians and only the intervention of the German guards prevented a brawl.

Onslow was mentioned in despatches on 1st January 1918.[1] He was interned in Holland on 7 October 1918 and repatriated eight days later. He remained in the Army after the war and was promoted to major before retiring to Victoria, Australia.[2]

'W' *(PAGES 61, 128)*

'W' who lectured in appreciation of George Bernard Shaw was Captain Hugh Stewart Walker (1888-1958), Cameron Highlanders who went to France on 1 July 1915. Will Harvey and Walker were similar characters who developed a strong friendship, despite their opposing views on George Bernard Shaw. They were the same age and Walker only outlived his friend by a year.

Walker had been a Scottish International hockey player; a game much loved by Will Harvey. He played for Scotland in the 1908 Summer Olympics and scored in both their games. They won a bronze medal.

Harvey described Walker as:

'One of the most interesting and industrious men in the camp, schoolmaster, Scottish international, delightful companion, who added to his tunnelling activity a class of Russians, part management of games, and joint editorship of one of the prison papers.'

Walker commanded B Company of the 6th Battalion Cameron Highlanders and was captured at Hulloch on 27 February 1917, in a similar episode to Will Harvey's own capture. A patrol had left his lines and were unable to penetrate their own barbed-

---

1 London Gazette, 27 January 1920

2 London Gazette, 17 April 1936

wire defences. Walker investigated and found his way through. It was dark and, disorientated, he jumped into what he thought was his side's trench. Unfortunately, it was an enemy sap—a trench running from the German lines into No Man's Land. After a brief chase he was captured.

In Holland, as an internee, he improved his Russian and studied at Leiden University. He volunteered to join the British Red Cross who worked among Russian PoWs in Germany until the end of March 1919.

The British Army were seeking officers to serve with the Expeditionary Force in Russia and because of his Russian fluency he became of interest to military intelligence. He was at first considered for a posting to the Intelligence Corps in Turkey, but instead was posted to Vladivostock to work with the Russian counter-revolutionary White Army. The British and American missions in support of the White Russians were doomed to failure and the intervention became increasingly unpopular and difficult to sustain. The British mission in eastern Russia was forced to retreat with the White Army and eventually they abandoned the campaign altogether.

Consequently Walker left Vladivostock on May 4 1920. In *Comrades in Captivity,* written a year before this, Will Harvey had lamented Walker's disappearance to aid his friends 'the Russians' and had urged him to visit Minsterworth when he returned to England.

Will Harvey had also volunteered to serve in Russia. In the camps he had forsaken the opportunity to learn to speak Russian in favour of writing poetry, lessening his desirability as a recruit. His motive in volunteering could have been his attachment to Walker, or a reluctance to face the emotional impact of returning home. His brother Eric had been killed in September and he had stopped writing home.

Walker and Harvey were eventually reunited, and in 1947

Walker wrote an introduction to the collection of Harvey's poems called *Gloucestershire*. The strength of feeling and continuing friendship was reflected in the dedication to Walker with the words of Byron:

> 'To one whom I have known long and accompanied far, whom I have found watchful over my sickness and kind in my sorrow, glad in my prosperity and firm in my adversity, true in counsel and trusty in peril—to a friend often tried and never found wanting.'[3]

Walker attributed an escape attempt in a washing basket to Will Harvey. Harvey did not refer to this escape in *Comrades in Captivity*.[4]

'D.S.' *(PAGE 77)*

'D.S.' featured in a dream Will Harvey describes at the end of his lecture on George Bernard Shaw and later in the book he describes meeting D.S. in Holland. He was Sub-Lieutenant Cuthbert Henry Dolling-Smith who joined the Royal Naval Air Service on 24 April 1915.

On 29 July 1915 the seaplane in which he was an observer was reported missing. In August he was reported a PoW at Crefeld and was then moved to Gütersloh in November, where he met Will Harvey. Later he was moved back to Crefeld, then to Schwarmstedt and to Holzminden. On 9 April 1918 he was moved across the border into Holland and interned there. He was one of the jubilant characters who was to greet Will Harvey when he too was moved into Holland in October 1918. Dolling-Smith was repatriated to England and arrived at Hull on 18 November 1918.

---

3 Lord Byron's dedication to John Hobhouse in *Childe Harold's Pilgrimage*, Canto the Fourth.

4 Anthony Boden, *F.W. Harvey, Soldier, Poet* (Stroud: Sutton 1988) p.173.

BOBBIE *(PAGE 81)*

'Bobbie' from the parcel office, was Captain Robin Grey of the Warwickshire Royal Horse Artillery Territorial Force, Grenadier Guards and Royal Flying Corps. He had served in the ranks of the Imperial Yeomanry during the second Anglo-Boer War in 1900. He was the second flying officer of the war that was captured on 5 October 1915. In April 1915, Grey and thirty-eight other captured British officers were placed in solitary confinement as a reprisal for the treatment of captured German submarine crews in Britain. The Germans selected members of distinguished British families, which caused international outrage. Grey was chosen because he was a relative of the Foreign Secretary Sir Edward Grey. Captain Grey was interned in Holland on 6 February 1918 and repatriated on 4 October 1918. He was later mentioned in dispatches,[5] and awarded the Legion of Honour and the Distinguished Service Order.

JACKO *(PAGE 82,84)*

'Jacko' was Alexander Rochfort Jackson (1890-1969) of the East Kent Regiment. He arrived on the Western Front attached to the Loyal North Lancashire Regiment on 9 October 1914. He was born in Dublin and played international rugby for Ireland. In 1911 he was first capped against England. He scored three tries in ten internationals. His last match was against Wales in March 1914. He was interned in Holland in February 1918 and repatriated in September 1918.

JOCK *(PAGE 82, 96)*

'Jock' was probably Lieutenant James Bruce Turnbull of the Gordon Highlanders. He had gone to the Western Front in September 1915. *The Times* reported his repatriation on 2 December 1918.

---

5 London Gazette, 22 December 1919

Comrades in Captivity

PECK *(PAGE 83)*

'Peck' was Captain, later Major, Arthur John Peck (1877-1947), 2nd Battalion Royal Warwickshire Regiment. In 1900 he volunteered to serve in South Africa and went there to fight in the second Anglo-Boer War, in the ranks of the Imperial Yeomanry. He fought in battles at Bethlehem and Wittenberg. Interested in a military career, Arthur Peck became a Regular Army officer and was commissioned into the Royal Warwickshire Regiment in June 1902. He was reported missing in *The Times* on 16 November 1914 and was in the same battalion as 'Ony' or Captain Onslow[Ibid.]. He was made captain in May 1914 and was part of the British Expeditionary Force reinforcements that landed in France on 4 October 1914.

CAPTAIN CUMMINS *(PAGE 99)*

The Australian officer who obliged the company with 'Waltzing Matilda' was Captain George Cummins of the 55th Battalion Australian Imperial Force. He was from New South Wales. He enlisted on 23 August 1915, left Australia on 11 March 1916 and was missing and reported killed at Pozieres the following July. He was later found wounded, and hospitalised. Cummins was discharged to Gütersloh and followed the route of several others to Crefeld and Ströhen. On 17 June 1918 he was exchanged and became an internee in Holland. On 25 November 1918 he arrived in Southampton, suffering from pneumonia. He returned to Australia on 15 March 1919 where he had been a well known international footballer before the war.

MR BERNARD *(PAGE 103)*

The illustration 'Light Aus!' and others throughout the book were drawn by 'Mr Bernard.' Charles Edward Burton Bernard (1890-1977), was born in Yokohama, Japan on 21 June 1890.

He was commissioned into the West Yorkshire Regiment at the beginning of the war and first saw action at Gallipoli in September 1915. In August 1916 he was wounded at the Western Front, captured and became a prisoner of war. He returned to design and illustration after hostilities ended and contributed to books and magazine articles. He wrote and illustrated stories in publications such as *The Crusoe Magazine* and *Every Boy's Hobby Annual, 1927'* and *'Pixie Pranks'*. In 1927 he left Liverpool with his wife and family, for Boston, USA, and settled in Massachusetts. He died in 1977.

MOSSY *(PAGE 119)*

Will Harvey describes a chance encounter with 'Mossy' in Trafalgar Square. 'Peace Day' was Saturday 19 July 1919, a celebration originally planned for four days but reduced to one. To manage the expected influx of thousands, a temporary camp was constructed in Kensington Gardens. Crowds slept along the route to reserve a view. By ten o'clock in the morning Trafalgar Square was packed. 15,000 servicemen took part and were led by the Allied commanders. In Whitehall the parade saluted a temporary monument that was erected where the Cenotaph now stands.

'Mossy' was Captain Frederick Moysey, Suffolk Regiment, later Sudan Defence Force. Moysey famously illustrated the walls of their Holzminden camp room with ducks in a pond surrounded by reeds. The inspiration for Harvey's famous poem 'Ducks.' Moysey continued a successful military career, becoming a lieutenant colonel and being awarded the DSO.

Moysey was an inveterate escaper and was wounded in the same escape attempt that led to the fatal shooting of William Graveley Morritt at Holzminden Camp on 27 June 1917. The technical notes regarding progress of the Gütersloh tunnel are courtesy of 'Mossy's ' diary.

JACKSON *(PAGE 141)*

Gerald Goddard Jackson (1878-1941) was an artist before being commissioned into the Oxfordshire and Buckinghamshire Light Infantry in 1911. He served in the Buckinghamshire Battalion and was promoted Captain in September 1914. Jackson was captured on 21 July 1916. He provided Will Harvey with a pen and ink sketch intended for the cover of his book of poems, mainly written in Gütersloh and sent to England from Crefeld. The crefeld commandant refused to allow the sketch to be sent home because the barbs on the wire had been drawn 'too big' creating the 'wrong' impression. Will Harvey used it for *Comrades in Captivity*. Another pen and ink sketch by Jackson, 'Officers Washing, Schwarmstedt, West Germany'and dated 1917, is in Manchester Art Gallery.

Jackson, aged 40, was repatriated on 1 November 1918. Nineteen days later, he married the Honourable Hildred Mosley. She was the daughter of Tonman Mosley, the first and last Baron Anslow, who was the brother of Sir Oswald Mosley. Jackson resigned his commission on 9 August 1922 and retained the rank of Captain. In 1924 *The Times* carried news of his divorce. There were no children from the marriage. Jackson died in 1941 aged 63 years.

LIEUTENANT FREDERICK RAY NORTH *(PAGE 126)*

The diary of 'Mossy' revealed that two English prisoners had cut the wire on 29 December but failed to escape. One of these men was Lieutenant Frederick Ray North (1886-1948), of the Duke of Cornwall Light Infantry (DCLI). North, from a Devonshire farming family, had been commissioned into the DCLI and arrived on the Western Front in May 1916. North was reported as repatriated to England on 30 November 1918.

'H' *(PAGE 128)*

'H' was Lieutenant, later Major Cecil Beckham Harcourt, 28th Punjabis, Indian Army (1880-1930). He was born in Darjeeling, India. The Indian Army played a significant role on the Western Front in the early part of the Great War. Harcourt was thirty-eight years of age and captured in September 1915. He did not expect to survive because he had understood Germans executed colonial soldiers and their officers. Harcourt was detained in Gütersloh, Crefeld, Augustabad, Eutin and Bad-Colberg where he was the senior British officer before removal to Aachen with Will Harvey in March 1918. He expected to be repatriated in an exchange, but this did not happen until September. He arrived in Boston, Lincolnshire the same month and he worried over the conditions of prisoner comrades he had left behind.[6] In May 1923 he resigned his commission because of ill health. He died in London in 1930.

COMRADES AND CHARACTERS FROM CREFELD, 20 MARCH 1917

COMMANDANT OBERST COURT *(PAGE 141)*

Will Harvey does not describe events at Crefeld in any detail. The commandant of the camp is described as 'jolly' with a large, colourful alcoholic nose. He was also considered a gentleman to whom Will Harvey was grateful for allowing his book of poems to be sent back to England. The commandant was Oberst Court and his sympathies may have been influenced by the fact that his wife was English.

---

6 The National Archives, F.O. 383/273

Pte. Mulcahy *(PAGE 148)*

Pte. Mulcahy is described as a sturdy little orderly of Celtic origin. He is the only orderly mentioned in *Comrades*.

Pte. Mulcahy rescued 'N' and 'O' when they were buried in a tunnel collapse. 'O' was Captain O. A. Owen. 'N' was Captain, later Major John Andrew Vernatti Noel of the Royal Artillery and Royal Flying Corps (1893-1966). He was the son of a naval officer, Captain Robert Lascelles Gambier Noel, and attended Cheltenham College, before joining the Military Academy at Woolwich. He was commissioned into the Royal Artillery in July 1913 and was later attached as a captain to the Royal Flying Corps and arrived in France in January 1917. He also served in the Second World War.

Comrades and Characters from Schwarmstedt

'M' *(PAGE 163)*

'M' was Captain William Graveley Morritt of the East Surrey Regiment (1892-1917). He was a Regular officer commissioned into the East Surrey Regiment in February 1912 and landed in France on 16 August 1914. He was captured a few days later on 23 August after being shot in the wrist, knee and calf. At Schwarmstedt, Morritt was part of an escape plan involving a tunnel and six other officers; Captains; Weir, Morritt, Moysey, Owen, Mullaly, and Lieutenant Dodgson. A tunnel leading to a ditch just outside the wire was completed and the party attempted to escape on 27 June 1917. There are varying accounts of what happened. It seems Moysey led the escape followed by Morritt, but the next escapee, Mullaly became stuck in the tunnel, which blocked the others' exit. A guard spotted Moysey and later claimed that he shouted a challenge to stop. As Morritt stood up the guard fired, killing him. Moysey was also fired upon, but he escaped, wounded in the arm. He returned injured to the camp where he was arrested. He observed that the German officers he surrendered himself to in the early hours of the morning were fully dressed and concluded they had anticipated the attempted escape.

There were several issues about the shooting that provoked outrage. The first was the strong suspicion that the camp authorities knew about the escape, and the shooting was planned as a deterrent to future attempts. The second was the belief that the guard had not, as he claimed, called to Morritt to warn him of his intent to shoot. The Prussian Ministry of War defended the guard's claims. The repercussions in Britain were protracted and in August 1918 Lord Newton was urging the Army Council to raise an order to shoot German escapees without a warning as a reprisal. However, in November, the Prisoner of War Department replied, stating that they thought it unadvisable to alter the existing order of challenging escaping German PoWs before firing on them.

Morritt left a wife, Alice, and a son. The shooting of Morritt caused a major reaction because it was witnessed and reported widely. In July 1919 Morritt's grieving mother wrote to the War Office from Lahore, India, demanding justice. Will Harvey dedicated the poem 'Requiescat' to Morritt:

(*W.M. Shot, June 1917, Schwarmstedt Camp*)

Were men but men, and Christians not at all:
Mere Pagans and quick of sense
To feel the sun's great blind beneficence:
The kind hand of the breeze:- nay but to see
Only the brotherly blue that's over all,

> And realise that calm immensity
> So far enfolding, softly bright and still,
> Feel only that:- Surely they would not kill!
> Beside a new-digged grave beneath the trees
> I kneel. The brotherly sky is over all.
> It seems to me so strange wars do not cease.

Captain William Gravely Morritt, aged 24, was buried outside the camp in the grave described by Will Harvey.

In 1923 the remains of Allied servicemen who were buried in different locations scattered across Germany were concentrated in four cemeteries. Those from 120 sites in Schleswig-Holstein, Mecklenburg, Oldenburg, Hanover, Saxony, Brunswick and Westphalia were brought to Hamburg. Morritt and 300 other men, most of whom died as prisoners of war, are buried together in Hamburg cemetery.

The officer stuck in the tunnel during the fatal escape attempt was Captain John Clive Mullaly. He came from a long line of army officers, his grandfather served in the Zhob Valley Expedition in 1884 and his father was awarded the DSO as a major in the Tibet Mission in 1904. He was commissioned into the Indian Army in 1912 and captured serving with the 3rd Brahmans in 1915. He was interned in Holland in 1918, and while still in the Hague he married Joan Mary Warner on 20 November 1918.

'P' (*PAGE 164*)

'P' was Captain Garthshore Tindal Porter of the Royal Artillery attached to the Royal Flying Corps (1887-1957). He was born in Queensland, Australia, where his father was a government surveyor. He was commissioned into the Royal Artillery in July 1906. He became one of the early aviators when attached to the Air Battalion, Royal Engineers in April 1912. In May 1912 the battalion was integrated into the newly formed Royal Flying Corps. He gained his aviator's certificate (169) flying a Bristol Biplane at Salisbury Plain in January 1912. He was one of the earliest entrants into the war, landing in France on 13 August 1914. He was taken prisoner of war on 27 December 1915.

PERCY FRYER *(Page 167)*

The occupant with cramp was possibly Major Percy Spencer Fryer of the 1st Battalion West Yorkshire Regiment (1879-1927). Percy Fryer was commissioned into the West Yorks Regiment in October 1899. He served with the Ladysmith Relief Force in the Second Anglo-Boer War and took part in several battles was severely wounded and mentioned in despatches.[7] He embarked for France with the BEF on 9 September 1914.

'G' *(PAGE 169)*

'G', the escaper who demonstrated how to climb the fence, was Lieutenant John Prefect Gulland (1888-1955) of the Indian Army. In *The Times* of 11 October 1915 he was reported killed, serving with the 69th Punjabis. The newspaper published his obituary before it was known he was a PoW. He was interned in Holland in 1918 and after the Armistice he returned to his career in the Indian Army. He retired a Colonel but returned to service in the Second World War.

JACKY *(PAGE 170)*

Escapers from Schwarmstedt were encouraged to consult Jacky's map for escape routes, particularly for Weser-Ems and its surroundings. Jacky was Captain Jack Stanford of the Royal Field Artillery (RFA). Stanford must have been an unsuccessful escaper but had used his artillery mapping skills to provide a map for the locality. Stanford was reported in *The Times* as

---

7 London Gazette, 25 July 1902.

repatriated on 30 November 1918. He returned to the RFA and the Army of Occupation in Germany. He retired a major living at the Tudor Court Hotel, Cromwell Road, London.

CAUNTER *(PAGE 179)*

Will Harvey describes the successful escape of Fox and Caunter. John Alan Lyde Caunter was a Regular Army officer, educated at Uppingham School Leicestershire and the Royal Military College, Sandhurst. He served in India and went to France with the 1st Battalion Gloucestershire Regiment on 14 August 1914. He was captured on 31 October 1914. He was promoted to captain (1915) and awarded the Military Cross (MC) (1916) while in captivity. In 1917 he escaped from Schwarmstedt prison camp, Germany and returned home via Holland. He saw further service on the Western Front, Turkey and the Black Sea and was awarded a bar to his MC in 1918. He wrote a book about his PoW escape, *13 days – the Chronicle of an Escape from a German Prison Camp*. Harvey was still a prisoner when this book was published, which included a few lines from *Gloucestershire Friends*. Caunter continued his military career as a staff officer between the wars. He commanded an armoured brigade in North Africa in World War Two and was awarded the CBE in 1941. He retired and became a councillor in Cornwall and wrote: *A Short Guide to Shark Angling at Looe, and other places in SW England* (Published by the author, Looe, Cornwall, 1958) and *Shark Angling in Great Britain* (George Allen and Unwin, London, 1961). He died in 1981.

COMRADES IN STRÖHEN

LITTLE MAN *(PAGE 205)*

Will Harvey was never a prisoner at Ströhen. His account of events there were provided by a friend. The Ströhen camp received a number of his comrades when the occupants of Crefeld were dispersed. It was a purposely constructed camp of thirty wooden huts surrounded by two parallel ten-foot high barbed-wire fences, four or five yards apart. The perimeter was patrolled by sentries and a machine-gun turret stood at each of the four corners. The most troublesome escapers were concentrated at Ströhen, which was known as a reprisal camp. The account of escapes and life at Ströhen were written by 'Little Man' who was most likely Captain George Warner Holloway of the West Yorkshire Regiment, attached to the 8th Northumberland Fusiliers. Holloway had first seen action in Gallipoli in September 1915. He then went to the Western Front. The *Stroud News* reported him missing on 18 August 1916. He lived in Amberley, Stroud, Gloucestershire.

LIEUTENANT KNIGHT *(PAGE 209)*

The camp was notorious for ruthless discipline and the 'blood and iron' policy of shooting escapees caught in the act. There were incidents of bayoneting disobedient prisoners. Two of the worst noted in London were the wounding of Lt. Knight and Downes. Both men were bayoneted by guards 'controlling crowds' on the direction of German senior officers. Downes was bayoneted in his front and back which caused a collapsed lung and Knight was stabbed in his leg.

Lieutenant Gerald Featherstone Knight of the Devonshire Regiment attached to the Royal Flying Corps had been a student at the University of Toronto when war was declared. He returned and was commissioned, becoming a flying officer.

He was shot down and captured at Bapaume on 9 November 1916. He was bayoneted in the leg by a Landstrum Wilhelm Bornkamp and was hospitalised for two weeks. After his escape he urged the British authorities to carry out reprisals at British camps for the way in which officers were being treated.[8] He was awarded the Military Cross. He died from cancer, aged 24, in the RAF Hospital, Eaton Square on 30 October 1919, He is buried in Marylebone Cemetery.

STRÖHEN ESCAPES

The sandy soil and vigilance of the guards made tunnelling very difficult. The most famous Ströhen escapes occurred from a bath complex situated outside the wire and to which prisoners were escorted. On August 16 1917 Knight was sufficiently recovered to construct a false wall in the shower room and successfully escape. Harrison, a determined and famous 'escaper', led a group of three, which included Claude Templar, a comrade he admired for his gallantry and with whom he had made his first escape attempt in 1915. Templar had brought along his friend Stuart Insall and another officer who decided not to escape and rather created a diversion by cutting wire to mislead the guards about the route taken by the escapees.[9] They escaped on 20 August and after travelling 90 miles crossed the frontier into Holland. They returned to England on 12 September 1917.

CAPTAIN HARRISON *(PAGE 209)*

Captain Michael Charles Cooper Harrison was commissioned into the Royal Irish Regiment in 1906. He was captain and adjutant when his battalion joined the British Expeditionary Force in 1914. He was severely wounded and taken prisoner in October 1914. He made six escape attempts. After his success-

---

8 The National Archive F.O. 383/272

9 *Escapers All,* page 173.

ful escape in September 1917 he rejoined his old Battalion in France in December 1917. He became a Lieutenant-Colonel in March 1918, was wounded twice, mentioned in despatches three times and awarded the Italian Silver Medal for Military Valour, DSO, MC and bar. He commanded the 5th Battalion Royal Irish Regiment in the Army of Rhine 1919. He became a Sandhurst instructor and later joined the Royal Tank Corps. He was joint author, with H.A. Cartwright, of *Within Four Walls.*

CAPTAIN STUART MARTIN INSALL *(page 209)*

Captain Stuart Martin Insall VC, MC (1894-1972) won his VC at Achiet, France on 7 November 1915 for destroying a German aeroplane over enemy trenches and bringing his Vickers plane home through difficult circumstances. He was shot down and taken prisoner on 14 December 1915. After the war Insall remained in the RAF where his aerial photography led to the rediscovery of Woodhenge (1925) and Arminghall Henge (1929).

CAPTAIN CLAUD TEMPLER *(PAGE 209)*

Captain Claud Templer (1895-1918) was born in India and educated at Wellington and Paris. He was commissioned from Sandhurst into the 1st Battalion Gloucestershire Regiment and joined them on the Western Front on 12 November 1914. On 22 December 1915 he was leading a patrol and advanced ahead of his platoon to reconnoitre a German trench. He was discovered and knocked unconscious.

He made twelve escape attempts. After his first escape he was recaptured with seven Russians. Following his successful escape in September 1917 he rejoined his battalion on 29 March 1918. On the night of 4 June 1918 he led a raid on German trenches but was struck by a shell and killed when returning to his own lines. His family published a detailed account of his escapes and poetry and writings from captivity: *Poems and Imaginings,* (Paris: Editions Bossard, 1920).

Following the successful escape by Knight, Harrison, Templer and Insall, five more officers (Colquhoun, Horrocks, Greenhow, Heppel and Onslow) attempted an escape using the same washroom floor exit. They were discovered and arrested.

LIEUTENANT BRIAN HORROCKS

Lieutenant Brian Horrocks (1895-1985) was one of the unsuccessful escapees. He made numerous escape attempts, one of which involved him walking two hundred and thirteen miles in ten nights, (escapers usually travelled at night). He was severely wounded and captured at Ypres on 21 October 1914. At his first camp he was nicknamed 'the Pup' because of his youthfulness. On his 21st birthday a camp dinner was held in his honour where he was formally renamed 'Dog'.

Horrocks was moved around most of the camps in Germany and was well known to all the prisoners. In early 1918 he refused to be interned in Holland or repatriated much to the annoyance of his captors. He eventually agreed to be moved to Aachen where he escaped, but he was recaptured. Cartwright, who was a friend of Horrocks, succeeded shortly afterwards. He never did manage to escape and was finally repatriated after the Armistice. Frustrated by his three-and-a-half years of imprisonment, but able to speak Russian, he travelled to Siberia and persuaded the C.O. of the mission there, to offer him a job. The situation in Siberia deteriorated and he was captured by the Bolsheviks.

Brian Horrocks later competed in the 1924 Paris Olympics. He is remembered as the commander of XXX Corps in Operation Market Garden and other operations during the Second World War. He retired Lieutenant-General Sir Brian Horrocks, KCB, KBE, DSO, MC. He then became a television presenter, authored books on military history, and was Black

Rod in the House of Lords for fourteen years. His prison experiences and his life are described in *A Full Life,* his autobiography published in 1960.

LIEUTENANT WILLIAM LEEFE ROBINSON *(PAGE 212)*

There is a reference to an attempted escape by four officers; Lyon, Marshall, Wingfield and Robinson. They escaped by cutting the wire but were recaptured.

Lieutenant William Leefe Robinson, VC (1895–1918) was commissioned from Sandhurst into the Worcestershire Regiment in 1914. He transferred to the Royal Flying Corps and went to France in march 1916 as an observer. He was wounded and returned to England where he trained to fly. He was attached to No. 39 Squadron Royal Flying Corps, a night-flying squadron at based in Essex. On the night of 2/3 September 1916 flying over Cuffley in a converted B.E.2c a home defence night-fighter, he sighted and attacked a German army Schütte-Lanz airship—one of 16 airships that had left Germany for a raid over England. Robison attacked from 1,500 feet—a high, difficult and dangerous altitude for the flimsy and underpowered B.E.2c. At just after two-o'clock in the morning, he shot the airship down, the first brought down over Britain. His daring feat was witnessed by many joyful Londoners who were reassured that the menace of raiding airships could be countered. Robinson returned to Suttons Farm Airfield to discover his aeroplane peppered with bullet holes from the airship's guns. As a result he became a national celebrity and was awarded the Victoria Cross by the king at Windsor Castle.

In April 1917 Robinson was posted as a flight commander with 48 Squadron. On his first mission he was wounded and shot down after an encounter with a squadron of German Albatros 'planes led by the 'Red Baron' Manfred von Richthofen. Robinson was notorious to the Germans and it was reported that he was treated very badly. He was kept in Holzminden but transferred to Fort Zorndorf because of his escape attempts. He was repatriated in a very weak condition, as like Will Harvey, he had caught the pandemic Spanish 'flu. He has a restaurant, a pub and a road near the site of Suttons Farm Airfield named after him.

He died on 31 December, 1918 at the Stanmore home of his sister, the Baroness Heyking. Robinson has a memorial erected near where the airship crashed.

FITZGERALD, HARDING, SOMERVILLE AND COLLIER *(PAGE 212)*

'Little Man' describes the escapes of Fitzgerald, Harding, Somerville and Collier. Collier was recaptured.

Lieutenant Geoffrey Parker Harding (b. 1895), 1st Cheshire Regiment attached to the RFC had been shot down on 1 May 1917 at Vimy while flying a RAF F.E.2b. He wrote, *Escape Fever,* which described his escape to Holland. Lieutenant Roy James Fitzgerald, 12th Gloucestershire Regiment, was taken prisoner at Fresnoy on May 8 1917. He was born in Wellington, New Zealand in 1890 and was working in Warmley, Bristol before enlistment. When Harding and Fitzgerald arrived in Holland on 29 September they each gave intelligence reports.[10] Fitzgerald observed that cigarettes had been banned because the Germans feared that the French were using them to import chemicals to damage crops. He also noted that when Captains Crossman and Grinnell-Milne were recaptured following an escape on 1 August 1917, the Germans believed the Horlicks milk tablets in their possession contained bacteria or anthrax for contaminating the countryside. After his escape Fitzgerald was attached to the RFC and was killed as the observer in a Bristol F.2b Fighter on 1 July 1918 He had been mentioned in dispatches and awarded the MC.

---

10 The National Archives F.O. 383/273

MAJOR TOOGOOD *(PAGE 210)*

Ströhen camp was a focus of criticism and concern for the British Legation in the Netherlands. In the late autumn of 1917 the German commandant and the senior British commander, Major Toogood were removed. Toogood was deemed ineffectual and disrespected by fellow officers. The internment and repatriation process progressed and in early 1918 the camp was closed.[11]

MORE CHARACTERS FROM SCHWARMSTEDT

OLD PIN *(PAGE 215)*

'Old Pin' was Lieutenant Frank George Pinder (b.1886) Royal Flying Corps. Pinder born Victoria, British Columbia, had enlisted in Canada where he was a mining engineer. He gained his flying certificate at Brookland in October 1915. His repatriation to England was reported in *The Times* in April 1918.

LIEUTENANT HARRY CLIVE HINWOOD *(PAGE 216)*

Will Harvey takes the opportunity to describe the diverse professional backgrounds of his comrades who were not Regular Army officers. The 'medical student' he mentioned was Lieutenant Harry Clive Hinwood. He had undertaken six years' medical training and had also been in his university Officer Training Corps for a similar period when war broke out. He joined the Royal Field Artillery and was a forward observing officer, finding targets and ranges for artillery, often in very perilous positions. At St Eloi on 14 March 1915 he was on the 'Mound,' with a platoon of the Duke of Cornwall's Light Infantry at an elevated position that overlooked the German lines only 100

11 The National Archives F.O. 383/273

yards away. He was unaware that the Germans had tunnelled under his platoon's position. At 4 pm that day, a huge mine exploded. Half the platoon was buried alive, and as Hinwood was treating eight wounded, they were all taken prisoner. He assumed medical responsibilities in the PoW camp but was invalided to Switzerland and then repatriated to England in March 1918. On return he was transferred to the Royal Army Medical Corps, since the terms of his repatriation meant that he had to forfeit the right to be a combatant. After the war he became a general practitioner in Hightown, Manchester.[12]

LIEUTENANT JASON GURNEY (*PAGE 219*)
The young man who had sailed around the Horn of Africa in a windjammer was Lieutenant Jason Gurney of the 8th Battalion London Regiment. He went to the Western Front in February 1916. He concluded the war as a captain. *The Times* reported his repatriation on 2 December 1918.

THE IRISHMAN (*PAGE 220*)
Will Harvey tells a remarkable story about an adventurer with a 'predilection for noir at roulette.' 'The Irishman' he describes was Captain Albert Bernard O'Donnell, Royal Warwickshire Regiment. He enlisted as a sergeant in the Natal Light Horse in East Africa, a private in King Edwards Horse in Europe and was commissioned into the Royal Warwickshire Regiment. He was promoted to captain, and awarded the DSO, French Cross and was twice mentioned in despatches.[13] He returned to Kenya after the war.

---

12 The National Archive W.O. 339/28689

13 London Gazette, 26 September 1916 and 4 January 1917.

THE CANADIAN VC *(PAGE 220)*

'The Canadian VC' was possibly Edward Donald Bellew (1882-1961) of the 7th Battalion British Columbia Regiment, CEF. He was a Canadian recipient of the Victoria Cross. Bellew was educated at Blundell's School before attending Sandhurst Military Academy. He was thirty-two, and a lieutenant when he held up an enemy advance at Ypres on Saturday 24 April 1915, where the Canadians were suffering heavy casualties. The advance of the enemy was temporarily stayed by Lieutenant Bellew, the battalion machine-gun officer. With the enemy less than 100 yards away and no further assistance in sight, Lieutenant Bellew and a Sergeant Peerless decided to fight it out. The sergeant was killed and Lieutenant Bellew wounded. Nevertheless, he maintained his fire until his ammunition failed and he was taken prisoner. His captors sentenced him to death for firing after part of his unit had surrendered. He was about to be summarily executed by firing squad when his sentence was commuted.

COMRADES IN HOLZMINDEN

CAPON *(PAGE 245)*

Will Harvey describes a character called 'Capon,' who gave a lecture about astronomy. Lieutenant Robert Stanley Capon (1886-1975), was the son of a Liverpool dentist. He took up medical training, studied music in Berlin and finally took a mathematics degree at Oxford University. He was a very successful student and was published in his field. He became interested in astronomy and studied under the most eminent astronomers of the time in Britain and America. He returned following the outbreak of war and joined the ranks of the

London Regiment. He fought on the Western Front and was commissioned at the end of 1915 and applied to join the Royal Flying Corps. Accepted, he was employed as an assistant equipment officer before he learned to fly. In August 1916 he joined 24 Squadron and flew missions over the Somme. Later the same month he was wounded when shot through the knee. He recovered and in 1917 was posted to 66 Squadron. He was shot down by enemy aircraft on 24 April 1917, flying a Sopwith Camel, while escorting bombers near Cambrai. He was first detained at Karlsruhe, then Ströhen where he was involved in a tunnelling escape. Before the tunnel was completed he also attempted an escape from the wash house, as previously managed by Knight and then Harrison, Templer and Insall. His attempt failed and after solitary confinement he was transferred in late 1917 to Holzminden where Will Harvey would have known him. He was involved in escape plans at Holzminden but was moved to Clausthal where he teamed up with another pilot, Hamilton E. Hervey. Hervey, Capon and several others prepared to escape in July 1918 via a tunnel. Capon's role was to play the piano to hide the noise and warn about the approach of guards by playing a distinctive tune. He never did escape but was repatriated to England on 30 December 1918.

He remained in the newly formed Royal Air Force as a pilot and tester of new equipment. He later became Principal Scientific Officer and then superintendent of scientific research at Farnborough.

In 1931 he was awarded an OBE for his services in research and development. He became Deputy Director of Research and Development in Armament at the Air Ministry where he acted as director for short periods. He retired in 1946 and two years later retired to Melbourne, Australia where he returned to the academic study of mathematics. He died in 1975.

FLUFFY *(PAGE 248)*

'Fluffy,' was almost certainly Lieutenant Hamilton E. Hervey MC. He was a 1st Class Air Mechanic commissioned in June 1916, serving with the Royal Flying Corps. He became a committed escaper at both Holzminden and Clausthal and later wrote *Cage Birds,* a book about his exploits. In his book he reluctantly acknowledged his nickname 'Flossie' and, for a camp cabaret, he wore 'two charming evening frocks, 'undies', wigs and considerable padding'.

Hervey had joined the Royal Flying Corps from a university course in aeronautical engineering. He went to France in August 1915 as a rigger and air gunner. Following his commission he served as Flying Officer Observer and then Flying Officer Pilot. He was awarded the Military Cross and bar.

In April 1917, the arrival of the German Albatross aeroplane had given the Germans air superiority and there were heavy British and French aircraft losses. He was shot down and wounded. He was mentioned in despatches for his many escape attempts but was always unsuccessful in reaching the frontier.

Hervey was repatriated in December 1918 and demobilised in September 1919. He emigrated to Australia to work as a fruit grower and then a commercial pilot. In 1935 he returned to England and became manager and instructor at the London Gliding Club. In January 1940 he rejoined the Royal Air Force and helped in the use of gliders in airbourne assaults. Hervey died in Oxford in 1990, aged 94 years.

COMRADES AND EVENTS IN BAD-COLDBERG

THE CLEMENCEAU-CZERIN REVELATIONS *(PAGE 270)*

Will Harvey in his treatise on secret diplomacy mentions the Clemenceau-Czerin revelations. This is a reference to the 'Sixtus Affair' of April 1918. The Hungarian diplomat Czerin had entered into secret negotiations to withdraw the Austria-Hungary Empire from the Great War in March 1917. They failed and in April 1918 the French Prime Minister, Georges Clemenceau revealed Czerin's role, destroying his credibility and forcing his resignation.

'M' AND 'W' *(PAGE 290)*

One of the most painful recollections for Will Harvey was the killing of 'M' and 'W' at Bad-Coldberg. 'M' was Second Lieutenant Harold William Medlicott of the Royal Air Force, aged 25 years. 'W' was Captain Joseph Stanley Walter of the 7th Battalion Queen's (Royal West Surrey) Regiment.

Medlicott was another inveterate and daring escaper. He had made a reputation for himself as a flying officer in the Royal Flying Corps. His escape attempts were legendary. Imprisoned in a fort at Vasel, he was locked in a high tower. Although the base of the tower was wider than the top, the walls were practically vertical and it was deemed pointless to bar the windows. Medicott climbed out of his and slid down the wall. He survived the fall and escaped but was recaptured a few days later.

The German account of the deaths of Medlicott and Walter were widely disbelieved at time. They stated that after recapture, and almost on return to the camp, they fled their guards and both were shot. Stories circulated that both bodies had multiple gunshot and bayonet wounds but there were no witnesses to substantiate these claims. It was unusual for officers recaptured in such circumstances to flee. Once caught they would normally behave as instructed.

Harold Medlicott and Joseph Walter are buried in the Niederzwehren Cemetery, near Kessel, approximately 165 kilometres south of Hanover.[14]

GENERAL D *(PAGE 297)*

Will Harvey describes a General D, brought into Bad-Colberg around May 1918, who played rounders and was a great asset to the camp because of his firmness in 'dealing with the Huns.' If the 'D' is a reliable clue, it is either Brigadier-General Frederick Stuart Dawson, General Officer Commanding (GOC) South African Brigade, 9th (Scottish) Division, captured on 24 March 1918 at Marrieres Wood, or Brigadier-General James Keith Dick-Cunyngham, GOC 152 Brigade, 51st (Highland) Division, captured 12 April 1918 together with his Brigade HQ near Merville.

COMRADES AND EVENTS IN AACHEN

THE KONIGEN REGENTES *(PAGE 301)*

Will Harvey attributed the delay in his repatriation to the sinking of the *Konigen Regentes*. In January 1918 the British and German Governments agreed a prisoner repatriation scheme that operated via Holland. In June 1918, Will Harvey antici-

---

14 The cemetery was begun by the Germans in 1915 for the burial of prisoners of war who died at the local camp. During the war almost 3,000 Allied soldiers and civilians, including French, Russian and Commonwealth, were buried there In 1922-23 it became one of the four permanent cemeteries in Germany and more than 1,500 graves were brought into the cemetery from the surrounding area including Bad-Colberg.

pated being part of the exchange when he was moved close to the Dutch border. This failed to happen.

The *S.S. Konigen Regentes* was a steam paddle ship that had operated between England and Holland since 1985 as part of the Zealand line and became involved in the transport of prisoners returning home. On June 6 1918 the ship, in convoy with *Zealand* and *Sindoro*, left Boston Lincolnshire. On entering the North Sea, 20 miles east of the Leman Bank lightship. At 1.15 pm, the ship exploded and sank within a few minutes, with the loss of seven crew. It had hit a mine or been torpedoed. The ship was flying a neutral flag and there would have been a very significant loss of life if it had been carrying German prisoners. The British Government in accepting responsibility compensated the Zealand Shipping Co., 600,000 Francs in February 1919.

'A CAPTAIN' *(PAGE 303)*

'A Captain', taken in the first few months of the war and because of his prolonged years of captivity given the opportunity to escape in preference to Will Harvey and others, was Captain Henry Antrobus Cartwright of the Middlesex Regiment (1887-1957). He was commissioned in 1906 and became a lieutenant in 1909. He arrived in France with the British Expeditionary Forces on 14th August 1914. He was awarded the Legion d'Honneur in 1914, the Military Cross in 1918 and the Croix de Guerre Czechoslovaque in 1919. He was a determined escaper and refused repatriation because it would have obliged him to be a non-combatant. He was later the joint author, with M.C.C. Harrison, of *Within Four Walls*, which includes an account of events in Aachen, including his escape. He retired from the Army in 1922.

Colonel Henry Antrobus Cartwright, CMG, MC died in 1957. His account of events in Aachen, including his escape, can be read in *Within Four Walls*.

COMRADES IN STRALSUND

'E' *(PAGE 303)*

Will Harvey left his friend, identified only as 'E', in Stralsund when he left for Aachen again on 22 October 1918. In the incident after the Armistice on 5 December 1918, a guard opened fire on two officers walking outside the wire. Will Harvey described this as follows: 'an American officer was shot dead by a sentry for wandering about the island outside the wire—surely not a very serious crime after the signing of an armistice!' The irony reflects will Harvey's anger at the injustice of this shooting and his lingering bitterness at the killings of Medlicott, Walter and Morritt.

Second Lieutenant Colheeny of the Royal Lancaster Regiment was the officer killed. He was a United States citizen who had come to Europe and enlisted as a private in the Dragoons before being commissioned in June 1917. A second officer, Lieutenant J.G. Colver, was wounded in the incident. At the time of the shooting the camp was in the hands of the 'Workers' and Soldiers' Council' who had taken over the running of the camp in the confusion following the Armistice and the abdication of the Kaiser.

F.W. HARVEY AND HIS COMRADES

Will Harvey, 'The Poet,' was described by his friend, Hugh Walker, as an opportunistic escaper.[15] Although close to the P.T., the Gütersloh tunnelling party, he did not have enthusiasm for tunnelling. The escapers were frequently discouraged from their attempts by senior officers who feared 'strafing' and repris-

---

15 'A Portrait of Will Harvey by his Friends' BBC Broadcast 1958

als from the camp guards. Nevertheless, they persisted. They wanted to get home and were also aware of the cost to the enemy who had to commit valuable men and resources guarding them. Thus, even though unarmed, by being troublesome they were still fighting the war; sometimes at a terrible cost. If they managed to escape they then had to face a hazardous journey across a hostile country, sometimes at the cost of their lives. Those that found their way home were then returned to battle, once again to put their lives at risk. Captain J. Hardy, one of the most determined escapers, finally succeeded, was returned to his regiment and almost died at Ypres, where he lost a leg. Templer and others escaped, returned to the fighting and were killed.

Faced with such difficulties and physical challenges it was the moral challenges that often proved most difficult. Will Harvey – tongue in cheek as usual, points out the awful dilemma that faced the P.T., who were unable to use their tunnel and with just a day left in camp. Should they attempt to use it part finished, or leave it for the use of their successors? It is this glimpse of moral dilemma and debate that demonstrates the human qualities of the escapers. Will Harvey's remarkable ability to see the humour in the situation and the search for the right thing to do, is just one aspect of his remarkable insight and understanding of his fellow man.

Thanks to Eric Nicholls and Captain Eric Montague Onslow for providing clues to the identity of F.W. Harvey's comrades.